MW00752864

A Woman Soldier's Own Story

A Woman Soldier's Own Story

THE AUTOBIOGRAPHY OF XIE BINGYING

Xie Bingying

TRANSLATED BY

Lily Chia Brissman & Barry Brissman

COLUMBIA UNIVERSITY PRESS   NEW YORK

COLUMBIA UNIVERSITY PRESS

Publishers Since 1893

New York   Chichester, West Sussex

Copyright © 2001 Lily Chia Brissman and Barry Brissman
All rights reserved
Library of Congress Cataloging-in-Publication Data

Xie, Bingying, 1906–2000
[Nü bing zi zhuan. English]
A woman soldier's own story : the autobiography of Xie Bingying / Xie Bingying ;
translated by Lily Chia Brissman and Barry Brissman.
p. cm.
ISBN 0-231-12250-0 (alk. paper)
1. Xie, Bingying, 1906–2000. 2. Authors, Chinese—20th century—Biography.
I. Brissman, Lily Chia.   II. Brissman, Barry, 1942–   III. Title.

PL2765.I45 Z5213 2001
895.1′85109—dc21   2001023514

Casebound editions of Columbia University Press books are
printed on permanent and durable acid-free paper.
Printed in the United States of America
Designed by Lisa Hamm
c 10 9 8 7 6 5 4 3 2 1

Contents

Illustrations follow page 146

Preface to the New Translation
of My Autobiography

Xie Bingying

WHEN I WAS YOUNG, I COULD NOT UNDERSTAND WHY REBELLING against my parents was such a bad thing. I only wanted to be educated, just like my brothers, and to escape the feudal traditions of having my feet bound and my marriage arranged. I joined the Northern Expedition and fought the warlords partly to gain my country's freedom, partly to gain my own. This book describes the first thirty-two years of my life. It is the story of a Chinese girl who wanted to choose her own destiny in a country bound up in tradition and prejudice. I began the autobiography at the suggestion of Lin Yutang, who wished to publish it in *Universal Wind*, a magazine he edited at that time. I began writing it when I was in Changsha and I completed the first volume in the spring of 1936.

Many newspapers in Shanghai and Nanjing gave the book favorable reviews when it appeared, calling it a sincere and truthful description of a young girl's struggle to educate herself and to rebel against suffocating feudal traditions. In those days many young girls were in the same situation as I, but often they were not as lucky as I in gaining their freedom—yet they continued to struggle. As a result of their efforts, most modern Chinese women do not suffer the pain of bound feet, and many have escaped the shame of arranged marriages. Also, many now receive an education equal to that which men receive. All these are signs of human progress.

My father was a scholar from the last years of the Qing dynasty, and for thirty-seven years he served as the principal of Xinhua County Middle School. He respected the doctrines of Confucius and Mencius, loved his family, loved his country, and favored equality between males and females. My mother was a strong-willed woman whose motto was "No failure allowed, only success"—a spirit she transmitted to her children. As for my brothers, they were pleased when my autobiography was published and glad to have a female writer in the family. Even so, they disapproved of my having become a rebel and run away from home.

But all that was many years ago. I hope that now, at last, my parents are happy and at peace under the Nine Fountains.

My daughter Lily has worked closely with me to preserve the spirit and sense of my book as she has translated it into English. I hope that you, my new audience, will find in it many pleasures, both historical and literary.

San Francisco
AUGUST 1996

Introduction

Barry Brissman & Lily Chia Brissman

FOR MORE THAN SEVENTY YEARS XIE BINGYING WAS A LEADING Chinese writer. During that time the list of her published works grew to include a multitude of diaries, novels, short stories, children's books, travel books, and essays. But her reputation has always rested primarily on her autobiographical works, perhaps because they contain her most poetic and historically important writing and her most dramatic portrayal of women fighting to free themselves from the bondage of ancient Chinese tradition.

Xie Bingying lived through a period during which people of all classes in China were groping their way toward an uncertain future. After the Qing dynasty vanished in 1912, Sun Yat-sen, Chiang Kai-shek, Mao Zedong, and many others struggled to build a new China. Internal confusion and external threats unsettled the country. Warlords stepped in and filled the power vacuum in many provinces, including hers. And people everywhere were anguished (as they had been for years) about the humiliation that China continued to suffer at the hands of imperialist Japan and imperialist nations of the West.

This was also a period in which many young women were struggling to find a way to play more fulfilling roles in China's ancient society. Some young Chinese women, like Xie Bingying, did succeed in changing their lives. Many others failed. Her autobiography, *A Woman Soldier's Own Story*, illustrates that women's struggle for equality is something that has been going on for a long time in both East and West.

Xie Bingying was born in 1906 in a small village in Hunan Province. Even as a child she resisted the traditional values of her strong-willed mother, for she was like her mother in willfulness. She went to school (with the help and encouragement of her sympathetic older brothers), but then broke off her studies in 1926 to join the National Revolutionary Army in its Northern Expedition against warlords who controlled much of China at that time. From the war front she sent back personal reflections to a Hankou newspaper, and these writings became her first book, *War Diary*, published in 1928. After the war she, like many other young Chinese women in similar circumstances, was ostracized by much of society. People who had once supported her as she marched off to war were now contemptuous of her modern lifestyle and considered her a short-haired radical. Penniless, she returned to her native village. There she attempted to dissolve the marriage contract that her parents had drawn up when she was a toddler—but her mother would not allow her to do this. In fact, her mother locked her up and kept her a prisoner in the family home.

Xie Bingying made three attempts to run away. All three failed. At last she was forced to go through with the ancient wedding ceremony her family had arranged, but she did so only as part of a scheme to break free of her family. The scheme worked. Her marriage was never consummated and Xie Bingying escaped to Changsha. From there she took a boat to Shanghai to begin a new life. All this she tells in the first volume of her autobiography.

In Shanghai, Xie Bingying lived the bohemian life of a poor artist, studying and writing. After several months she moved to Beijing, but rumors that she was politically undesirable eventually forced her to leave her teaching position there and to resign her editorial responsibilities at a women's monthly publication. She later traveled to Tokyo to study Japanese, for she intended to devote herself to bringing classics of Western literature to her countrymen by translating them from the Japanese into Chinese. Before she could begin her task, she was thrown into prison when Puyi, the last emperor of the Qing dynasty, visited Japan and she refused to acknowledge him as a legitimate ruler in China—an experience she recounts in a book called *Inside Japanese Prison*. She returned to China and in 1937, eleven years after her first military experience in the Northern Expedition, she again went to war, this time to fight the invading Japanese. She organized the Hunan Women's War Zone Service Corps and led these women to the front lines, where they worked for months under terrible conditions to help the wounded and the dying. The second volume of her autobiography ends as she lies ill in a hospital, looking out the window toward the front lines where cannon fire touches the sky.

Her war experience was the first great adventure of her adult life, and it remained a source of excitement and inspiration to her as long as she lived. Even her bohemian life in Shanghai—those years of grinding poverty, of many lovers, of intellectual ferment, of new books discovered in the shops on Fourth Avenue—did not affect her as deeply as her experiences on the firing line. The death, excitement, camaraderie, hardships, patriotism, and idealism of war so lit her life that even as a woman of ninety she could be found inciting a group of American children to shout "Yi, er, san, si!"— one, two, three, four—as they pretended to march off to war through the imaginary hills of Hubei.

From 1938 to 1948 Xie Bingying published novels, short stories, and essays, plus the second volume of her autobiography and two other important autobiographical works, *New War Diary* and *Inside Japanese Prison*. During this period she worked at a number of jobs, including editing a literary magazine in Xian, editing a daily news supplement in Hankou, and teaching school in Chengdu. In 1938, when she was in her early thirties, she married Jia Yizhen, whom she had first met in Beijing at a student meeting. Their son was born in 1940; their daughter, in 1943. In 1945 Xie Bingying moved to Beijing to teach at Beijing Normal University. In 1948, shortly before the fall of the Guomindang, she left for Taiwan. In her diary for October 13, 1948, she writes, "Tonight is my last night in Beijing, and I feel unspeakable nostalgia. When will I ever return?" She could not have known that she would never return, either to Beijing—the city that had played so large a part in her life—or to mainland China. She traveled to Shanghai and from there took the boat to Jilong Harbor in Taiwan. Traveling with her was her five-year-old daughter—one of the translators of this book. Jia Yizhen, their son, and his son from his first marriage soon joined mother and daughter in Taiwan. Xie Bingying took a job as a professor of Chinese literature at Taiwan Normal University in Taipei.

She had lived much of her life in harsh conditions, often without proper food or clothing, and her first years in Taiwan also were financially difficult. Yet her generosity was spontaneous, natural, irrepressible. At the door of the family's small house in Taiwan arrived a steady flow of poor acquaintances and struggling students, many of them looking for meals, shelter, and moral support. She stinted nothing. What she had, she gave. From her earliest childhood all who had known her had been struck by her courage and her generosity, and these traits seemed to spring from her passionate nature. She embraced each passing moment with such enthusiasm that the future and all its dangers seem scarcely ever to have entered her mind. Often in her life she gave away, almost literally, her last penny. When outraged by injustice (which was often), she spoke against it without considering consequences to herself. When her country was threatened, she rushed away to war with the breathless enthusiasm of one who never ponders risks.

This same passionate style may explain her political and feminist attitudes, which were not always quite what they seemed to be. At first glance she seems to have been the quintessential political activist and feminist thinker, always in the thick of things, organizing student protests at school, marching off to war, participating in political rallies, giving speeches, writing in support of this cause or that. It is certainly true that from childhood on she spent much of her energy opposing feudal traditions unfair to women. It is also true that she was a conscious critic of the society, a person willing to do what even her brothers dared not do: debate with her parents. Her parents might be "as big as the sky," and the society might be bigger still, but she was seldom daunted by the odds. At every instant she was ready to let fly with all her outrages and enthusiasms. Sometimes she succeeded in changing things, sometimes not. Her clever tongue and clever pen got her into many a scrape—and out of many another. She was, in this sense, political, polemical, and practical.

Yet her nature was almost the opposite of political, something quite different. She knew this herself: "I was a lover of freedom and did not wish to join any party whatever, or to be swept into any political whirlpool. I utterly disdained those politicians who hung up a sheep's head to sell dog meat, and those opportunist revolutionaries who supported this party today and purged that party tomorrow."

A love of freedom and a terrible sympathy for each passing moment were the wellsprings of her nature. Though she spoke often of the necessity for army discipline, and though she talked of giving up reading Goethe's *The Sorrows of Young Werther* (and other such romantic nonsense) in order to dedicate herself to the practical world of revolution, the truth is that she was not a practical person and she never gave up her romantic love of freedom. As a child in her village in Hunan Province, she *would* run outside with the boys despite the scoldings of her mother, and as a woman of nearly ninety in San Francisco she *would* still run excitedly for buses, laughing and waving her cane, despite the remonstrances of just about everybody. Her nature was to be passionate and impetuous, to focus on the pleasure or problem at hand, not on theoretical hopes or fears that might never materialize. The moment was always *now*. In the fight for women's equality Xie Bingying was less a tactician than an inspiration.

In 1957 Xie Bingying and her husband moved from Taiwan to Malaysia, where they both taught high school in Taiping. Their daughter went with them. After several years they returned to Taiwan and Xie Bingying resumed her post at the university. In 1974, when she was sixty-seven, she and her husband moved to San Francisco. For the next quarter century she wrote books and articles, edited and organized her own work, wrote a newspaper column for children called "Letters to Grandma," and carried on an extensive correspondence with students, journalists, and scholars from all over the world, many of whom came to visit her in their small apartment. Her husband died in 1988. Xie Bingying died in San Francisco on January 5, 2000, nearly seventy-two years after her *War Diary* had been published in Shanghai and had set her on a literary path she was to follow for the rest of her life.

A Woman Soldier's Own Story was her most famous book. The first volume was published in Shanghai in 1936; the second, in Hankou in 1946. Subsequently, the two volumes were combined and published in Taiwan, but the Taiwan edition omitted a number of passages that appeared in the original editions. Evidently, some passages were dropped because of aesthetic imperfections, others because they did not suit the political or moral climate in Taiwan. In our translation we have retained nearly all the original material, excluding only passages that seemed to us (and to the author) to be cumbersome. Ours is the first English translation of the entire autobiography and the last version in any language to be authorized by Xie Bingying.

Within the constraints natural to all translations, we have striven to stay close to Xie Bingying's text, for she wrote with a freshness of style that has captivated readers for more than half a century. Our aim has been to render her freshness in colloquial American English, for the most part. On occasion we have felt it right to let a little of her world's strangeness appear in her language, as a shadow on a paper screen. Xie Bingying lived in a society far more formal than ours, and often a hint of that formality is felt in the way her people speak. In those few passages where a formal and even rigid manner of speaking seems important, we have tried not to completely obscure it, for it represents the very thing that Xie Bingying struggled against all her life.

Xie Bingying's impetuous style, like her impetuous nature, is both disconcerting and charming. She is usually accurate in describing dates, people, geography, and events, yet her exuberant focus on each passing moment, and her emphasis on immediate feeling rather than wide perspective, often make her narrative as edgy and disorienting as life itself. Reading her autobiography is sometimes like watching live video shot by a camera that slides through the world on Xie Bingying's shoulder: new characters appear suddenly and act out brief scenes, then vanish; landscapes explode into view—mountains in mist or cities in flame—then quickly dissolve before one is entirely certain where Bingying has been or is going. We have tried to give readers enough notes and maps to keep them oriented, but not so many as to slow their journey or dampen Xie's spontaneous style.

Xie Bingying's autobiography is about the passing of the old and the beginning of the new, the story of one woman's journey from Old China into a new world. In her small way Xie Bingying was always an adventurer, always walking a little ahead of most of her comrades, her family, her friends, always wide-eyed for the next experience.

Several years ago at a friend's country house in Wisconsin she said she wanted to climb up the ladder into the children's tree house. Others thought this might not be such a great idea for someone nearly ninety. They tried to dissuade her.

"I can! I can!" she said.

And up she went.

Main Events in Xie Bingying's Life

1906   Born in the village of Xietuoshan, Hunan Province. Her father is a scholar, writer, and school principal. The youngest of five children, she has one sister and three brothers.

1909   Betrothed to Xiao Ming, son of a family friend.

1911   Learns from her father to read ancient literature and recite poems from the Tang dynasty.

1914   Undergoes the binding of her feet.

1916   Enrolls as the only girl in a private boys' school in the village.

1918   Enters Datong Girls School after threatening suicide if she is not allowed to attend.

1919   Enters Xinhua County Girls School. Receives from her second-oldest brother Chinese translations of works by the French writers Alphonse Daudet and Guy de Maupassant.

1920   Attends Xinyi Girls School in Yiyang. Is sent home for not complying with missionary school rules and for instigating a parade on National Shame Day. Attends Changsha First Provincial Girls Teacher Training School. Reads Zola, Tolstoy, Goethe, Dickens. Edits the school's monthly magazine.

1921   Her essay "Momentary Impression" appears in a Changsha newspaper—her first published writing.

1926   Encouraged by her second brother, reads books on revolutionary theory instead of romances and emancipates herself from the old society by joining the class of female cadets at the Central Military and Political School in Wuhan.

1927   Works in the propaganda regiment of the army led by Chiang Kai-shek during the Northern Expedition. Sends her dairies from this period to a newspaper in Hankou. (These writings later become her first book, *War Diary*.) Returns home after her military unit is disbanded, and there is imprisoned by her mother for refusing to marry Xiao Ming. Tries to escape but is forced to go through with the marriage ceremony.

1928   Escapes to Changsha and has the marriage annulled. Is suspected of being a Communist and is imprisoned. Teaches grade school in Hengyang. Goes to Shanghai and enrolls in the Chinese literature department of the Shanghai Academy of Art. *War Diary*, her first book, is published in Shanghai.

1930   Gives birth to daughter in Beijing; her lover, Qi, is imprisoned for political reasons. She is suspected of leaning to the Left and advised to leave Beijing.

1931   Makes first visit to Japan but is sent home because she attends a meeting of Chinese students protesting the Japanese invasion of China's northeastern provinces. Returns to Shanghai.

1932   Edits *Women's Light*, a weekly, and works in an ambulance corps in Shanghai after Japanese attack the city.

1933   Visits Longyan and Gutian in western Fujian Province. Founds a monthly literary publication, *Lighthouse*, in Xiamen. Moves to Changsha and begins writing *A Woman Soldier's Own Story*.

1935   Makes second visit to Japan, intending to study Japanese and translate world literature from Japanese into Chinese. Is imprisoned for three weeks for refusing to welcome Puyi, the last emperor of the Qing dynasty, on his visit to Japan.

1936   Sees publication in Shanghai of her ninth book, *A Woman Soldier's Own Story* (vol. 1).

1937   Suffers the death of her mother. Organizes the Hunan Women's War Zone Service Corps in Changsha and leads the corps to the front to nurse troops fighting the invading Japanese. Begins to write *New War Diary*.

1938   Marries Jia Yizhen in Xian. Publishes *New War Diary*.

1940   Gives birth to son, Wenxiang. Publishes *Inside Japanese Prison*. Serves as editor-in-chief for *Huanghe* magazine in Xian.

1942   Suffers death of her father.

1943   Teaches school in Chengdu. Gives birth to daughter Wenrong (Lily).

1945   Becomes chief editor for the supplement to *Peace Daily News* in Hankou.

1946   Establishes a day-care center in Hankou. Publishes the second volume of *A Woman Soldier's Own Story* in Hankou.

1947   Teaches at Beijing Normal University and at Huabei Cultural Academy.

1948   Leaves Beijing, moves to Taiwan, and teaches at Taiwan Normal University in Taipei.

1956   Publishes the Taiwan edition of her autobiography (a volume comprising most of the two separate volumes published in Shanghai and Hankou).

1957   Moves to Malaysia and teaches at Hualian High School in Taiping.

1960   Returns to Taipei to teach at Taiwan Normal University.

1968   First visits the United States.

1974   Moves to San Francisco with her husband and writes books, articles, and a newspaper column for children.

1988   Suffers the death of her husband.

2000   Dies on January 5 in San Francisco.

A Note on Chinese Names

Chinese names in this book are transliterated using the pinyin system. Many pinyin letters are pronounced nearly as they are in English, but here are a few notable exceptions:

c = ts
e = eh
i = ee
q = ch
x = sh
zh = j

For example, *Xie Bingying* is pronounced *Shee-eh Bingying*. Big Sister *Tie* is pronounced *Tee-eh*. *Qi* is pronounced *Chee*.

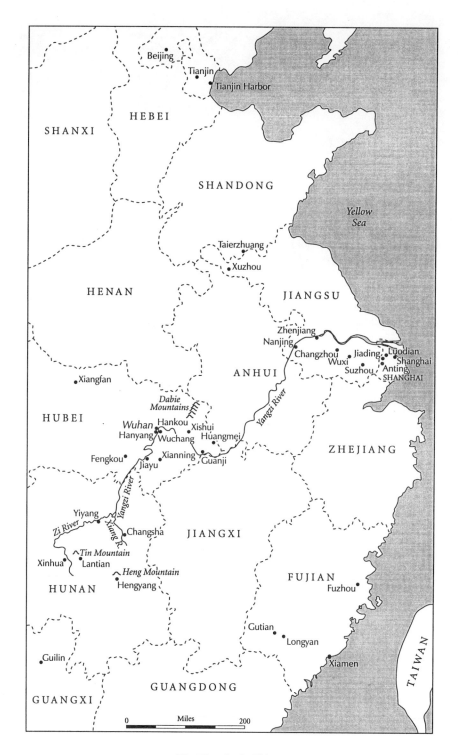

Xie Bingying's China

Xinhua Area of Hunan Province

Xie Bingying's home village of Xietuoshan was in the neighborhood of Tin Mountain, not far from Lantian, on a stream running into the Zi River, and thirty-two miles from Xinhua over a road that crossed two high mountains. The translators have not been able to determine the exact location of Xietuoshan.

A Woman Soldier's Own Story

Volume One

PART I Childhood

THE NEW AUTUMN SEEMED ALMOST HOTTER THAN SUMMER. EVENING breeze blew gently through the torn paper window, yet my body was covered in sweat as Grandma held me to her bosom. Earlier in the day my mother had beaten me with a wooden stick. Now silvery moonlight revealed blood streaks on my skin and shone whitely on my pale and worried face.

My stifled sobs turned suddenly into loud crying.

"Crying will awaken your mother, and she will come again to beat you. Don't cry, my precious little Phoenix."

Grandmother spoke these scary words, patting me lightly to put me to sleep.

"I . . . I'm not afraid of beating. Why doesn't she beat me to death?"

I spoke loudly, almost as if I wanted my mother to know what I felt. But Mother, sleeping on the other side of the wall, kept her temper and made no sound.

"Precious, don't be naughty anymore," said Grandmother. "Your mother has suffered I don't know how much distress for your sake. Remember the time you put a copper coin in your throat and could neither spit it out nor swallow it? Your eyes rolled far up in your head and went white. All day long saliva gushed from your mouth as if you were suffocating. Your mother was filled with anxiety as she climbed seven miles up a high mountain to get the doctor. In front of total strangers she kowtowed like a crazy person, crying out, 'If only someone will save my child, he can have my life if he wishes it.'

"Later, you managed to swallow the coin and it fell into your stomach. Then your mother feared the copper would absorb blood and endanger your life, so she sent someone to Baoqing to buy fifteen or twenty pounds of plant roots for you to eat—and she constantly examined your feces to see if the copper coin had come out.

"And then there was the time you fell from a ladder while fooling with a swallow's nest in the rafters—you injured your face, stopped breathing, and your whole body turned icy cold. You were knocked completely sense-less. Your mother cried streams of tears. First she called for the doctor. Then she knelt before the Goddess of Mercy and prayed by the bowl of magic water, saying, 'Oh, Goddess, please let misfortune descend on me instead of my precious Phoenix. I only ask you to protect her health and her high spirits. Take my life in exchange for all her misfortunes.'

"Precious . . . do you remember all these things?"

I stopped crying. Silently, I listened to Grandma tell my story.

"Alas, my sweetheart." Grandma sighed—a very long sigh. "You really are too troublesome—I just don't know where you came from. In the same month that you were conceived, your mother began to vomit everything she swallowed, even a single sip of water. If she ate so much as a single bean, she threw it up. Each day she felt lightheaded and her stomach ached. Dur-ing the last two or three months of her pregnancy she suffered so much that she considered suicide, yet she always remembered that she had three sons and one daughter who needed her care, so her thoughts turned again to life.

"Finally came her fateful moment: you were about to descend to earth. Your mother told me that her stomach was so painful she could not even get out of bed. No use talking about eating—she could not even swallow water. For two days she tossed and tumbled in pain. Then suddenly your head appeared. I thought you would come out immediately, and my heart was full of hope. I stared, waiting to receive you as you were born. Unfor-tunately, I watched one whole day and one whole night, and still your little head full of black hair stayed at the same place. Your mother could not last much longer. To make matters worse, your father was not home. I was alone and dared not move one step away from her. At last I asked your great aunt to go and get the midwife. Ah—this business of the midwife makes me angry every time I think about it. Already your mother had given birth to four children, and not one of them had required a midwife. Each had been born in an hour, at the most. But *this* time . . . who could have known that after three days and three nights you still would not descend? The midwife came, looked, and shook her head: 'No hope, you should at once prepare for the funeral.' That's actually what she said to us.

"Next your great aunt began to insist that the midwife must get the child out. 'No matter what happens,' she said, 'we must save the adult—it doesn't matter if we sacrifice the little child.'

"By then I was totally frantic. I had no idea what to do. Yet your mother was still clearheaded, and she sobbed to me, 'Mother, quickly go to the Nanyue god and promise incense on my behalf—if the child is a male he will return to burn incense when he is sixteen, and if it is a girl I will take her myself the moment she is twenty.'

"So I did what your mother said. I knelt in front of the Nanyue god and promised Blood Basin Incense.*

"As a result," continued Grandmother, "just at the moment of dawn there came a *WHAaa* sound and you descended to earth. Your voice was unusually loud. Almost everyone in the courtyard was startled from sleep. Your eyes were like two brightly lit lanterns, and your eyeballs were moving extremely quickly. A pair of little fists and two legs moved nonstop. Your great aunt sighed and said, 'Too bad it's a girl. If it were a boy he surely would become a big official—you see this lively pair of eyes?'

"At that comment your mother was most unhappy. She replied, 'Son, daughter, all the same.'

"From this you can see that your mother loves you very much, despite all the hardship she has suffered for your sake. In future, Precious, do not make your mother sad again. You should appreciate her hard work and her love."

I listened silently. I was only six.

---

*The superstition in my village was that if a childbirth was difficult, someone had to go before the Heng Mountain's Nanyue god and promise Blood Basin Incense. The child later had to return with the incense, wearing a red shirt, red pants, and a red scarf wrapped round the head.

Grandma feared I had fallen asleep. Actually, I was quite clear: on one side my brain played the sad scene of my mother's difficult delivery, while on the other side was deeply imprinted the scene earlier that day when my mother had beaten me with all her strength. A most curious feeling. Also, I had a suspicion that when Grandma told me what my great aunt had said just before I was born—that I must be sacrificed to save my mother—she really was describing her own words. But I knew that Grandma loved me very much, so I did not settle accounts with her.

Hah! But if Mother loves me so much, why did she beat me so hard? Isn't a child a person? Doesn't she have her own ideas? Must she obey an adult's every word? (These words ran round and round inside my brain.) Yes, I am a naughty child. I often anger Mother—she who manipulates everybody, men and women, young and old. She manipulates the entire village of Xietuoshan. But to catch up with me, naughty and strange little creature, this is Mother's most unhappy task.

Sometimes Mother's anger reached the limit and she told Father vindictively, "You take her away from me forever. This child could not have been born to me." Or else she would say, "I'll marry her off early and avoid trouble."

Pitiful child. By the time I was three, I had already been promised as a wife to the son of my father's friend. Who could predict the fate of this little life, already so carefully arranged?

⁂

GRANDMOTHER OFTEN TOLD the story of her marriage to Grandfather: "My own family was very poor, but when I came to your grandfather's family I found he was poorer still, with neither rice to eat nor two bowls to eat it from."

"How can that be?" I always asked her, whenever she told this tale.

"Be patient and I will tell you. Your great-grandfather had six sons. Your grandfather was the second of them. When the old man died, each son received one pound of rice, one bench, and one bowl. That was all the inheritance he left them. Your grandfather, like all the other sons, had only a single bowl. So after I came into the family, what were we to do?"

"Go buy one!" I said.

"Right. Your grandfather was an honest and hardworking farmer, and whenever he worked for others the boss treated him very well. He not only earned enough money to buy another bowl but every year was able to save part of his salary. When I came here to live with him I washed clothes and did hard labor for other people every day, so I was able to earn a bit of rice. Eventually we were able to buy farm tools. We borrowed money to buy a buffalo, and we rented several acres to cultivate. Ah! Speaking of farming reminds me of your father.

"Even when he was only a boy of seven or eight, your father loved to read books. Each day when he tended our buffalo he secretly carried a book along with him, hidden in his shirt. After reaching open country, he sat down to read it. No matter where the buffalo wandered, and no matter whose wheat, vegetables, or beans the buffalo ate . . . well, your father paid no attention. One time the buffalo got lost, and for a whole day your father was too scared to go home. He cried in desperation. On the second day a neighbor found the buffalo. When your grandfather asked your father why he had been so absentminded, he replied that he had forgotten about the buffalo because he was reading a book. Your grandfather then realized this boy was no herder: he was a born book idiot.

"So your grandfather agreed to send him to school. He said that if your father excelled in his studies, he could take the national scholars test. On hearing these words, your father became crazy with happiness. He read books all day and all night. On moonless nights he read by the light of lit pine branches, and sometimes he burned his fingers, scorched his skin— but he did not even notice.

"In the year 1903 he went to take the provincial scholars test. He did not have proper clothes for the journey so I made him a new set of outer clothes, and I gave him some of my own torn clothing to wear under them. Your grandfather carried your father's bundles of luggage for him, which was why shop people along the way paid no attention to your grandfather and treated him like a servant. Afterward your father became a scholar. Who would have dreamed that the old porter was actually the scholar's father? Ha!" Grandmother laughed.

I knew many tales about my father. I knew that he had attended Zhang Zhidong's Academy of Hunan and Hubei, and that his thinking was entirely sympathetic to that of Confucius and Mencius. I also knew that he preferred studying the words of Song dynasty scholars. In the last year of the Qing dynasty he was one of six people invited to the capital to take a special exam in economics, sponsored by the governor of Guangdong and Guangxi Provinces, for a government post.* All the others went but not Father. He had high ethical standards and would have nothing to do with politics. He believed in traditional morality, including absolute obedience to parents. He was even more reverent than the philosopher Zeng Zi when it came to honoring his parents. Everyone liked being with Father, for he was easygoing and polite. To his children he could be stricter than the strictest teacher in all matters related to schooling and character, yet in his love for them he was gentler and kinder than Mother. Strange to say, he did not oppose new ideas, although his own thinking was quite old-fashioned. When my second-oldest brother wanted to study English in middle school, for instance, my father encouraged him and urged him to work hard. And Father always engaged new graduates to teach courses at the Xinhua County Middle School, where he served as principal for thirty-seven years.† Of course, he still enthusiastically promoted ancient literature and traditional morality, and that was why I, when still a child in my father's bosom, had already begun to chant poetry and read ancient literature.

As for Mother? She was a woman of great courage and character, afraid of neither heaven nor earth.

Her own mother had had no sons, just three daughters. Mother was the oldest of the three, so family matters fell entirely under her sway. At sixteen she married my father and quickly became famous in Xietuoshan as someone exceedingly clever. She was endowed with a talent for managing things and was brimming with notions about how a proper wife and a proper woman should behave. She believed absolutely in the notion that a female should be humble and should respect the male. She paid particular attention to the fine points of traditional manners, which were almost more important to her than her own life. She was Xietuoshan's Mussolini: whether at home or out in society, she was always telling people what to do. Almost

---

*The last full year of the Qing dynasty was 1911; the dynasty ended in February 1912.—trans.

†Middle school included grades seven to twelve.—trans.

everyone in the village, adult or child, listened to what she said. Community property was kept by her, for she never took advantage of anyone and she always worked enthusiastically for the common welfare. Village politicians could not get along without her. Whenever the members of the village council could not find a solution to a situation, they had only to invite her to speak a few words and all questions were answered.

She was strong and capable, born with an unbending and unwavering spirit. Everyone feared her and obeyed her—and not just in the village. Even in her own family she was the dictator, treating her children as an emperor treats slaves who must listen to her every pronouncement and obey her every order. One time my big brother took his wife to Yiyang, a town 170 miles away, to start his own little family. Unfortunately, he did not get Mother's consent beforehand. So Mother sent someone to find him and bring him back. She punished him by making him kneel on the ground with a large foot basin full of water on top of his head. Whenever he moved only slightly, the water spilled, and then Mother would spank his bottom. After many people tried to intercede for him, she finally allowed the foot basin to be set down. On another occasion my second brother wanted to divorce his mean, unfeeling, tiny-footed wife, but Mother slapped the table and scolded him loudly, "You thing! The idea of returning from your studies to try to pull such a shameful and immoral trick. Really. Don't you care about the honor of your ancestors? If you want a divorce, kill me first and then talk about divorce. So long as I am alive, I will not allow this loss of face." My brother knew her character and believed that if he got a divorce she would kill herself, so he suffered the bitterness of his marriage and did nothing. From that moment until the day he died from spitting blood, my brother remained utterly alone and never had a romantic relationship with a woman.

My sister was even more obedient. She was actually like a little lamb in front of Mother, and spoke in a whisper. She married someone named Liang at eighteen, and suffered the ill treatment of her husband and her in-laws without complaint. Whenever she came home she went out of her way to tell us how well her husband treated her, for she knew if she did not say this, our mother would scold her for not waiting on him. Many times I caught my sister crying in the toilet, and often at night I was awakened from my dreams by the sound of her sobbing. My youngest brother obeyed

Mother and Father, but he was stronger than my second brother. Sometimes he actually argued with Mother. He had ways of touching our parents' hearts so they would not oppose what he wished to do.

As for me?

Ah—I regret to say I was a completely rebellious child.

I WAS MOTHER'S YOUNGEST. My sister, ten years older, was married off when I was eight. By then my oldest brother was already working as a teacher.

My other two brothers went away with Father each school term to study in the town of Xinhua. Twice a year, at winter and summer vacations, they came back home. Those were the happy times when we were reunited. During the winter Mother prepared lots of dried fish and dried meat and stored it away for their return. I always envied my brothers for the way she treated them as guests. As soon as we received a letter telling us that my father and brothers were on their way home, Mother became so happy that she could not sleep for one or two nights. She cooked up rice and dishes of food. She changed me into clean clothes and would always say, "Precious, don't get dirty. When Father returns he will bring you candy, and your brothers will give you many toys."

The journey from Xinhua to our home was thirty-two miles along a road that climbed over two high mountains. Father rode in a sedan chair and hired a porter for the trip, but my brothers huffed and puffed along on foot, wearing short shirts and straw shoes just like coal deliverers' children.

Mother always took my hand, and we stood watching at our gate from five o'clock in the afternoon until finally, at twilight, we could see the sedan chair coming in the distance.

"Precious, your father is returning!"

Then she ran back into the house to boil water and steep tea. Meanwhile, the little black dog and I raced three hundred yards to welcome them. By then Father was always walking, for he customarily got off his sedan chair about three miles from home, just at the place in the road where he passed near the homes of some elderly people and the graves of our ancestors.

"Father! Candy?" Like a little monkey going up a tree, I quickly climbed until my two little hands held tightly to Father's neck.

The little black dog wagged his tail and leaped on Father—and my second brother hit the dog with a stick. Father quickly said, "Don't beat it, don't beat it. It's welcoming us, just like Precious."

Even the porter laughed.

I only twisted my lips tight and made no sound. I was unhappy that Father compared me to the little dog.

Whenever I welcomed Father, he carried me home. In winter as soon as he entered the gate he wrapped me in a leather coat, afraid I would catch cold. My brothers bustled about, giving me many toys they had made themselves—tiny boxes, toy sparrows, little boats, pencil holders—as well as blue ink bottles and broken glass vessels from their chemistry lab. I especially loved those glass vessels. In summer I caught many lightning bugs and put them inside the glass, and the bugs moved up and down like a golden dragon, flickering. Most intriguing.

Father had bought flavorful candy for Grandmother and pretty little round pepper cakes especially for me. Mother was afraid I would take all the cakes and share them with other children, so she always kept them and gave them to me just a few at a time. But she didn't know about the candy I got from Grandmother, or how I sometimes stole cakes and biscuits that had been prepared for our guests, put them into my pockets, and took them outside to divide among my little friends.

On one occasion Mother was too busy to sew a pocket on my old shirt, but I insisted that she do it right away. Because of this she chased me with a wooden stick. I ran so fast that her little feet could not keep up with me, however hard she tried. She ordered me: "Stop!" I ignored her and ran even faster.

Suddenly I heard a noise, *poo-tunk*: Mother had fallen and her two little feet were plunged in a mud field. She could not pull them out for a long while. Pitiful. Taking advantage of this opportunity, I escaped home and cried out for my sister-in-law to save me. But Mother soon returned, locked me in a dark room, and used a thistle stick to beat me. On that night my grandma told me several stories, for I ran to her bed to sleep and nurse my wounds.

Father loved most of all to plant flowers. Behind our house was his garden. In spring and summer, winter and fall, this garden was bursting with many kinds and colors of flowers, as well as with pomelos, oranges, cherries, plums, pears, loquats—all sorts of fruit trees—and here were many bamboos and pines, and when the thorny bright roses opened up, the entire garden sparkled, and all day long the yellow oriole cried . . . this beautiful garden, I don't know how much happiness and hope it gave me.

When he was home, Father spent his days in the garden. If he was not pulling weeds, he was using a watering can to sprinkle the flowers and trees. In evenings, beneath a vegetable oil lamp with a bean-size flame, he instructed my brothers in ancient literature and taught me to chant poetry, while nearby my mother and sister-in-law spun their yarn. The sound of Father chanting poetry frequently intertwined with the sound of the spinning wheel, all harmonizing in a drunken music. On many such nights I lay in Father's arms and fell asleep . . . and one morning when I awoke, he asked me to recite a poem by heart.

With a red face I answered:

> "Father held Precious,
> His voice so deep;
> Next thing Precious
> Fell asleep."

"Who taught you this poem?" Father pretended to be upset. Yet I knew his anger was fake, for a smile floated at the corners of his mouth.

"Precious self."

While speaking, I slipped away like a little sparrow.

SPRING ARRIVED.

Paths in the fields were green with grass and filled with red and white flowers. Water ran slowly in the stream. Frogs in the field cried *guh-guh* nonstop. This was the time for farmers to plant and for children to catch fish and shrimp. Every spring the barefoot farmers, wearing coir raincoats,* stood bent at the waist in their fields, beneath the drizzling fine rain, from early morning until skyblack.

---

*Raincoats made of coconut husks.—trans.

When I saw our foreman returning with little carp strung on thin reeds, I knew it was time for me to go out to play. I took off my shoes and socks and put on a bamboo rain hat, just like the farmers, and ventured out with a few naughty boys. In a muddy stream we competed at catching shrimp and little fish. Sometimes the stream was moving so fast we couldn't catch anything, and then the boys discussed stealing fish from the fields. Raising fish in fields was a secondary farming business, and stealing a few little carp was no problem as long as you did not encounter anyone. But my goal was shrimps and crabs, not fish—and, anyway, I definitely did not want to be a little thief.

I liked snails too. When I picked up snails, my legs often were bitten by leeches and began to bleed, all my clothes got wet, and my face got all muddy. Whenever I went crying to the house, Mother scolded me: "You know you are a girl, don't you? Why play outside with such dirty, knock-about boys?"

"Can't girls play outside?"

"Not outside, no! Only in the house."

"No, no! I must be outside. . . ."

Then followed the mingled sounds of Mother scolding, me crying.

OFTEN I IGNORED Mother's words and spent the daylight hours playing outside, refusing to sit home and behave myself. So Mother gave me a job: every day after breakfast I had to go to the field to pick tea leaves. The road stretched more than half a mile between our house and the tea field, so our lunch was put into a basket and sent with a servant. At twilight my sister-in-law and I, and many other girls who picked tea, returned home.

Because I had no experience picking tea leaves, I often broke the tea branches. At last my sister-in-law jumped up in great distress and said, "Sister, you might as well go catch your butterflies and not damage the tea trees. If Mother finds out, she will scold you again."

"No, I must pick. You were not born knowing how to pick, were you? You must have learned."

She was tongue-tied, as usual, and could not answer me.

When I speak of my tea picking I should really say flower picking, for always my little basket was full of flowers when the time came to return home. As we crossed the sixty-foot stone bridge, I threw my flowers beneath it so the stream would carry them to Dongting Lake, and as they floated away I reminded them: "Flowers, you be sure to float to the palace of the Dragon King, where his beautiful princess is waiting to become a new bride." I said this because of a story I had heard long before, when I was very young, from the carpenter who had made my sister's dowry. He told me that the Dragon King's daughter was an extraordinarily beautiful maiden and that when her wedding day arrived the entire earth would be flooded and everyone in the world would be floating on water. I happily hoped to see such a scene—the earth's surface completely covered with whitecaps. So I wished for the Dragon King's daughter to be married off soon.

More than half the young girls who picked tea leaves were children being kept to be daughters-in-law. Their lives were full of hardship. Every day each girl had to pick at least 140 or 150 pounds of tea leaves, yet her pay was only twenty or so copper coins. She had to give this money to her future mother-in-law. If a girl was discovered holding back a coin or two for herself, her mother-in-law would burn her entire body with a red-hot iron.

These girls seldom ate a full meal. They ate either sweet potatoes or very coarse wheat cakes, and they never tasted a single piece of meat except during the New Year Festival. Arriving at the tea field, they looked as skinny as skeletons and each one took a turn telling how her mother-in-law cruelly crushed her spirit. Whenever the girl who was speaking reached a heartbreaking point in her tale, tears would stream down onto the tea trees and sparkle like drops of dew.

"Why don't you run away if she treats you so cruelly?" I said this to a little girl whose face was blood-streaked from a beating. Her name was Chunxiang.

"Run away? How would I dare? My mother-in-law always manages to hurt me. I will die in her hands." She began to cry, and I cried with her.

A bigger girl, Xiuying, advised her, "Crying is useless. You had better hurry up and pick tea leaves. If you don't return home with two hundred pounds by the time the sky turns black, you will be beaten again."

Sister Lian's eyes were swollen from crying, but still she comforted herself. "Oh—we can only blame our bitter fate that we are born to live a life not even as good as the lives of cows or horses. We must suffer till we die. In the next life we will surely be happier."

From that time on I knew a little bit about life's bitterness and pains. Often I felt anger at how unfairly these children were treated while being kept as future daughters-in-law. Whenever we picked tea leaves, I helped them with their work.

As twilight approached and night's black curtain slowly descended, we collected our tea knives, our benches, our tea canisters, and, carrying our baskets on our backs, we sang:

> "In the month of March we pick the tea,
> Pick the green tea leaves,
> And pairs of sisters, old and young,
> Embroider handkerchieves—
> Embroider on each border bright
> The flowers for all to see—
> And in between a picture of
> A fellow picking tea."

AUTUMN WIND BLEW subtle fragrance of cassia. Moon threw brilliant light. Stars sparkled at the edges of the sky. Children raced with shadows in the yard, playing hide-and-seek. And me? A little girl of eight, I had already begun to do the work of an adult.

Spinning with me under the moon were my sister-in-law, two distant aunts, and a neighbor named Miss Zhen.

When a girl who was born and raised in our village reached seven or eight years of age, she was taught to spin cotton and flax, and she was taught to sew. The poor girls spun for other people and received a wage of twenty copper coins for every pound of spun cotton. The quickest spinners could spin no more than four ounces a day, but two or three ounces was more usual. So the girls earned only three or four copper coins a day, on average. I was spinning for my own use and had no set quota. Mother said, "You just be sure to work hard at your spinning and if we do not have enough of our family's homegrown cotton to supply you, we will go to Lantian to buy some."

"No, I don't like spinning, and I cannot wear this much fabric anyway," I replied.

"It is not for you to wear now but for your trousseau. If you spin more enthusiastically, you will someday have twenty cases of clothes to carry to your in-laws—how you will impress them!"

I knew that my marriage had been arranged long ago, when I was sucking my mother's nipple. But I did not really understand what this meant, so when I heard Mother's words I felt no pain at all. I continued spinning happily. Especially when we sat outside beneath the moon, I really could not have been happier.

When we spun inside the house in winter, we suffered several inconveniences, for in order to save oil Mother always refused to light the lamp. So we had to borrow light from the fire in order to spin, and the result was that not only did we end up spinning in darkness anyway, but our backs felt cold.

But in autumn the weather was warm and we sat outside, and the moon was especially pure and clear. Added to this were Grandmother's stories about the cowherd and the spinning maiden and about the goddess in the moon and the goddess's mother. These stories made our spinning even more enchanting. Sometimes we became so entranced by her tales that we all stopped our spinning wheels, and all fought to ask, "How did it end?"

"How did it end? Lazy little girls all stopped working!" Grandmother's humorous answer made everyone laugh.

Soft and loud was the sound of spinning wheels singing late in the night when people were quiet—like the sound of a lute drifting up from the empty valley. Gentle breeze blew by our heads, bringing fragrant smells of flowers.

Drunk, we were drunk with the lovely colors of night.

BAD RUMORS ABOUT ME reached Mother's ears. People in the village were saying that I was too old to have my feet still unbound and that my future in-laws certainly would not want me. They also said it was not proper for an eight- or nine-year-old girl to be playing with the boys—making clay Buddhas and throwing stones and pretending to be a military commander.* The people of the village said that, according to ancient custom, boys and girls must not sit together after they are four years old. My mother was a woman who read books, they said, so why could she not understand even this simple point?

Truth be told, Mother loved me very much. She felt her own small feet were too short and very inconvenient for walking. And my sister's little feet, which Mother had bound very small, were truly like little red peppers. My sister was beautiful to look at, but she could walk only two steps before she had to lean on a wall, nearly disabled. So Mother decided to delay binding my feet. She hoped to avoid breaking my foot bones, as my sister's had been. At the same time, Mother thought that if she did not begin to bind my feet now, the bones would develop day by day, and then it would be difficult to bind them into small feet. In our village the custom was that no one would marry a girl with large feet. Also, whoever saw such a girl would scold her, saying, "Is your mother dead? Your fan-like feet are as ugly as death."

Then came the day that Mother asked me to make a pair of small red pointy-tipped shoes to hang on the incense burner for Buddha. I did not understand what was going on.

"Precious," she said—for my mother called me this name till I was more than ten years old—"today I must bind your feet for you. Come, pray to the Goddess of Mercy. She will protect you, so it will not hurt at all, even if they are bound very small."

Mother's hand lit incense and burned paper money as she waited for me to kneel.

"Mama, I do not want my feet bound." I stood very far away, watching her, not daring to move closer. Two small tears suddenly rolled down, and my heart began to taste the flavor of fright and pain.

"Come quickly, come quickly. The bodhisattva will protect you." She dragged me over and made me kneel on the ground.

Ah, she had prepared everything—pointy shoes with embroidered plum flowers on the front, and two pieces of very long blue binding cloth that was

---

*I had organized the children of the village into a squadron of soldiers, and every day we carried sticks and marched "one, two, three, four." I called myself the commander.

three inches wide. I trembled when I saw this. I carefully picked up the flower shoes to look at them. They were made of scarlet silk and had thin bottoms, and they were very beautiful. I had no idea when Mother had made them, for I had never seen her making embroidered flower shoes.

"Mama, binding feet is too painful. I won't be able to walk. Don't hurt me," I begged her amid terrified cries.

"It is because I love you that I bind your feet. Not binding them would truly hurt you. How do you think a young girl with large feet would ever be married off?" As she spoke, Mother sprayed from her mouth the holy water that she had gotten by kneeling in front of the Goddess of Mercy—she sprayed it right onto my feet. She also flicked some red ash between my toes. Now I began to cry loudly and cause a big commotion.

"Ma, it is as painful as death. I would rather never marry. I do not want my feet bound."

"You little thing! Even before they are bound you are already crying with pain—then I am determined to bind them even tighter, to show you what pain really is."

The binding cloth was already wound around my feet, but my feet were wildly kicking and my hands were grabbing the bandage from Mother's hands and throwing the shoes on the ground. Mother was very angry. She quickly called for my sister-in-law and had her hold my hands. First, they began to bind my left foot, with my right foot caught between Mother's legs. Like a bound prisoner entering the place of execution, I screamed and hollered. All the neighbors ran over to see the commotion.

When my great aunt came through the door she said, "My dear, don't cry. After your feet are bound, I will carry you on my back to see a monkey play." Those who were watching all laughed stupidly. No one was sympathetic. Nobody was moved by my cries. Oh, I thought. These women are Mother's gang. They are all executioners.

Now my two feet wore red shoes. Already my entire body was numb. Mother lifted me down to help me try to walk. I felt sharp pain as if my bones were broken. I let out a cry and fell to the ground. . . .

�֍

FROM THEN ON each day I could only sit by the stove and spin yarn or slowly stroll in the living room. I felt as if I were carrying shackles on my feet and could not move, and would never again see beautiful flowers and grass and lively fish and shrimp.

On the day of the Flower Festival, Mother pierced each of my ears while I was sound asleep. By the time the pain had awakened me from my dream, she had already hung a red silk thread through each earlobe.

"Good. I have accomplished two of the three most important things in your life," said Mother very happily.

Apparently she was responsible for doing three important tasks for her daughter: binding her feet, piercing her ears, and marrying her off.

"Yes," I said angrily, "the one job you have not done is to kill me." And this made her scold me again.

When my sister had gotten married, Mother had borrowed money and provided her with a large dowry, and she had invited a flower lady to come to our house to embroider flowers on sixteen silk blankets. She had also arranged for thirty-six loads of wooden household articles to be constructed. Among these were eight large trunks that later were filled with clothes and shoes and stockings, all embroidered with flowers. Sister had begun to embroider when she was eight years old and had continued until she was eighteen, the year she got married. She never left the house. Each day she was shut in a small room where she embroidered from six in the morning straight through until six in the afternoon, when at last she was allowed to stop. In the evening she had to spin. Poor her. She was so tired that she could not breathe. She could only sigh secretly, not daring to utter a single word of complaint to Mother.

Mother naturally wished that I would be like my sister and would embroider a huge quantity of flowers that someday could be carried to my mother-in-law's house. But I told her, "I do not want anything like that, I only want to study."

"What! A girl thinking about study? Really, then heaven and earth are turning topsy-turvy. Studying is your brothers' business. You should have been shut away in the maiden's chamber after you were born. Think: what use is it for a woman to study? There is no rank of 'female scholar' that can be attained."

But despite all her opposition, in the end I would enter school.

PART 2 School

MY NATIVE VILLAGE WAS AN ISOLATED FARMING COMMUNITY FAR OFF the beaten track, surrounded by mountain peaks. From the Zi River a small stream flowed endlessly, and its waters played enchanting music all year round, *tsung-tsung-tsung.* When spring arrived and windows were open, you could see the deep blue heavens, green mountains, beautiful flowers and plants, and little birds flitting to and fro in the sky. Truly, it was a village of green mountains and luxuriant water, a paradise to make one drunk on its beauty.

More than two hundred families lived in our village. Most of the men were farmers or miners. Xinhua was China's coal-producing region, and the tin of Tin Mountain was world famous.

Day and night, miners lived coal-black lives on their hands and knees. Their skin was dyed black by the coal, and so were the insides of their nostrils, their ears, and their mouths. Even their spit was black. That was why the upper class belittled them, calling them "black stomachs."

All the village girls had feet like three-inch golden lotus flowers. The poorer ones were given away as future daughters-in-law, which improved their condition a little, and when they were fifteen or sixteen they were married off. Then each day they had to cook for the family, mend clothes, do washing, care for the children, and help their husbands dig in the fields, pulling weeds and planting vegetables. But they never entered the coal mines, for it was said the miners were naked, so women were not allowed.

Naturally, the girls born in this village never dreamed of entering school. A private school was just a third of a mile from my house, but it was for boys only: girls would not think of crossing its doorway.

BY THE TIME I was five years old I had begun to read. Father was a writer who composed in the old style (he had written more than fifty works). During the winter and summer vacations when he returned home from Xinhua County Middle School, he taught me to read poetry. There were many words I did not recognize at that time. As for understanding the meaning of the phrases and sentences, do not even mention it. But just as I knew how to imitate Grandmother when she sang "Bright Moon," so I imitated Father when he recited poetry. By the time I was eight I had memorized half the book of *Poems by Girl Poets of Suiyuan* and half of *Three Hundred Poems from the Tang Dynasty*. Every day I increased the number of words that I recognized.

Mother always taught me to read such things as *Teach Your Daughter Traditional Rules, Memoirs of Female Martyrs,* and *The Daughter's Classic Book.* But for some strange reason—I did not know why—I felt the words were dry and tasteless. I did not like to read books such as those. So I began to ask Mother to send me to the private school. But she said girls did not need to go to school, that it was enough if girls could recognize a few words, could understand a few stories about virtuous women, could keep accounts, and could read contracts. She was hoping, apparently, that I would become a good housewife. Yet because of my repeated requests she allowed me, in the year I turned ten, to enter that private school.

I really never imagined it would be so difficult for a girl to get an education. The teacher and many others were opposed to the idea and would not accept it. In my native village they had never seen girls going to school, certainly not to the same school as the boys. The most violently opposed to the idea was a flat-nosed woman whom everyone called the "sharp-mouthed old dame." She was known by old and young as a fierce person. Her only son studied at this private school, and when she heard that I was going to enroll there she busily proclaimed her views, saying that girls would steal all the wisdom if boys and girls studied together. She said that the boys, one by one, would turn stupid, staring, and dumb. She blamed Mother for not understanding the rules and for not seeing what everyone else already knew, that males and females are different—especially since I was no longer just a little girl.

Although most people agreed with her, they discussed the matter only on the quiet. They were afraid of Mother and dared not confront her to try to prevent me from going to school. But the sharp-mouthed old dame was a different sort, bold and fearless and quite willing to confront Mother and cause trouble. She told Mother that she should not send me to school but instead should hire an elderly tutor to teach me at home. The old dame threatened that if Mother would not do this, she would have the school disbanded immediately.

But Mother was the tougher of the two women. Having heard the old dame's threats, she was even more determined to send me to study at that private school. She swore in anger and promptly picked up a basket containing the best incense paper (this was used to honor Confucius) and took me straight to the private school. The teacher did not want to accept me as his only girl student, but he quickly put a smile on his face and dared not speak a single word of protest—for Mother was the dictator of Xietuoshan.

After I went through the ceremony of bowing before the picture of Confucius four times and bowing before the teacher twice, I officially became a student.

Our teacher had such poor sight that whenever he taught he had to paste his entire face to the book. Sometimes, if the words were very small (as in books about ethics or books by Mencius), he actually flattened his nose against the page. Most disturbing of all was that he let snot from his nose and spit from his mouth drop onto our pages. In doing this, he dirtied every student's books.

Sometimes when he did this he'd be embarrassed, wipe the book with his sleeve, and make apologies. But none of the students forgave him. We nicknamed him "the dirty blind one."

Inside our classroom he had his bed set up, and we never once saw him make that bed. It had a black coverlet. Often he had such bad body odor that it made a person want to vomit. But only behind his back did we dare accuse him of never taking a bath in his life. In front of him we were afraid to make a sound.

More than forty boy students attended our school. I could not sit with them because I was a girl. Instead, I sat right in front of the teacher. So everything that happened in the classroom each morning had to pass by my eyes and ears—whether it was our teacher reading and pointing at his book or students reciting from memory. Whenever my classmates had not fully prepared their readings and were unable to recite from memory, I prompted them with a few words. For doing this I suffered many scoldings.

In that first year I finished reading eight books of girls' literature and one book of girls' classics. In secret I also read half a book of miscellaneous elementary studies and a book of the analects of Confucius. Unfortunately, I did not entirely understand what these books said, for the teacher never explained them in his lectures.

Our poor-sighted teacher told my mother that I had great talent, but he followed his praise by sighing and saying, "Unfortunately, she is very naughty."

Mother, of course, was not happy to hear him praise me at all. She had hoped that I would cut class or not study hard, so she could use these as excuses to stop me from going to school.

I disliked the poor-sighted teacher more than my classmates did, for, being a girl, I naturally cared more about cleanliness than they did. The boys' books were often smeared with ink stains; mine I had covered with white paper. Inside my books the only marks were the red dots made by the teacher's pen—but nine times out of ten, when he pointed to my book and wanted me to read to him, he dripped spit or snot onto it. Filthy.

"Teacher, first you cure your nose, then teach me, OK?" Once I actually dared say this to him.

"What? What did you say?" He raised his head and roared and frightened me so I almost fell off the bench.

My classmates all looked at me and laughed out loud.

※

THAT WINTER MOTHER received a letter from my oldest brother, who was in Changsha. In the letter he wrote a few words about me:

"Sister Phoenix has unusual talent and great potential. Next spring we could send her to Datong Girls School, where she can study and prepare to take the entrance exam for the Girls Teacher Training School. Recently, the restrictions on women have been lifted: schools for women are sprouting like forests. Our family has a tradition of learning, kind Mother, so I hope you will not refuse my sister just because she is a girl."

I was grateful to my big brother, though I really could not understand why he was so kind to me. Anyway, suddenly my future was bright with hope. I was so happy I couldn't sleep that night. I could only think of going to Datong Girls School as soon as New Year was past.

"When I get there, I will study even harder than I do now, and I will read more books than my brothers"—often I dreamed this.

At this time my father and my younger brothers had not yet returned. My sister was home with her child and all day long she cried and wore a mournful face, for she had hoped to hire a wet nurse but Mother refused to allow it.

One night I was reading a book while Mother was spinning by the stove and my sister was feeding milk to the baby, and suddenly I thought of my brother's letter. I said to Mother very earnestly, "Ma, next spring I must go to Datong Girls School to study."

"Still wanting to study? Girls who have read as many books as you have, have already read enough. You are not a man. What is the use of reading so many books?" She lectured me impatiently and just would not take my words seriously.

"Didn't Big Brother write a letter about sending me to Datong Girls School?" I spoke in a gentler tone.

"What does he know? A girl is controlled by her mother, and you are going to start embroidering next year—not to mention that your feet are still not bound small, and when you are married off and go to your mother-in-law's house they will surely say your mother never trained you."

"Ma, I want to study. Am I not a person like my brothers?"

"What a joke! A person like them? After they study, they can become officials and earn money. You are a girl. You can only be a virtuous wife and a good mother who waits on her in-laws and takes care of the family property. Think again—of what use would study be to *you*?"

At that time I really could not say why I wanted to study. I did not understand the inequality between male and female, and certainly I had no idea what work a woman might eventually do in society after she had completed her schooling. I only felt that I needed to study and acquire knowledge—

just like I needed to eat meals and wear clothes. I could not understand why after a girl is born she can only become someone's wife, bear her husband a son, and suffer the ill treatment of her father- and mother-in-law—which is just what happened to my sister.

Two bean-size tears fell from my eyes. My weak heart was trembling. I could not imagine that Mother would treat me this way. This was the first time in my life that I had seen cruelty in her face.

"Already you are unlike a girl." Mother gave me a sidelong glance and then continued: "You are more fierce than any boy. Everyone in the schoolhouse speaks of your naughtiness. The teacher is strict, but even he does not know what to do with you. What do you expect to do by continuing your education, become a saint?"

From then on I did not dare mention the topic of my schooling. I knew Mother would not do me any favors. I could only wait until Father returned . . . maybe there was still a chance. But no—Father was so afraid of Mother that he listened to her every word. Ugh! So far as studying was concerned, I was completely without hope.

Now the God of Spring came to earth and every living thing grew luxuriantly. Yet as all the rest of the world started moving toward birth, I began to prepare my journey toward death.

First, Father and Grandmother tried to persuade Mother to send me to study for another half-year, but Mother refused and swore she would die first. Then my sister, my sister-in-law, and my aunts begged her, but still she would not agree. When I knew there was no more hope, I decided to commit suicide.

In our village I knew only the following ways of doing it: one, hang yourself by the neck; two, jump into the river; three, eat the heads of matches; four, eat opium; five, swallow rings; six, slash your throat with a sharp knife.

I thought, day after day, about which method I would use to end my life. I came to these conclusions.

First, I thought of the time I had seen Yidi hanging dead by the neck with her tongue sticking out—a tragic and frightening scene. So I did not dare hang myself.

Second, if I jumped into the river, my stomach would blow up like a drum full of water and men would strip off my clothes to draw out the water—so I did not want to do this.

Third, the smell of matchsticks was too foul.

Fourth, I had no way to buy opium.

Fifth, I had no ring, and even if I had one, I would not dare swallow it, for I still remembered the pain from the time when I swallowed the copper coin.

Sixth, if I slashed my throat unsuccessfully, and they saved me, wouldn't it be extremely painful and also a big mess?

So at last I decided I would not eat. I would just lie on my bed and die of hunger—yes, die effortlessly of hunger. I slept for two whole days and everyone in the house thought I was ill. Mother at once asked the doctor to come examine me.

"Not sick," the doctor said. (In fact, he was the poor-sighted teacher.)

My sister noticed that I had not eaten a single thing all day, that I only cried. Many times she came to my bed to comfort me: "Good sister, whatever you want, just tell me and I will do it for you."

"No one can do it for me," I said, shedding more tears.

"Tell me, what's wrong?"

"I . . . I . . . I want to go to school."

After a struggle those words came out. Then my sister cried with me. Lacking milk for her child, she was already desperate, and now my difficult problem had made her even more heartbroken.

Mother deliberately ignored me—almost as if she knew that I refused to eat just because I wanted to study. This only increased my determination to kill myself. If a mother is supposed to love her children more than anything, then why wouldn't she agree to my request when I was but a step from death? I began to doubt Mother's love.

On the third day Mother agreed to my demand. Perhaps she saw that I was obstinate and there was no alternative. But she said two years must pass before she would send me to school. During those two years she would test my temper. If it changed for the better, she would go along with my request—otherwise, she would move my marriage date ahead.

By this ray of hope my fragile little life was saved.

I ENTERED DATONG GIRLS SCHOOL when I was twelve. As I stepped through the school gate I saw so many lively and unaffected girls bouncing balls and jumping rope that I thought I had gone to heaven. I went crazy. My heart was filled with happiness and hope. But one thing pained me deeply: my feet were still bound tightly by bandages.

Actually, I could loosen them, but Mother said that if my feet were not bound, she would not allow me to continue studying. So what could I do? Many girls at the school had tiny feet like mine, and they all suffered the same torture. At first I preferred to put up with the pain, for I wished to study. But when I saw other girls with large feet, and saw that mine were but five inches long, like golden lotus flowers, I could not help feeling ashamed.

Two older classmates, Zufen and Shixian, had natural feet. They used scissors to cut off our foot cloths. In the end I let them burn all my foot bandages. Afterward they came around every day to check whether my feet had returned to normal.

Soon heavy rains fell, filling our school courtyard with pools of water.

I played barefoot in the puddles, just like all the others.

THE SCHOOL HAD two superintendents, both of whom had once lived in Changsha. In those days they were the only village women who had ever so much as set foot in Changsha. Their husbands were dead, and Mrs. Jiang was especially lonesome and pitiable, for she had not even a child to keep her company.

We affectionately called them Teacher Jiang and Teacher Zhou, for they treated us like their own children. Really, they were better than our own mothers. Often they encouraged us to study hard and to not bind our feet.

Life was happy there. We schoolmates were more affectionate and honest with one another than we were with our own families. Whenever questions arose, the little kids asked the big kids, the newcomers asked the old-timers. When we had finished our homework, we all went off together to play on Zhongjia Hill or Sanqi Bridge. All day long this group of worry-free little angels knew only jumping and laughing and never thought of life's pain and sorrow. But those happy and placid days were rocked by a small wave when suddenly Mr. Zhong, the painting and science teacher, resigned—and as a result Teacher Jiang was run out of the school.

The whole thing began like this.

Mr. Zhong was a young man with a temperament gentler than a woman's. He never raised his voice, whether lecturing or conversing. Happy smiles forever floated upon his face. He liked to play with children, and he treated the students like his own brothers and sisters. Students were not afraid of him and looked at him not as a solemn teacher but as a dear friend. Then one day Teacher Jiang suddenly called in all the students of our A class and warned us not to talk too much with this male teacher, Mr. Zhong. She said that our demeanor during his class must be serious, with eyes not wandering east and west. "Mr. Zhong is too young and likes to smile, and he is not a suitable teacher for female students. You are all yellow flower girls and are required to study hard and behave properly.* You are forbidden to be too free and easy."

We all felt that her words were belittling, and soon the entire school was stirred up over what she had said. Within three days the unrest had spread and the entire town was agitated, everything topsy-turvy. But we were only a group of pure and innocent children—how could we know the dark, despotic ways of society?

The next morning we all went to Mr. Zhong's science class, our first class of the day, and we all sat sternly in our seats and scarcely made a sound.

"Do you have your books out?" asked Mr. Zhong, wearing his usual smile.

Not a voice answered him.

But he paid no heed, opening his book. "What kind of corolla does the rape plant have? How many pistils and stamens has it? Minggang!"

He called my name but I did not answer. (This was my school name, chosen by my father.)

"What? You cannot answer? Yongsheng, you answer."

Like me, she did not reply. She just looked at him.

"Have you all become mute? Very strange."

He was now a little angry, yet his face was piled full of smiles.

"Teacher," said Hesheng, standing up bravely. (We all admired her

---

* "Yellow flower girls" means " virgins."—trans.

courage. Our eyes converged on her.) "Teacher, we are not mute. It is because we do not dare to answer you and—"

"Why?" He quickly interrupted her, and the color of his face suddenly changed.

"It is a long story, Teacher," Hesheng said. "But I can briefly tell you, Teacher. It is because Teacher Jiang does not allow us to speak to Teacher. So in order to avoid suspicion we do not even dare to answer your questions. Please forgive us, Teacher."

"Good, then I will resign. I am not qualified to teach you." His face flushed bright red. He immediately picked up his book and walked out in anger.

Teacher Jiang pretended to know nothing. She came and asked us why Mr. Zhong had left before the dismissal bell had been rung.

"You go and ask him," we said in one voice.

So she actually went to the boys' school and asked Mr. Zhong to come and hold class but on one condition: he must not smile at young girls, since people would see him and call it improper.

"Huh? Not smile? Only if I am dead." Mr. Zhong now really exploded. "From the time I was little I liked to smile, and when I grew big I smiled at everything. Even when faced with cats or dogs, with grass or trees or birds or beasts, I would smile. What is so terrible about a smile? It is not a poisonous snake, a vicious animal. . . ."

Mr. Zhong insisted on resigning, which caused the students from the B and C classes to make big trouble. They all said Mr. Zhong's teaching methods were excellent, and they insisted he must stay and teach us. The principal wanted us to send two representatives from each class to ask Mr. Zhong to stay, but beyond that he refused to discuss the matter despite all our arguments. The morning of the third day Mr. Zhong suddenly stepped onto the lecture platform, and we thought perhaps the problem had been solved. Who would have thought he had come to say goodbye?

"Schoolmates, one and all." His voice sounded somber and serious. His expression was unsmiling, face pale, forehead lined with green veins. The classroom was crammed full of our schoolmates—even the sick had crawled out of bed to attend.

"Today is our last conversation, and I have nothing to say. Angry as I am, I find it difficult to say anything at all. My only hope is that you will study diligently and someday find a way to change this bad situation and create a better one. You and males are identical, both human, so why should you suffer and be manipulated by ancient customs? You came to school intending to gain knowledge—but what have you gained? You are not even free to ask questions and converse with a teacher. So much as a single sentence—a single smile—brings intervention. Why is this? You have just been taught a lesson by this school, which I hope you will never forget: you must rebel against ancient customs to gain your freedom. Farewell. I hope you will strive for brilliance and for freedom."

What a pity. As soon as we heard he was leaving, we began to tremble. We could only watch with tearful eyes as he went away. What could we say? Mr. Zhong left us. Our kind, affectionate, dignified, and courteous Mr. Zhong had left us alone, like a garden of peaches and plums suddenly denied the spring breeze. Dear Mr. Zhong, when are you going to return?

Unrest grew. The boys' school quickly became involved and asked Mr. Zhong to return. Soon the principal lost control of the situation. Already we had taken the initiative by refusing to attend classes. Now we demanded that Teacher Jiang restore our reputation by apologizing, and we also demanded that she be discharged. Otherwise, we would all quit school.

Eventually she was forced to leave, using the fake excuse that she was ill.

We unwillingly attended two weeks of classes. Then we all left for home in low spirits. Fortunately, the news of the disturbance at school did not reach my mother's ears. If it had, my future as a student might have been cut short.

FALL ARRIVED, TIME again for school to open. When Mother saw that my small feet had changed into big feet, she scolded me for disobeying her orders and blamed the school for disregarding the reputation of the parents. Of course, from her point of view large feet were terribly disgraceful, especially after she had toiled so energetically to bind my feet so they were five inches small. She absolutely refused to send me away to school, which left me no choice but to beg my father. He already knew that I had received the best marks in the A class, so he allowed me to continue my studies. I changed schools that semester and entered the county's upper-level grade school for girls. There I was the only girl from the Datong township, and because I was not conversant in the local dialect I had hardly a friend in the first two months. I saw other girls laughing and chatting together about everything under the sun, but I dared not break in. After classes I always hid alone in the bedroom, not doing homework but reading *Youth Magazine* and books like *Little Friend* that I had borrowed from the library. I also loved detective novels full of adventures.

One day I noticed my name posted on the bulletin board outside the school office. In small characters beside it was a one-line message asking me to pick up some books. I instantly tore down the note and hurried into the office. With a single glance I saw that the package of books had been mailed from Shanxi by my second brother. I carefully opened the package and found two wrapped, brand-new volumes, one a collection of modern speeches and the other a collection of short stories. I was mad with joy. Whenever I saw schoolmates I foolishly said—whether they listened or not—"My brother sent me some books, posted with many stamps and mailed from Shanxi!"

When I saw the title of one of the books, *Collection of Speeches,* my head began to ache. The very thought of stepping onto a platform to give a speech made my face turn green from fright. Read a book like that? Don't even mention it.

That same night I began reading the short stories. They were so fluently translated by the scholar Hu Shi that I finished half the book in a single breath. "Last Lesson" and "Two Fishermen" moved me the most. I began to feel boundless sympathy and admiration for modern literature. I read this thin collection of short stories three times without stopping, and still I felt unsatisfied—as if the more I read them, the more intrigued I became, and the more unwilling to put them down.

At that time students with good grades in subjects such as composition, drawing, calligraphy, and handicraft had their work exhibited. My calligraphy was ugly and never received an A and not once did it appear on the wall. But often several of my crooked compositions were posted. Father made a special point of buying me books that illustrated Zhou and Yan calligraphy. He wanted me to choose one style or the other and imitate it. But I never opened either book. Once, when I wrote him a letter, he was so upset by my ugly writing that he came across the river just to scold me, saying, "Which kind of calligraphy are you practicing? These words are odd and ugly."

"I . . . I . . ."

"Which calligraphy?"

Father furrowed his eyebrows and raised a hand as if to slap me.

"Minggang calligraphy."

"What?"

"Pa, I am not copying any style of calligraphy. I am writing my own words."

Then he saw that I was teasing, and he began to laugh.

WHEN I FIRST HEARD the news that Mother would allow me to go to Yiyang to continue my studies, I refused to believe it until she told me herself.

"Your big brother is a principal at Yiyang, and your sister-in-law has no wish to come back here. Well, every day you argue about studying. So go to your brother and ask him to give you an education."

I did not know how to thank Mother. I felt she was the best, most considerate, and most loving mother in the world. I had heard that from our house to Yiyang it was more than two hundred miles by water, a voyage of at least four days on even the fastest passenger boat. I would not have dreamed it possible that she would let me go on so long a journey.

Perhaps at my birth the Fates had decided I must be a wanderer, someone who would leave her family without sadness or regret and travel to faraway and unfamiliar places. As I boarded the boat and saw my sister and mother and grandmother crying, I could not help but cry too. Yet my heart instantly lightened when the boat began to move: I silently admired the passing scenery.

On the third day after I arrived at Yiyang, my brother escorted me to the Xinyi Girls School, which was the most complete school in Yiyang, one that offered a grade school, middle school, teacher-training school, and university. All had very good teachers and equipment. The school was run by an old maid from Norway named Anna. More than two thousand students attended. I had already completed the fifth grade, so naturally I wanted to enter the sixth. But I never imagined that a missionary school would give such a stiff entrance exam. The English and math were too difficult for me. The test required using both active and passive tenses in English, whereas I had learned only very simple sentences. And in mathematics I had not studied fractions and ratios. In short, the test results showed I could enter only at the level of fifth grade, second semester.

Being a village girl, and now suddenly living in a four-story foreign-style building, I was almost happier than a beggar who has become a king. The school did not require us to pay tuition and actually gave spending money to poor students. Because my circumstances were relatively good, I paid ten yuan per semester for food. Really, no one is unhappy when studying in a comfortable, cost-free school. The rooms were quiet and spacious, and the air was especially fresh. The Zi River looped around the back of the school, and even when summer was at its hottest, the cooling breeze often blew upon us, making us sway like fairies. When the sun sank in the west and its last red beams began to ripple in the water, we schoolmates would climb up three stories and stand in groups of three or five, shoulder to shoulder, looking afar at the sailboats coming in: fishermen sang cheerful songs, slowly rowing their light boats as they returned. Gentle river breezes, one by one, brought in the thick scent of flowers. Sailboats drifted lightly as seagulls over water, and on the far shore lofty mountain peaks were covered by a thin gray curtain. Here was a painting rich with poetry.

Summer mornings were the most beautiful. Little birds on branches sang morning songs, the river breeze blew over the fresh green willows and gracefully swaying grasses, and the sun climbed out of her deep blue eastern clouds like a young girl coming out of her bath, shy and smiling, moving slowly. In a little while her brilliant rays darted into the river: instantly the water turned blood red. Gradually, the cluster of mountains turned gold to crimson. Ah, what a beautiful sun. Its brilliance was splendid, powerful, filling the sky and the earth and all the world.

I loved to see the sun rise more than anything else, and if it was not raining, I always got up early. I was never disappointed, even if the sun was hidden, for I could breathe the air that had not yet been breathed by others. I exercised with dumbbells every day, and my body became strong as steel.

All my schoolmates treated me very well and liked to play with me. All my teachers said that I was smart. Even when I did not follow the wishes of my Chinese literature teacher, and expressed my dissatisfaction with imperialism in an essay called "The Sun Often Shines on the British Flag," he did not reprimand me. My classmates all playfully called me a sprite because I did not fret about homework. All day long I laughed, played, and skipped like a little sparrow. But no one knew of the deep and heartfelt pain that had pressed on me from the first day I entered school, all because I did not like reading the Bible, neither the Old nor the New Testament.

Because I did not like to pray, I preferred to suffer by hiding in the toilet every morning and evening and at mealtimes. When Teacher Wu realized that I was often late to meals, she called me to the disciplinary office and asked, "Why do you always arrive at every meal later than everyone else?"

"I never hear the bell ring."

"Why not? What are you doing?"

"Reading the Bible."

"Is it true, are you studying so hard? I thought you were the one who didn't like the Bible."

"Why shouldn't it be true? Who said I don't like the Bible? In the past I did not feel any pleasure in the book, but now I feel that God is the world's only savior. I must believe in Him and I must worship Him."

"Don't lie in front of God. From now on you must come and pray at every meal." She smiled and patted my head.

"OK," my mouth replied. But my heart thought: ha-ha, only God knows. . . .

In those childish days my brain was simple and I never debated deep or lofty theories with schoolmates. Yet I often doubted the philosophy that all those who believe in God will be saved. If that were so, why were there so many poor people in ragged clothes attending the service each Sunday? Would they stay poor like this forever, with no food to eat? God was unable to grant them clothing or food or lodging, or cure their illnesses, or even help them find work. I really could not believe that God would be so petty as to punish these poor people, even if they *had* sinned. So I believed that all depends on a person's own efforts, that really a human being is the god who creates the world.

When my brother heard that I did not believe in God and did not attend services, he came at once to give me a warning: "Sister, you should not cause trouble or else the school will expel you. If that happens, I can only send you home. Then don't ever dream of studying again."

That night I could not sleep. If it were true that the school would expel me because I did not want to be baptized, I would have to let them expel me.

MAY SEVENTH, THE tragic day commemorating our national disgrace, had arrived.* Nearly every school, every group, and every organization joined in a parade on this holiday. Two days earlier our school had received a letter from the United Students Association asking us to organize a group and meet on the grounds of the Board of Education at eight o'clock on the morning of the seventh. This letter had been posted for us to read, yet our school had not declared a holiday. Instead, we had classes as usual.

When I heard the school bell ring on the morning of the seventh, I asked a classmate, "Why are we not having a holiday today?"

"What holiday?" She had actually forgotten what day it was.

"You don't even know? It is the day to remember our national disgrace."

"We have never had such a holiday here."

"You mean we are not going to join in the parade?"

"Of course not. We are not allowed to go."

"But we must go!" I almost jumped up.

"We will all go!" came a shout from the entire class. "We want a holiday to commemorate our national disgrace."

At first, two classmates and I were the only ones who went around protesting, but eventually our entire class protested attending classes, and before long the entire grade school responded. When the students in the teacher-training program saw us children causing such a big disturbance, even *they* began to agitate. The first, second, and third grades stopped attending classes, but the fourth grade did not join our protest, just locked its doors and listened to lectures.

In the end, our classes were suspended for the day.

Yet the school still would not allow us to join in the parade. We were not even excused to go home or to go on outings. Our first thought was

---

*The Day of National Shame commemorates the day in 1915 when Japan forced upon China "Twenty-one Demands" for special rights for Japanese in Shandong Province.—trans.

to continue protesting strenuously against our school policy, but the older schoolmates said, "This is the first time ever that classes have been stopped—if you continue to cause trouble, you leaders will be expelled at once."

"Then we will hold a memorial ceremony right at our own school," I said.

To my surprise, more than half my schoolmates agreed with this plan.

Outside, we heard the mingled sounds of beating drums and blowing bugles, together with cries of "Down with Japanese imperialism!" Inside, we wrote slogans on calligraphy papers and wrapped them around chopsticks to make flags. We marched from downstairs to upstairs, shouting slogans just as fanatically and enthusiastically and loudly as the groups of students outside:

"Down with imperialism!"

"Oppose Christianity!"

"Fight for freedom of speech!"

"Join the United Students Association!"

"Swear to wash clean our national disgrace!"

Unfortunately, the principal's spy, Teacher Tang, heard these slogans and reported us. The principal flew into a rage and immediately rang the bell and convened us. She lectured us, calling us disturbing elements who should be struck from the school register.

"What do I fear?" I said to my good friend Jizhen, who was in a lower grade than I. "Let her go ahead and expel me. Is it conceivable that we should turn our backs on our own country?"

"Of course not, we are not afraid of anything."

"I would be willing to let her kill me," I added.

In the end, the power of the massed students was so great that the principal did not dare expel us, yet she did not want to keep us in school, either. To deal with me she contrived a cruel and clever tactic: she sent Teacher Wu to talk to my brother and to convince him to send me home.

Teacher Wu spoke deceptively: "Your sister is too cunning. She specializes in causing trouble at school. This time the disturbance was unspeakable. According to regulations, we must expel her. But you, sir, have a reputation, and we know it is your sister's nature to be clever and energetic—she really is a lovable child. To avoid jeopardizing her future studies, we will not openly expel her. Instead, we ask you to take her home where she can be supervised."

To my big brother this was like hearing thunder in a clear sky. My fate was decided. At twilight that day I departed God's school, rewarded with expulsion only because I loved my country.

I MUST GIVE special thanks to my father and mother. At the request of my second brother and my youngest brother, Mother permitted me to take the entrance test at the First Provincial Girls Teacher Training School, which was in Changsha. This public school provided students with tuition as well as with money for food and books. Each year two students from each village were chosen to attend.

Father even took me to Changsha himself. He was very concerned about me because I had not graduated from grade school. He was certain I would fail the test, especially since there were so many applicants. Luckily, though, I passed.

Because I was coming to middle school (seventh grade) from fifth grade, it was almost impossible for me to catch up in classes other than Chinese literature, history, and geography. Fortunately, I was willing to study diligently, and within two months I no longer had difficulties. My schoolmates were fond of me and protected me; they all became my good friends shortly after I entered the school. Our life was much happier than that of most students, for we had a principal who loved and protected us as if we were his own children.

Principal Xu was a truly extraordinary educator. Because of his influence, schoolmates who were natural bookworms became as lively as little birds in spring. We all called him "grandmother" because he loved us very much and treated us in every way like his own nieces. Yet in certain ways he was very strict: he forbade us to eat hot peppers or to wear tight little vests, and he did not allow us to read books after the private study period in the evening. Often he was still up at one o'clock in the morning, checking every bedroom to see if someone was talking. If a person got up in the middle of the night to go to the lavatory, he would say, "Why are you not asleep? I prefer that you get up early—so don't put off going to sleep."

When it was time for exams we all were afraid of him because no matter which dark corner you stood in, he would shine the flashlight on you and urge you to go to sleep. Many schoolmates did not dare light candles to study. They just stood under lampposts or went into the lavatory to read their books. But Grandmother chased them off every time.

One night I said to him, "Grandmother, it is three o'clock in the morning, so why are you not sleeping?"

"I cannot rest until each one of you has gone to sleep." He pointed urgently to the bedroom, directing me to hurry to bed. But as soon as I entered the door, another classmate came out.

Because Grandmother controlled us so very strictly, we decided to give him trouble. Several other scheming students and I arranged to read novels in different spots around the school, and we made Grandmother chase us from east to west, from west to east until four o'clock in the morning. This time we had purposely disobeyed the school regulations, so everyone involved received a large demerit.

As soon as winter arrived a coal stove was lit in the classroom. Every day the principal reminded us to wear more clothes and not catch cold. In the summer he would open the windows for us so the air would circulate. In those days it was fashionable for students to eat broad beans at school: schoolmates enjoyed strolling together through the school in twos or threes, shelling the broad beans as they walked, until the entire school ground was covered with scattered shells. When Grandmother saw this, he scolded no one. Instead, he quietly bent down and picked up the shells, one by one. Of course, the students were eating with great delight and never imagined that a Grandmother-turned-servant was following behind them, sweeping the ground for them with his hands. He waited until they had walked a long way before he said softly (for fear of startling them), "Throw slightly fewer shells, for my old waist is already in pain from bending."

When they heard Grandmother's voice, they immediately stopped—frightened—and when they turned around they saw that he was holding their discarded shells. Their faces turned red and they could not speak even half a sentence. From then on we did not dare throw broad-bean shells or peanut shells on the ground, and no one dared toss away even a slip of paper. He was an educator who influenced his students by his character and example. How could we not admire and obey him?

On another occasion he found out that two students were misbehaving. One night one of them did not return to school, and although she had been given leave to go home, Grandmother knew where she had gone that night. The next day he called her in for a talk. At first, the student insisted she had gone home. When Grandmother saw that she dared not tell the truth for fear of being dismissed, he immediately changed his tone: "I have been to your home, and your mother said you did not go back there. I know where you were last night. It doesn't matter. Just tell me honestly, why did you go to the hotel? Are you suffering some sort of hardship? Tell me frankly, without reservation. I will forgive you."

The student cried. From the expression on her face Grandmother knew she was a girl to be pitied. Quickly he spoke comforting words and told her she would not be expelled. By and by she began to speak in detail about her family's poverty, and why she walked this path. Grandmother was quick to make her a promise, saying, "I will help your family meet their expenses by giving them twenty yuan each month. Starting today, you only need to study hard in school. I won't allow you to go out and behave recklessly."

He used a similar method to educate the other student. Later on, they both devoted their energy to studying, and their foul reputations—for which they had once been despised by their classmates—were now washed clean.

Because he gave his money to poor students and bought books to donate to the library, Grandmother could never send any of his salary home. He always wore a torn long gown and over his bed he spread a torn coverlet. In the spring of 1926 an army led by someone named Ye surrounded and attacked the school. The soldiers ignored Grandma as though he were a servant. But they took Dean Xia, who wore Western clothes and leather shoes, and beat him till his head broke and bled.

When the semester ended, several students who were older than the rest of us did not have passing marks, but Grandmother did not reprimand them for not studying hard. Instead, he called them in to his office and told them the story of his own schooling.

"It wasn't until I was forty-seven years old that I went to France to study. I had not learned French grammar, or even a single French word, and yet I went and sat in the same class with children who were six or seven years old. We began by learning the alphabet. The children all called me 'old grandfather,' and some of them sat on my lap and played with my beard. But I did not feel the least ashamed. I knew that if I was willing to study hard, my bad memory would not matter. I knew that if I learned just 1 word a day, I would know 365 words in a year. There is no need to worry about your age. Worry only if you don't work hard, or don't make progress."

His daughter had had a failed romance with someone, and she had published a book called *Love's Melancholy*. A perverted class of people who read the book said it was Xu's disgrace to have such a daughter, but he cared nothing at all for what they said. In fact, he replied that his daughter had the revolutionary spirit: "My daughter is very open. She is unlike you who have been injected with the poison of feudal thinking, and who allow your surroundings to manipulate you. What does it matter if she lost her love? Having suffered one defeat, she will be able to find a better lover."

Our school's library could be called the most complete of any in the province's middle schools. It contained a large number of books and in particular it was well stocked with newly published books and newspapers and magazines devoted to scholarship and new ideas. Grandmother often said, "I'd rather not eat for a day than not read for a day, for it is easy to get food but difficult to get good books."

At that time we managed the library ourselves. Each class elected two librarians who took turns doing the work. Luckily, I was elected. I accepted the post without hesitation, for this meant I would be able to read more books.

Best of all I liked reading novels, whether new or old, Chinese or foreign. I did not care what the stories were about—I must find and read them. Among the old novels, I liked *Outlaws of the Marsh* best.* *Dream of the Red Chamber* was a classic, yet it did not catch my interest: I disliked the incessant crying of Lin Daiyu, the main female character, and I disliked even more the empty thoughts of Jia Baoyu, the main male character, who did nothing but fool around with girls all day. I admired every hero described in *Outlaws of the Marsh*. Their bold and heroic spirit influenced me greatly in my decision to join the military in later years.

Shuihu, also translated in English as *The Water Margin* and *All Men Are Brothers*.—trans.

China gave birth to its modern literature at the time of the May Fourth movement, and my favorite books were by writers published by the Creation Society at that time—Guo Moruo, Yu Dafu, and Cheng Fangwu.* As for foreign writers, I loved reading works by Maupassant, Zola, Tolstoy, Dostoyevsky, and Eroshenko. Though Lu Yin and Bing Xin were women writers with long-standing reputations, their works did not impress me as deeply as the works by Bai Wei. Bai Wei had been suppressed by the feudal society, and her *Fighting out of the Ghost Tower* was filled with the spirit of rebellion and struggle. My thoughts were very unsettled in those days and I went through many phases. I also liked reading Oscar Wilde's *Salomé* and Su Manzhu's *The Lone Swan.* I read Goethe's *The Sorrows of Young Werther* five times straight through without stopping. The descriptions in that book were most profound and moving.

Sometimes when I was on duty in the library I became so engrossed in my reading that I paid no attention when schoolmates came in to borrow books. Not until they had shouted and scolded me did I hastily put down what I was reading and make my apologies.

I BEGAN TO WRITE stories in my second year at the First Provincial Girls Teacher Training School, when I had just reached the age of fifteen. One day two old grade-school friends and I went to eat at the home of some people from our native village. These people had just purchased a thirteen-year-old maidservant. The servant girl's face was yellow and streaked with tears, and her body was small and thin. Yet her eyes were so large and dark and sparkling that they made her lovable. I pitied her.

Our hostess was the wife of a division commander. She ordered the girl to walk before us. Then she invited us to criticize the manner in which the

---

*The May Fourth movement was a political, cultural, and literary movement aimed at protesting China's subservient international position and at introducing social values based on the Western concepts of individualism, equality, and democracy. The movement began on May 4, 1919, when students from thirteen area colleges and universities met and demonstrated in Beijing's Tiananmen Square to protest the humiliating terms of the Treaty of Versailles as they related to the rights of Japan in Shandong Province in northeastern China.—trans.

girl carried herself. She asked us to tell her whether we thought the girl was suitable to be a servant in the household of a division commander.

My two schoolmates actually gazed at the girl with critical eyes, but my eyes were on fire at seeing this injustice. I hated our hostess for her inhumanity—she actually treated this girl as if she were an animal. I was so angry I could not eat. I excused myself, saying I had to return to school.

Immediately I wrote an essay that I called "Momentary Impression." Using "Busybody" as a pen name, I mailed it to the editor of the *Dagong News*, Mr. Li Baoyi.

Three days later I walked into the newspaper reading room and chanced to see my own writing. My joy at that moment cannot be described with pen and ink.

"Have you seen today's paper?" I asked a fellow student.

"No. Does it have one of your masterpieces?" She made a face.

"How would I dare to . . . ?"

Like a stream of smoke, I slipped away.

Truthfully, I had very contradictory feelings. On the one hand, I hoped my schoolmates would know I had written the story; on the other, I felt very embarrassed.

Yongsheng scolded me: "You deserve to die for this. How could you write a story about Mrs. Tang's inviting us to look over her maidservant? Aren't you afraid she will be angry?"

"Who cares about her? If she can buy and sell a human, do you mean to say I don't have the freedom to speak? I will never go to her home again."

Yongsheng later became that division commander's mistress.

I never learned what happened to that pitiful little maidservant.

AT THE TIME we did not really know the meaning of the term "homosexual love." Yet it was very strange how all our friends paired up in couples, inseparable whether in action or at rest. When two people met they fell in love. From love they moved to "marriage" (when they slept together they were married).

One day when I returned from visiting my second brother, I saw a letter without postage lying on my bed. The handwriting was elegant and firm.

As soon as I saw it, I knew it was written by a smart girl. I quickly opened it and read it—

Minggang, you whom I admire and love,

Please forgive me for taking the liberty of addressing you in this way. This is a letter which has been written for a long time, but I have not dared to give it to you until now. I cannot suppress it any longer, so I must bring it to you personally, without fear. I hope you are not home because it will be embarrassing if I have to give it to you in person.

Your friend and my classmate, Luo, introduced your writing to me the first day I came to school. What beautiful words! I was intoxicated to the point of delirium. From that day onward I grew to know you, but you only gave me a smile and walked away. Minggang, please forgive my second intrusion. I have often chased your shadow. I have often wanted to talk with you, to be near you. Would you be willing to accept this innocent child as your friend, at some level? I wait here earnestly for your reply.

With admiration,
Love, Kun

This was the first time in my life that I had received such a letter. Naturally, I was surprised and flattered. Yet I did not feel happy, for I knew that here was trouble. I humbly answered her, saying in my letter that we could have a *literary* relationship. So we did not converse much, but we wrote to each other frequently. Many of her writings were published in the school monthly, and I liked her because she was a richly talented writer and she studied very hard. Still, I did not wish to talk to her much, though this was unfair to her. She spoke with the nasal accent of our county, which sounded like *nahn-nahn*, and I honestly did not like hearing it.

Just when everyone was ridiculing me for having a literary friend, a new wave of misfortune rolled in. In the fifteenth class were actually two classmates who loved me. One was Miss Dan Xiuxia, who loved me single-mindedly and who had written many poems to me and burned them. The other was Miss Chen. She loved me even more deeply than Dan, and in her composition notebook she boldly wrote poetry telling her thoughts of me, and she told others how adorable I was. Of course, this became new material for conversation among her classmates. Then one evening several classmates acted like bandits and dragged me to Chen's room.

Honestly, I had never dreamed that such a thing could happen to an honest person like me—though it was a common trick they played whenever the bell for bed had rung.

"What? What are you doing?" I cried loudly, surprised.

"Please join in the fun," answered a classmate whom I did not know.

"Please sleep here tonight," said a girl named Li, her face a little red. She looked at me earnestly and then dropped her gaze to Chen's face. Chen lowered her head shyly and wriggled uneasily, like a new bride seeing her groom at her wedding night. Her cheeks were as red as blood. She quickly turned her back to me.

"This is not my room," I answered in a rough voice, for I meant to bully them and frighten them. "Why must I sleep here?"

"This room is the same as your room."

"What are you saying?"

"Because Chen's bed is your bed! Ha! Ha! Ha!" They began to take my shoes off.

"You see how Miss Chen loves you. Her eyes are always nailed on you."

"Why does Miss Chen love me like this?" I asked stubbornly, not caring that Chen would be angry when she heard me. "I don't even know her."

"But she knows you and loves you," said someone, with a laugh. "Who knows how many dreams of longing she has had!"

"Go to hell!" I heard Chen say. She must have been very angry because of my outburst.

"Don't be angry. We'll leave you two in peace so you can talk about love."

As they were leaving they held me down on the bed and took off my shoes. (This was the only way they could handle someone whom they had dragged in.) *Ping!* They hooked the door.

What am I going to do? I can only jump out the window . . . I pondered my predicament silently, sitting on the edge of the bed feeling terrible. I didn't know what to do.

Suddenly the light went off.

Four others were in the same room. They were quietly listening to see whether we were talking; occasionally I could hear light sounds of laughter. "Have courage to speak of love, Miss Chen. We won't eavesdrop."

"Go ahead and talk, I don't have anything to say," I said. I remained sitting, like an idiot, for half an hour after Chen had gone to bed. And then I lay down.

I was truly scared, as if sleeping in a tiger's den. I scarcely dared breathe. I leaned against the side of the bed. Didn't dare use the bed cover. My entire body was icy cold.

How am I going to pass the night? I must jump out of the window, or else! Otherwise, I will certainly lose sleep and tomorrow morning I must take a test in biology, for which I have not prepared. . . .

Thinking this, I wanted to jump out the window right away. But I was afraid they would chase me and also afraid I would fall. Besides, I did not have shoes. I would not have minded sacrificing my socks, but mostly I feared the fall. The window was far above ground, and jumping seemed dangerous.

"Ahh," I sighed lightly, still not daring to turn over. I heard the sound of the third gong.* Heavens! How am I going to last this long and endless night?

Chen couldn't sleep either. I heard her breathe and realized her head was next to mine—but we were back to back, a foot between us. We didn't speak a word.

I didn't dare open my eyes. It seemed to me that her face was covered with tears. I thought I heard her sob. I was too ungrateful to her. She loved me so much, longed for me, yet I treated her coldly and did not even look at her. I had insulted her for no reason, but what else could I do? I entirely disagreed with the idea of dragging friends around—not to mention that I had no feelings for her.

I now appreciated the pain of people who sleep together with a spouse they do not love. I thought, "Yes, aren't they just like me at this moment?" I actually treated Chen like my enemy, feared her and hated her. "If it were not for this episode, perhaps we could have become friends, slowly. But they dragged me in here and because of that I have no feeling for you whatsoever." I felt like saying this to her but I didn't have courage to open my

---

*The third gong sounded at 11 P.M.—trans.

mouth. By chance it was raining that night. I never completely closed my eyes. When I heard the *shhhi-li shhhi-li* sound of the rain, my heart felt even sadder. Several times I thought of drumming up my courage to ask her, "Have you slept?" Or to comfort her by saying, "I am very sorry." But, I don't know why, I couldn't make a sound. After the six o'clock wake-up bell sounded, someone came to give me my shoes.

"You must have spent the whole night talking of love," Miss Li said. She looked at us with a seductive smile.

"Thank you for ruining my whole night's sleep," I said resentfully—and then I slipped away.

From then on, I did not dare to walk past that door. When I went to the toilet, I always made a big circle. Whenever I met Chen on the exercise field or in the food hall, we both involuntarily lowered our heads. She would walk shyly by, as if she were avoiding her fiancé. And though I did not behave as she did, I felt uncomfortable.

"NOW THAT WE have invited the translator, Mr. Li Qingya, to teach literature, I hope you will work particularly hard at your literary studies. I think you all know that Mr. Li has translated stories by Maupassant. . . ."

After the director of studies made this introduction, we all showed sincere respect as we welcomed the newly arrived Mr. Li to our school.

The director of studies had separated humanities and science into two divisions, and we were grateful to him for paying special attention to hiring a teacher of Chinese literature. We already had another teacher who was quite good, Mr. Zhou Dongyuan, but he was responsible for too many classes. So Mr. Li was specially engaged, and we all hoped he would prove a good teacher. Even students who normally did not care for literature had decided to work hard in his class.

I was particularly enthusiastic and decided to be very daring in the practice of novel writing, for I was dead certain that Mr. Li would not only correct my work but do his utmost to guide me in all the intricacies of novel construction, including content, structure, technique, and word choice. For my first composition I wrote—with the greatest of ease—a novelette of more than ten thousand words. I called it "First Love." I asked Mr. Li to correct it. Who could have guessed that two months later my roll of paper would still be sleeping in his drawer, its pages unturned? He never did return my novelette. Several times I asked him for it. Then I realized he was the sort of person who is capable but busy. Mr. Li was responsible for teaching classes at four schools. Every day his hired ricksha raced *ding-dong, ding-dong* through the streets. When he returned home and was surrounded by his children, he held congenial conversations with his family—on top of which Mr. Li was busy doing translations. Naturally, he did not have time to correct my crooked sentences.

"Mr. Li, have you still not corrected my paper?"

"To be honest, I haven't had time. I really am very sorry." He answered quite pleasantly.

"Then I don't need to write any more?"

"Well, of course I could correct a paper of a few hundred words. Otherwise, please excuse me for not obliging."

"What will I do? I don't know why, but I have always liked to write long essays. Without realizing it, I frequently write several thousand words as soon as my pen touches the paper."

"The length of an essay does not count, only the brilliance."

"But how does one attain brilliance? Teacher, can you tell me?"

"Practice slowly. After you have written an essay, make corrections on it constantly. This will lead to brilliance."

After we had this conversation in his home, I felt distraught, and when I returned to school I felt listless, lamenting to myself, "Why can't I meet a teacher like Flaubert? I haven't the talent of Maupassant, but must Fate always follow Talent?"

Mr. Li gave us a lecture on Flaubert's *Madame Bovary*. In the beginning we listened with concentration, but later we all felt our interest flagging. We had hoped he would speak of literary theories, of novel-writing techniques, of literary trends, but we were totally disappointed. Of course, how could we blame him? Amid his numerous duties, how could he pay attention to the requests of us children?

"What? Your composition received a zero?" Semester exams were over, and my good friend Huang Shukun ran in alarm to tell me this news—news that surprised me very much, and stupefied almost the entire class.

"You have already seen the marks for the semester?"

"I saw only the results for Chinese literature. We were picking up our mail at the registrar's office just now, and it happened that Mister Li's messenger was bringing in the grades. And we stole a glance."

"There is no reason for this—how could he give me a zero? Didn't I turn in a book of compositions? Hah! I will go and negotiate with him."

I felt disgraced and angry. Really, zero is such a shameful thing.

Shukun waited a bit before continuing. "There is something else you don't know. You will die from anger when you find out."

"What? You speak up! Even if I got zero in all my classes, I won't die of anger. I didn't come here to study for grades."

"The research paper you wrote for Miss Wang in a quarter of an hour received eighty-five points. It was the only paper she turned in this semester."

"So what? Ha! Doesn't that mean *I* have eighty-five points? So why did you say I have zero?"

Then she too laughed.

STUDENTS FROM EVERY SCHOOL in Changsha lined up to join the parade on the day after the tragic incident of "June First."* All were petitioning the provincial government to arrest the criminals involved in the incident, to eliminate the twenty-one articles, and to compensate the families of the dead. With piercing shouts we screamed the slogan "Pay back life!" and we held our banners high and shouted "Down with imperialism!" While the rest of us waited outside the government office, representatives from each school went in to petition the provincial governor. Ten minutes later we heard loud shouts and cries inside, and then we learned that all the representatives were being put in jail. Everyone started crowding into the building. More than a hundred people were arrested and locked up in the jail

---

*On May 30, 1925, British forces in the Shanghai International Settlement fired on students and workers who were protesting against militarism and foreign imperialism, and who were demanding the release of six Chinese students held by the British. Eleven protesters were killed and twenty were wounded. Outrage quickly spread throughout China. In many other cities demonstrations were held in support of the May Thirtieth Martyrs. Xie Bingying refers to it as the "June First" incident, perhaps because that was when the demonstration of support was held in Changsha.—trans.

guards' room, because the jail was full. In the end, even the jail's exercise field was filled with students who had been arrested. The military police were stern, but no one in the crowd outside was frightened; on the contrary, everyone rushed forward. Realizing the situation was getting ugly, a secretary of the provincial government came out and said to the crowd, "We are keeping the representatives here because we need to discuss many matters. Those of you who are not representatives should quickly return to your schools. Important national matters are, naturally, our responsibility. You need only work hard at your studies."

"Release the representatives! Release our arrested schoolmates!"

We refused to return to our schools until we had achieved our goal. This made it difficult for the secretary, who was forced to release one hundred or so students while still keeping the representatives locked inside. It was nine o'clock in the evening before we returned to school.

Early the next morning we formed propaganda groups to go out and give speeches to the public. All day we searched for crowds on big streets and in small lanes, telling them of the cruelty of the imperialists, telling them how to resist. Our stirring, public-spirited speeches filled the crowds with anger, and sometimes as we spoke our tears fell unconsciously, and the crowd would join us in crying. More and more people would join the throng to listen to us, and even after speaking continually for several hours, we felt no fatigue.

The tragedy of June First was like a bomb. It awoke countless hot-blooded young men and women. What is more, it awoke muddle-headed me, who until then had only known how to hide in the library every day to read *The Sorrows of Young Werther*.

Yes, a dangerous moment in my life. Had it not been for the second bombardment of 1926, which startled and awakened me, I might have become Werther number two.*

---

*At the end of *The Sorrows of Young Werther*, the novel that made Johann Wolfgang von Goethe famous in 1774, the hero shoots himself in despair over unrequited love. Most of Goethe's novel is written as a series of letters. These letters are dated but have neither salutations nor closings, and consequently they look very much like diary entries. Xie Bingying imitates Goethe's form and style in the diary passages that follow.—trans.

DIARY FRAGMENTS.

SEPTEMBER 7, 1926, 2 P.M.

I am too self-tortured and frustrated. Why do I have only his shadow on my mind? My eyes see nothing but his smile, my ears hear only his voice. I pretend that letters from others are from him. I read them again and again. He fills my whole heart. How can this be good for me? I don't want to think anything, do anything. At class time or mealtime, sitting or sleeping, always I think of him. I hear not a single phrase when listening to a lecture, comprehend not a single word when reading a book. I can't do anything but quietly sit and think of him.

SEPTEMBER 15, 1926

Love? I do not know. Except for Father's and Mother's love, I have not tasted its flavor. I don't know if it is bitter or sweet, sour or spicy. I know only that toward him I have created a mysterious affection.

When first we met, his glance and mine for an instant touched. He easily sowed love seeds in my heart. My soul was attracted to his like iron to a magnet. Before that moment I was an innocent, unaffected child. Whenever schoolmates spoke of love, I ran off, saying, "Pooh!" When they said that I was but a child, unwise in the ways of the world, I replied that I hoped I would never be wise in the world's ways. But now, this sudden nameless suffering has overwhelmed me. What is happening?

I wish to kill myself. I can't understand why the shadowy image of a smiling youth stands ever before my eyes, preventing me from studying in peace, filling me with worry, robbing all life's sweetness. I hate him, hate also my third brother, who introduced us. Often I am awakened in the middle of the night by a bleak and frightening dream, and then I slap my head hard and scold myself: you useless thing, die quickly! His shadow, like a whirlwind, will sweep away your future—like a savage animal will swallow your life. Intellect? Emotion will still prevail. The shadowy image fails to fade, day by day looms larger in my brain.

I refuse to let him know how I feel about him, how I long for his affection. Each day I only write of my affection in my diary and poems. Sometimes I secretly drink wine till I am drunk. Sometimes I consider inviting several female friends to live with me and to study religion in an ancient temple, deep in the mountains. None of them knows my secret. Divine first love! How pure and unforgettable!

❧

SUDDENLY, THE ALARM CLOCK of that era rang: the Northern Expedition of 1926 exploded in our ears.* Brave young men and women one by one discarded their books, shed their long gowns, and joined the revolution. I, who had sunk in a swamp of love, was suddenly freed.

❊

ONE DAY HE appeared before me, face to face. His eyes filled with passion as he stared. "Have you received my letters? I wanted to find an opportunity to talk with you privately." His gentle voice was full of hope.

"Do you believe it? I am joining the military." My smile mingled with seriousness.

He looked surprised. "I don't believe it, are you joking?"

"No. It's true."

"But you won't be able to stand that hard life."

"I will train."

A gloomy, worried expression replaced his smile. "Have you really made up your mind?"

"I've already signed up."

"But first think, then decide—I want to speak with you about this in detail."

"There is nothing to consider. You should be totally in favor of my going."

He lowered his head in contemplation.

I knew that unspeakable pain pressed his heart, but strangely enough I felt not the least upset. I felt, instead, like a prisoner who had been condemned to die and who has been given a special pardon. Proudly, I smiled at him.

"Tomorrow I will go home." His voice touched me like a sad song. "Tell me, will we see each other again?"

---

*By the 1920s, China was so thoroughly dominated by warlords and foreign powers that many people feared it might cease to exist as a nation. In an effort to unify China, Sun Yat-sen's Nationalist Party, the Guomindang, joined forces with the Chinese Communist Party, which was supported by the Soviet Union. The two parties had very different long-range goals, but they agreed that the first step in implementing any political agenda was to eliminate the warlords who controlled

Suddenly I felt cold and lonely. "We will meet at the front. I hope you will join the army too."

He did not answer. His eyes were glittering and wet. So this was farewell. Without another word I saw him to the school gate. When I returned, my eyes were filled with hot tears.

---

much of China at that time. The Northern Expedition was their joint military effort aimed at doing this.

In June 1926 Chiang Kai-shek became commander in chief of the hybrid forces comprising the Northern Expedition. In August, Chiang's army successfully defeated the warlord general Wu Peifu in the tri-city area of Wuhan. Hanyang fell first, then Hankou, and then Wuchang. In late 1926 and the early months of 1927 Xie Bingying attended military school in Wuhan. In the spring of 1927 she marched away to war for the first time in her life.

The alliance of the Guomindang and the Chinese Communist Party was edgy, fraught with danger, and not destined to last long. The Guomindang was supported by the moneyed classes, while the Chinese Communist Party sought to put power in the hands of the people. Xie Bingying was often caught between these opposing and very uncertain political currents. As political power shifted this way and that, she frequently found herself persecuted for beliefs and activities that, a little earlier, people had praised.—trans.

PART 3 War

AS LONG AS I LIVE I'LL NEVER FORGET MY SECOND BROTHER, FOR IT was through his strength that I succeeded in becoming a soldier.

During the summer recess in 1926 I accompanied him to Yuelu Hill, where he went to convalesce from his tuberculosis. My mind was still overwhelmed by that smiling image of love, my spirits were drained, and all day long I scarcely spoke a sentence. I spent my time reading *Peony Pavilion*, *The Swallow Letter*, *Western Chamber*, *Story of the Lute*, and all sorts of silly books like that, and this made my brother so angry that one day he finally wrote Father a letter telling him of my behavior. He also scolded me so severely that even today his words burn in my brain: "Women are truly useless. The alarm bell for the era has rung, and yet here you are, still snoring in your dreams. All these books tell the same tale of dissipated scholars and beautiful women—you should have stopped reading such stuff long ago, and dumped it all. You are an intelligent young woman and very fond of modern literature—so why don't you read writings about revolution?"

He began to give me books about the ABCs of Communism and the basics of socialism, and other volumes about social sciences and revolutionary theory. As my interest in these books grew more intense, that love image in my mind began to slowly fade. Also, the subject of my writing changed. I had many opportunities to be in close contact with farmers in the village, and I began to write essays about their lives and their sufferings. Some of these were published in the *Popular Daily News,* of which my youngest brother was chief editor. Sometimes he corrected a few words for me. Other times not a single word was altered. My second brother said my writing was improving from essay to essay, and this made me extremely happy.

One morning, on the day before I was scheduled to take the entrance test at the military school, I met with my second and youngest brothers in the dormitory of the Mingde Middle School. We discussed the question of whether I should become a soldier.

"I am opposed to her going into the military," was my youngest brother's comment. "Military life is dry and mechanical, all absolute obedience, day after day—'stand at attention,' 'stand at ease.' Her brains will become slow and simple. Soldiering is hardly suitable for a person with literary talent— not to mention that she may not be strong enough to stand that sort of physical hardship."

"You are quite wrong," replied my second brother. "If she wants to create uncommon literature that is full of blood and energy, then she must live an uncommon life. Becoming a soldier is a good way to do that—a way to train her body, to nurture her thinking, and to supply her with material for her literary efforts. There would be only advantage, no harm whatever."

Naturally, his view was correct. My youngest brother did not argue. He was forced to abandon his view.

Anyway, I knew I had to go—even if they all opposed me. For otherwise, Mother would have forced me to get married that winter. To escape that fate I had to get away from Changsha. But where should I go? I was a child, not yet twenty, with not even half a coin in hand. Where could I head to?

My second brother was especially sympathetic, for he had suffered greatly from the pain inflicted by his arranged marriage. He strongly urged me to become a soldier. "This is the only way to free yourself," he said. "Only by joining the revolution will you solve your marriage problem and your problem of finding a future."

I believe that what motivated nine out of ten of my female schoolmates to become soldiers, in those days, was their wish to escape the pressure of their feudal families and to search for their own futures. Yet as soon as we had put on our uniforms and were holding guns and clubs, our motives changed. For who would not wish, in such a moment, to shoulder the burden of the people's revolution, to build a rich and strong Republic of China?

Without letting our families or schools know, we female students went secretly to take the test at the military school. Those of us who passed it had dancing faces. Our ecstasy could not be described in words.

I REMEMBER IT was an afternoon of pouring rain as 250 of us bold youths, both male and female, gathered at Changsha's East Station to await the train that would carry us away. Many old ladies and young girls came to send us off. Secretly they all wiped away tears with their handkerchieves, but we were not in the least sad. Chubby little Shurong told them, "You shouldn't cry. You should encourage us to dash ahead with bayonets and kill the enemy."

Just at that moment a young man all soaked by the heavy rain ran breathlessly up to me. To my surprise, he handed me a thick pink letter. He was a friend I had not known very long, an editor for the *Spark* magazine. I did not open his letter, not even after we had reached Wuchang, though I knew this was quite unfair of me.* Ever since the day I had determined to obliterate from my mind a certain beloved image, I had vowed that if ever again someone offered me his passion, I would smother it with ice water.

Fifty of us women crowded together in one boxcar with no place to sit. We used our suitcases as seats, as if we were refugees. The boxcar, which was built for hauling horses and freight, had two iron doors but not even one small window. We were suffering considerably from being caged in the dark, so we opened our throats and began to sing very loudly.

And as soon as we began to sing, the male students also took up our song. What commotion! We wanted to celebrate the beginning of a new life, a

---

*Wuchang, one of the three cities of the Wuhan tri-city area, is about 180 miles north of Changsha as the crow flies. The Central Military and Political School, which Xie Bingying hoped to attend, was located in Wuhan.—trans.

bright and splendid future. Everyone laughed like crazy, sang in high voices, leaped with joy. . . .

AT PERHAPS FIVE O'CLOCK in the afternoon the train stopped at a station without a name.

Shurong and I jumped off in a great hurry and ran toward the village. Many people stared at us in surprise, but no one intervened or tried to stop us.

We had courage enough to become soldiers, but we dared not ask where the toilet was. How utterly disgraceful that we lacked even the simplest knowledge of the world. What fools. It was our first train journey, but why were we so timid?

Three or four hundred feet from the station we used a toilet in someone's house. We hurried back outside but the train had vanished. Frantically—crazily—we ran onto the tracks to chase it. Our four eyes stared straight ahead. Our toes smacked rocks and our heels banged rails. Short and chubby Shurong fell down, barely managed to get up. After another couple steps she fell again. Kept falling. Pitiful! Can there really be idiots in this world who don't know they can't run as fast as a train?

"We can't catch it, let's go back," I said, disappointed.

We had no idea how far we had run. Already the station was out of sight. Dark and gloomy woods stood thick on either side of us. Not a house, not a person to be seen. Quickly we turned and headed back along the tracks the way we'd come. We were a little frightened, also disappointed, and blamed ourselves for being so foolish.

"Stupid pigs." Shurong was nearly in tears from anxiety. "Really, two stupid pigs."

"I am just a village fool," I said. "I have never ridden a train. But you are from Liling. So why didn't *you* know the train had no toilets, and how long it would stop at each station?"

My questions made her even more distressed. "It's really like bumping into a ghost," she said, "two village fools stumbling into each other—am I not just like you?"

Our spirits were crushed.

We went back to the house where we had just said our numerous thank-yous, and there the middle-aged woman remarked (in a tone that suggested she took pleasure in our predicament)—"Well, the train has left, so what are you going to do?"

"Wait for the next."

"Oh? Then, don't just stand there. Get back to the station."

Feeling tremendous gratitude for her advice, we instantly headed back toward the tracks, running just as we did when chasing the train, feeling like children lost in deep mountains who have suddenly seen a guiding star that seems to show them the way.

But at the station we waited an hour, two hours. Still no light of the Changsha train. Now earth was plunged in blackness. Again, we were frightened. Where could we sleep this night, two village maidens with empty pockets? Who would take us in? Many peddlers kidnap young women and sell them—what if we met such a person?

I thought I glimpsed a shadow rushing toward us with open arms. I drew back and said, with shaking voice, "Shurong, let's get out of here."

We held hands tightly and groped our way through darkness to another village.

"Lady shopkeeper, please open up."

Through a crack in the door we could see people eating by an oil lamp. We knocked lightly.

From inside came a voice, "Who's there? Don't stand at our door."

This cold, cruel, and severe voice had already smothered our considerable courage. My two legs suddenly went soft and couldn't move. "Let's try another house," I whispered.

Shurong said softly, "Lady shopkeeper, pity us. Please open the door."

Now came a voice from another house nearby: "Go somewhere else—we do not have food or money here." It was the voice of an old lady, a gentle voice.

"Granny, we are not beggars. We are girl students, just now dropped off the train."

Two men from some other house heard our voices and called in a leering manner, "Come to us!"

We immediately turned our backs on them and avoided their gaze, as if we had encountered a tiger. The two disgusting villains followed close behind us as we hurried to the door of another house to beg for help. This time we found our salvation. An old woman heard our voices and quickly opened the door—though her expression faltered when she saw us, and she suddenly looked very unhappy. The reason? Her daughter-in-law was about to give birth and, according to superstition, if a male entered the house at this moment, the new child would be a boy.

"Granny, may we stay the night here? We were unable to catch up with the train."

"No, we are busy and can't keep you. My daughter-in-law is giving birth. Go find another place."

"It is late; we don't know the road. Dogs will bite us. We have no idea where to go. Please tell us, Granny."

Perhaps she pitied us. Or maybe she just feared we would not leave her alone. In any case, she guided us to a store run by a widow and her daughter.

Many villagers gathered to gawk, as if we were two strange creatures dropped from the sky. The widow took us in. She was very courteous and treated us most affectionately. When we had eaten her excellent meal and were full, she put bedclothes on top of two counters so we could sleep. I was slightly relieved that we were sharing the room with both mother and daughter.

But we couldn't sleep, just talked the entire night until the sky was light.

Early in the morning I gave our hostess the only yuan in my pocket. Then, still acting like a couple of village fools, we timidly walked to the foreign-style building next to the railroad tracks. A man wearing dark glasses came out of his office and asked us, "Are you the students who were on your way to take an exam at the Central Military and Political School? Are you the ones who came on the train from Changsha yesterday afternoon, at two o'clock, and got off here?"

"Yes—but how did you know?"

"Well, why didn't you report here earlier? Every station along the line has been sending telegrams to ask about you two—and now people have been dispatched to come and find you. Go quickly and wait for the train. Don't be late. The Changsha express will be arriving soon."

Only then did we breathe easier. We kept bowing to him at a ninety-degree angle. But he didn't even notice. Already he had hurried off to send a telegram.

Soon we were jumping on the train. We spotted our schoolmate, Li, and we shouted happily, "What! You are here too?"

"Deputy Qiu sent me to find you. He said you are such excellent students that we cannot afford to lose you."

Shurong and I laughed until our guts hurt. Who would have thought that we two supposedly excellent students could also be such stupid and pathetic village fools?

IT SEEMS LAUGHABLE and unbelievable: I was expelled from the military school before I had so much as crossed through its gate.

The recruiting committee was supposed to accept only one hundred males and twenty females, but more than three thousand students took the exam and most passed it with high grades. So the applicants asked for the quota to be increased, and the committee finally agreed to accept two hundred males and fifty females as students. When we arrived at Wuchang, however, we were told that orders had just come down from the top stating that the specific purpose of this recruitment was to train talented people to be revolutionary leaders in each province, and this meant each province must have the same number of candidates in the program. Too many had been accepted from Hunan, so the number had to be cut back by about two-thirds—to just eighty males and twenty females. The committee decided to make the cut by giving a second exam.

When this news reached our ears we all felt stricken with despair, as if a death sentence had been proclaimed. Our brilliant future again seemed obscure.

"No, we absolutely refuse to be screened, and we demand that the entire group enter the school." A male schoolmate said this, and everyone followed his lead, saying, "We oppose a second exam. We want everyone to enter the school, unconditionally."

Big Sister Tie and a male schoolmate named Li gave the most stirring speeches. Big Sister Tie stood up from the crowd to thunderous applause and addressed us in a loud, hoarse voice:

"Fellow students, dear sisters! We came here to become soldiers after having committed ourselves to making this sacrifice. We escaped from our families in order to offer ourselves to the revolution. Our goal is to save the suffering people—and our suffering selves. The very fact that we female students are entering the military is an unprecedented example of breaking away from Chinese tradition.

"If the government now looks upon males and females as equals, and gives us the opportunity to devote our lives to our country and our people, then it will be a blessing for us as women as well as a glory for the entire human race. But now, just when everyone is exhilarated at this prospect, we suddenly receive news that there will be a reduction by 150 names. This greatly distresses us. Fellow students, let us consider. If in fact we are sent back home, what will we do? Our families won't recognize us as daughters, and our schools won't accept us as students. Where will we go?

"All of us have the revolutionary spirit, all of us have decided to sacrifice ourselves—and now is there suddenly no opportunity for us, no place for us? The revolution can only move forward. There can be no retreat. We are not willing to turn back—everyone must enter the military school."

These steely sentences roused every heart. All of us were opposed to taking another exam. We demanded that the entire student body be allowed to enter the school, unconditionally. Within five minutes we formed a committee to oppose a second exam. That afternoon the entire student body lined up and crossed the river to submit our petition to Secretary Tang of the Hankou military committee. The main body of our group stood outside while ten selected to serve as representatives went in to hand over the petition. We promptly received a satisfying and hopeful answer. He said that he would immediately send a telegram to Nanjing to ask for instructions. He also agreed to help us as best he could, so that we might all have an opportunity to join the revolution.

Three days passed. Still we heard no news. But on the morning of the fourth day a male schoolmate ran breathlessly to Gaosheng Inn, where we female students were staying. He said, "Not good, not good—all the students from Hunan must go to take the second exam. Those who don't will not be allowed to enter the school. Also, a notice has been posted announcing that the ten representatives have been expelled."

"What? The representatives are expelled? Then . . . I . . ." This was like hearing a thunderclap in the middle of the night. I was shocked speechless. I knew perfectly well that to have been selected as a representative, and to have acted for the benefit of everyone, had not been a reckless gesture—and that I would never regret sacrificing myself—yet my heart was filled with inexplicable sadness.

On the following day the newspaper published a story telling of the expulsion of the student representatives and announcing that the exam had been rescheduled for students from Hunan. I felt even more heartbroken when I saw my name in print. It seemed to me that if I now could not become a soldier, I would surely never find another future into which to escape.

My second brother read the news of my expulsion and became very anxious for me. He comforted me and then went to talk with the dean of the military school. But the dean's only response was, "No way. The order came down and I cannot retract it."

My brother kept insisting, "My sister is really a brave child, and she has no hope for a future unless she joins the revolution. Kindly think of some way to accept her."

"It is just not possible. Send her, instead, to take the test to get into the class in political training."

Nothing could be done. My brother was met with utter refusal. He had no choice but to leave.

The military committee was aware that the second exam to get into the military school had to weed out more than a hundred students from Hunan, yet the committee felt it would be a shame to dismiss us and force us to return home. To accommodate these future unnamed heroes, they opened the eight-month political-training class in Hankou. Big Sister Tie and the eight male representatives who had been expelled, plus those schoolmates who were not selected for the military school, went to take the test for the class, but I still lay in bed, fretting and feeling depressed, and awaiting news from my brother.

"Sister, I know a way!" my second brother cried, leaping with joy. "The large group of students from the North has not yet taken their exam—quickly, change your name and claim a new native province, and report to take the test."

Here was a rare and dangerous opportunity. If ever the school found out, I would surely be made to suffer. But so strong were my hopes for the future, and so ardent my desire to enter the military, that I could not have cared less.

I picked up the application form and sneaked off to register. I wrote down *Xie Bingying* in the space for my name, and *Beijing* as my native place.

"Why didn't you bring your school certificate?" the clerk in the military uniform asked sternly.

"I don't have it. Perhaps it will be here in two days. Our certificates of attendance are in the hands of a leader who will be arriving the day after tomorrow." I hoped I would get by this difficult barrier in peace.

Now another clerk, standing in front of me and watching me fill in the form, said, "You are from Beijing? Why do you speak the Hunan dialect?"

"Yes, I am from Beijing. I speak the Hunan dialect because I followed my father to Hunan when I was young and I grew up there."

"You are not one of those representatives who were expelled?" He stared at me like a detective.

"What are you saying? I don't understand." My manner was calm but I could not keep my heart from jumping.

Suddenly, just as my situation was becoming difficult, a big crowd of applicants arrived and the clerks no longer had time to continue questioning me. Luckily.

All my schoolmates from Hunan knew that I had falsified my native place and was taking the test a second time, but they were sympathetic. The school never learned a thing. On the day of the test more than a thousand young men and women from the North all crowded toward the examination hall; I sneaked in among them. The only sound I heard was the northern accent made with a curled tongue; I felt like I had arrived in Beijing. Nearly all the men and women were tall, with coarse dark skin that glowed with health and beauty. Their faces were full of friendly smiles, and my first impression of them was that they were earnest and sincere.

My character is like that of northerners, I thought. Except for the fact that I am short and small and that my skin is too white—and that my speech is different—I could easily pass as a northerner.

During the two-day exam I was always the first to turn in my papers, and I could not tell whether this was because I was answering too carelessly or because the questions were too easy. Each time I turned in my paper, a few proctors noticed me, swerving their eyes toward me as if on cue. At those moments I feared they might discover my secret. My heart felt as frightened and flighty as if it were hanging in the sky.

"Congratulations, you tested number one on the exam."

When Mr. Wang happily told me this news, I simply could not believe him. I feared he must be playing a joke on me—perhaps he meant exactly the reverse of number one.

With a happy and frightened heart I flew to the place where the results were posted, the Academy of Hunan and Hubei. I raised my head and, sure enough, I saw my name at the very top. From the depths of my heart rose a victorious smile.

Trooper, warrior! In a few days I would be starting the life of a soldier. What joy! On the way back I talked to myself, all smiles.

That evening my second brother invited me and a few of his friends to supper. He ordered extra food and asked me to drink wine with him. All this seemed beyond my wildest dreams—that I, who had been expelled, could on this day experience such happiness.

I REMEMBER IT all very clearly.

On the afternoon of November 25, 1926, we moved into the female company of the Central Military and Political School. As I entered the gate, I saw huddled groups of young women in flowery clothes. They were pressing their heads and ears close together as they talked. On some of their faces I saw expressions of sadness and distress. One girl was standing behind her friend, secretly wiping her tears on her sleeve.

"Why cry? If they won't let us go out today, we will wait for tomorrow."

I figured they were speaking about being allowed to go outside the school grounds. Softly, I asked a fellow student, one who had moved in earlier, "What's happening? You mean to say that even those of us who moved in today are not allowed to go out?"

"Right, no one can go out. Rumor has it we won't be allowed to go out until we have been here a month."

Just at that moment a fourteen- or fifteen-year-old private blew a bugle, *Di-di-di-DA-DA-DI-DA*. Three officers simultaneously walked out of their living quarters. I was transfixed: one of them was a woman dressed in a combat uniform. She wore yellow woolen puttees, just like the men.

The very tall male officer shouted for our group to line up. We all crowded into a chaotic line. A few schoolmates giggled as they watched the arrogant expression on the female officer's face.

"Hurry! No laughing. Line up quickly." This was the tall male officer speaking.

We stood for a whole hour before we were divided into three troops and lined up according to our height, tallest to the right. I was number thirty-three of the third troop. Many students were taller than I, but more than ten were shorter. I touched Zheng Meixian's shoulder and said, "You're so little, how can you carry a gun?"

"Ha! Do you think you are so terrifically big yourself? You're a little soldier, just like me."

We received a warning: "No talking."

All the others looked to their left. I lowered my head, feeling awful.

Five baskets of uniforms were carried out and each of us was issued gray cotton clothes, a hat, a pair of rubber-soled shoes, a pair of straw shoes, two pairs of black cotton socks, one pair of gray puttees, and a leather belt more than an inch wide. After these had been distributed, the tall male officer (I later learned he was the company commander) showed us how to put on the puttees, how to fasten the leather belt, how to wear the hat, and how to salute. "Now quickly return to your dormitory," he said. "Take off your young ladies' clothes and put on your military uniforms. From this moment on you are no longer pampered young ladies but woman soldiers." We all laughed, and the commander continued speaking: "Most important, you must wipe the makeup off your faces, leaving not a single trace. All hair must be cut uniformly short. In fact, it will be best if you shave your heads clean, like ours."

We all groaned in shock.

The commander quickly altered his amiable manner: "You must face the fact that in coming here you will not live the comfortable and romantic life of young ladies, as you did when you were studying literature. You are all soldiers entering the company, and the duty of a soldier is to obey rules, to obey officers, to be orderly, to be serious, to endure hardship, to do grueling work." The commander spoke in one breath, and suddenly everyone's spirit was lifted—for it was true that from today on we were part of a company of soldiers, where habits from the days of studying literature must be forgotten.

After we were dismissed we took the gray clothes to the dormitory to change, and there I heard many voices whining.

"I will be too cold if I take off my leather coat."

"The hat is like a farmer's bamboo rain hat."

"I have never in my life seen socks like these."

"Lord—the clothes are too big. I look like I'm singing in a puppet show."

At this last comment we all burst out laughing.

In the dining hall we finished our meal in ten minutes flat, but we could not leave until the officer-of-the-week shouted, "Stand up." We again lined up and then were dismissed.

That evening Captain Zheng of the female company gave a speech on discipline. He was tall and very thin, a little younger than forty, and his face was so pockmarked that, if I were to exaggerate, I would say it resembled a pineapple. He seemed very honest and refined, with manners not at all military. He had a very strange way of saluting: after the salute he flung his five fingers away from his face as if he meant to slap the ears of someone standing nearby. One schoolmate could not help laughing at this quirk, and the rest of us joined in. A warning glance from the company commander subdued us. The captain's voice was gentle, but he had one habit of speech we could not help smiling at: he ended almost every sentence with the word *time.* For instance, he said, "When each of you comrades arrived here you made up your mind to make sacrifices, that time. Now you must extinguish all romantic thoughts, this time. You must get rid of bad habits like dependency and laziness, this time."

Sometimes he even used the phrase "this time's time." When he did, we laughed until our stomachs hurt. Even the company commander had to bite his lower lip.

After the speech came roll call, and then—since we had just arrived and there would be no drill today, and because in the morning we would be required to get up at five-thirty—we were sent off early to bed. But how could one sleep? The eight o'clock night watch had just sounded, and I was lying in a barren room with more than forty strangers, and my bed was a hard plank. On the plank were white sheets, a gray blanket, a thin coverlet. A small white pillow matched the sheets and reminded me of the pillow in my cradle when I was three. Our beds were neat, clean. But a few of the young ladies had been accustomed to sleeping on spring beds with silken covers, and naturally they had complaints.

The female political director came in to check our dormitory. She seemed concerned about us and looked after us as tenderly as a mother. "No talking after lights out or you will be punished tomorrow." Instantly, the atmosphere turned still and serious. She shined her flashlight on each bed. She told us not to cover our mouths with the bedcover and not to kick off the bedclothes and not to catch cold.

That night we entered a new world.

Bong. Bong. Bong. I was startled awake by the watch in the dead of night. I opened my eyes. Pale moonlight whitened the room and made me feel as if I were lying in a cold and silent hospital. From each person's nose and mouth rose snoring sounds that mingled to create a night symphony. I could not sleep anymore. I thought how in only a few hours we would be carrying guns and sticks, marching to the cry of "one-two-three-four." *Soldier.* What a powerful word! I would not have believed that we Chinese women, repressed by ancient custom for thousands of years, would see the day when we would become soldiers. Now we must work hard to carry out our responsibility, to change society, to destroy the powers of feudalism.

A thousand beautiful and inexhaustible hopes rushed through my brain like shooting stars. If it had not been night, I would have jumped up and shouted.

My schoolmate in the next bed awoke when she heard me yawn. In a quiet voice she asked, "Do you know what time it is? Are we getting up soon?"

"Soon. Three o'clock has sounded."

At first only the two of us were talking. Then more and more people awoke. At last we all got up, fearing that ten minutes would be too little time for us to dress and make our beds and bind our legs and wash our faces. We all ran to the exercise field; it was not yet four in the morning.

"Hey! What is this? You are all up? The bugle call for reveille has not sounded yet. Too early, too early! Quickly, return to your dormitory." The company commander had come out of his bedroom. He was bewildered and almost frightened to see such a huge clump of black shadows where the entire company had gathered on the exercise field.

Someone replied, "Officer, we do not dare sleep anymore. We are afraid we won't awaken when the bugle calls."

(At that time we didn't know we were supposed to stand at attention and use the word *report* whenever we spoke to an officer.)

"You are very enthusiastic, which is a good sign. I hope you will never lose this spirit."

We began a life of four hours in class, four hours in drill. The rifle was quite heavy, probably weighing more than ten pounds. Six short people like Shurong were not as tall as the gun, and whenever the drill started, the tall people at the front of the line all watched them and laughed. Sometimes the short ones simply could not tug their guns along when we ran, but this happened only in the first few days. After a week they were all transformed into able and spirited sentries.

Strange. After growing used to the chaotic and free life of students, we had suddenly come to live this mechanical and rigorous military life marked by order and obedience. Yet none of us felt pain or discomfort; none of us considered deserting. We did, however, think that the rule restricting us to a single leave per month during our three-month training period was too strict.

WINTER. SNOWFLOWERS DRIFTED over the earth. While other people slept in sweet dreams, we stamped our neat footprints into clean snow. We opened our mouths wide and shouted, "One-two-three-four!"

AFTER WE HAD LEARNED the song of struggle, everyone went about singing it:

> "Study quickly, quickly drill,
> Strive to lead the people.
> Feudal shackles—smash them all,
> Smash romantic dreams.
> Fulfill the people's revolution
> Wonderful, wonderful women!"

When we sang the phrase "smash romantic dreams," we raised our voices to encourage ourselves and to warn the world that none must fall in love during the days of revolution.

The God of Spring sent breezes that made a person feel warm and drunk, wafting sweet love seeds and scattering them in the hearts of young men and women, blowing life's energy into their bodies. But loud cries of "Charge!" and "Slaughter the enemy!" awakened the young from their delusory dreams: one after another they rushed out of their pink palaces and strode toward society's battlefield, now strewn with countless skeletons and swept with the smell of blood. Discarding their selfish love, they replaced it with love of country and love of the people.

A few of our comrades did fall in love, but their first condition was that their mates must share their ideals, must be willing to sacrifice all for the revolution. In short, they practiced revolutionary romance.

Common sense would say that those who had tasted the repression and pain of ancient custom would feel a greater need for love's comfort once they were freed from their iron cages, but actually the opposite was true: they were not intrigued by the mystery of romance, did not even regard it as very important. Their most urgent desire was encompassed in a single word: *revolution.* They staked their future and their happiness on their revolutionary work. Romantic love, they believed, is mere selfishness. One's life ought to create happiness for all to enjoy. To those who believed strongly in offering their lives to their country and its people, romance seemed merely a toy for young ladies and young men of the idle class.

Such, in those revolutionary days, was our view of romance.

ONE MORNING DURING my second month in the company, the officer on duty handed me a thick letter. It was heavy, weighed like lead in my palm. My schoolmates smiled and watched me, thinking that here was another sweet love note from someone. The instant I saw the writing on the envelope my body turned numb. I felt as if I had been electrocuted. My mind whirled. At last our group was dismissed. I skulked off to a corner of the exercise field and tore open the letter.

What? When I saw that the paper was smeared with blood stains and sloppy writing, I hadn't the courage to read it. Quickly I put it into my pocket. Had it fallen into my hands two months earlier, I would have considered it precious. Now I was not in the mood. My views had changed utterly. I had dedicated my life to my country, had vowed to escape this selfish love that drains ambition. I felt like tearing the letter into pieces and tossing it into the wastebasket or burning it so not a trace would remain. And yet I was inconsistent: I did not have the courage to destroy it. In the end, I read it, this sad and passionate plea. He said that he hoped I would accept his sincere love, that he was willing to stand with me forever on the battle line to fight, that he was willing to sacrifice his life for our country. On the final page he had written the words *symbol of the tide of blood* in his own blood.

Seeing these words, I recalled what I had written in my own diary about my first love, and I felt very sad—but fortunately for only a split second. The bugle call to assembly sounded and I quickly ran to fall in with the troop.

Shurong whispered in my ear, "Whose love letter?"

I shook my head. Tears almost fell.

Shurong was my good friend. We told each other everything. That evening I let her read the letter. She sighed and said, "Ohhh, unfortunately, he's not a comrade. . . ."

From other sources I learned that his ideals were the reverse of mine. What was there to say? Finished! Finished!

Still, I was moved to write him a short letter, asking him to come to Wuhan immediately and join the military. Several months passed and I received no reply. At last I realized that his letter must have been written in the flush of momentary emotion, that he was not able to put down his pen and pick up a gun. Then I knew I could not love him, that I must let his memory fade forever from my mind.

RONGZHEN WAS A FEMALE SOLDIER who liked to put on a little powder and wear nice clothes. One day she sneaked away to see her lover without applying for leave, so the moment she returned she was sent to the isolation cell, where she was given neither food nor a single drop of water. The guard at her door didn't dare to give her food even though they were fellow students. And whenever the officer in charge saw us stopping to visit her after we had come out of the washroom, he would immediately stiffen his face and say, "You must be thinking about joining her. Good, I'll lock you up together."

She had been locked up for three days and still there was no news of her release. Everyone was anxious for her and felt that Commander Yang's punishment was perhaps a bit too harsh. We felt that he should be more lenient toward a female soldier—especially since she was only a first-time offender. Shurong and I were particularly sad. Sometimes we sneaked her steamed buns, and each time we did this we saw that her eyes were filled with tears. She lay on a hard plank and had only one gray blanket. Her toilet was in her cell. Every day she had only two bowls of white rice and one bowl of salt water. I went to the commander and asked why she was not given a dish of food to go with the rice. He replied, "Only those who have disobeyed rules are in the isolation cell. She is a criminal now and she must suffer this kind of treatment. If she lives and eats like you do, then everyone will want to break the rules."

"When will she be freed?"

"We only need her to admit her mistake. Then she will be released tomorrow."

The original regulation specified that she should be locked in isolation for three days. Who would have guessed that Rongzhen was so strong-minded that she would refuse to admit her mistake and that two more days would be added to her sentence? Then she got into trouble again by complaining about the toilet and asking for improvement in her bed and her food. The commander said that she was deliberately causing trouble, and he added another two days to her sentence. News spread throughout the school that Rongzhen was locked up for a week. All were very concerned that their day too would come. When she was released, her face seemed to have aged considerably and her spirit seemed less lively. We surrounded her and asked:

"What was the taste of life in the black room?"

"Did you sacrifice yourself for love?"

When we joined the company, we lived by this code: "Military orders are like a mountain, party regulations like iron." Every day at least two of us had to stand at attention as punishment for returning late from leave or for laughing while standing in the food line. Although I never stayed in the isolation cell, I was punished numerous times by being made to stand at attention.

I regret to say that I deserved punishment from the start. I had entered a military school that had strict rules and that treated us exactly as if we were already soldiers, yet I naturally loved the arts, loved freedom, and I refused to change my childlike disposition. On one occasion the commander found in my desk drawer little ducks, cats, foreign dolls, little drums, and cymbals. After that he often scolded me, saying, "Those who study literature are romantics—they cannot be revolutionaries."

This so provoked me that I not only let him confiscate my little toys but took several novels that I had brought from Changsha and flung them into the corners of the storage room and never read them. Every day my eyes encountered books about the problems of the farmers' revolution, the history of global revolution, about economics, politics, military affairs, and so on. One book in particular, *The Foot Soldier's Exercise Manual,* I read so often that I could nearly recite more than half of it from memory.

Perhaps I was proof of the old saying that rivers and mountains are easily moved but natural temperament cannot be altered. Though I was able to control my emotions, and though I had made up my mind to train my character like steel, I could never escape my childish spirit. I still remember the time we had field exercises and no sooner had the bugle sounded for us to rest than I immediately threw down my gun and decided to play. I climbed onto the back of a water buffalo.

Lieutenant Wang was furious. He came over to reprimand me. I answered him with a smile, "Lieutenant, the school has no horse for us to practice riding, so I can only ride on the buffalo."

These words made the lieutenant and all my schoolmates laugh.

IN 1927 WE PASSIONATELY celebrated the bright-red May, dyed with the blood of dead revolutionaries.* Apart from those cold-blooded animals

---

*As she describes the revolutionary events in Wuhan in 1927, Xie Bingying alludes to the revolutionaries who were killed in Shanghai by the British in the May Thirtieth incident of 1925.—trans.

who opposed the revolution, every person—old and young, even women with bound feet—raised their fists to urge defeat of the warlords and imperialists. All people stood beneath a single revolutionary flag waving in the sky. In all minds was deeply engraved the single belief that tomorrow is our world, a day when a new society would be born—for yesterday we had discarded the shackles of slavery and had become humans.

The overwhelming power of the masses was impossible to resist. The alliance of thousands and thousands of hearts allowed us to regain possession of the British Concession after only an hour. Laborers, students, soldiers, and the common people took over the land that had been tightly gripped by the imperialists, and they did so without wasting a single bullet or drop of blood. It was inspiring. More than ten foreign war vessels had dropped anchor in the Yangzi River, and their sailors had set up machine guns on the shore. But when they saw our united forces fiercely thrusting forward, these imperialists (not to mention their children and grandchildren to come) began vanishing, shitting and pissing with fear, and scattering to the far corners. They lost their machine guns to our forces. Their sailors—the executioners who had operated the machine guns—clambered back onto their vessels.

This was the first time I had witnessed the power of the masses.

This victory helped raise the confidence of every citizen. The final victory would surely belong to us, if only we were united and unafraid to sacrifice.

In bloody May the international workers' representatives arrived at Wuhan, the heart of the revolution. Leaders of labor revolts and peasant revolts also came. Every day we were busy welcoming them, drilling soldiers for military review, publishing special issues, writing slogans and handbills.

Huge red banners with slogans were hung in the schools and in the three towns of Wuhan.* On the day of the welcoming ceremony the revolutionary leaders from each country brought us love on behalf of their own brothers, and we gave our love in return, and our powers were united. Old Man Tom, who was in his seventies, pulled from his pocket a red silk cloth as large as a flag and waved it in the air after he had finished his speech. He jumped up and shouted, "Long live the success of world revolution!"

---

*The towns of the Wuhan tri-city area are Hankou, Hanyang, and Wuchang.—trans.

People on and off the platform also jumped and shouted.

The more than twenty thousand people standing on the vast field all went crazy, as if the world revolution would succeed tomorrow. They all forgot the darkness of repression and looked only at the brightness of revolution. No one felt pain; all knew only happiness. From each individual standing in the crowd a joyous heart flew upward into the sky, like a swallow.

In that bright red May, Isadora Duncan's dance company came to perform at Hankou's World of Bloody Flower Theater. Under pale green light a group of strong, energetic, and youthful women, all draped in blood-red silk, sang, "How we have suffered the pains of slavery and labor!" Their lively synchronized steps and their strong singing roused the passion of all who watched them, and the audience joined in and loudly sang, "The blazing stove completely dried our blood and sweat. . . ."

In the middle of the night countless people swarmed out of the theater, all praising the performance: "Extraordinary! This is the first time I have seen this kind of powerful revolutionary dance."

The moon shone brightly on the pavement. In the quiet night, people's humming filled the air.

Also in this bright-red May from factories and huts came young girls and old women with feet like four-inch golden lotus flowers, all going to a meeting at the Horse Parade Ground.

"Walk a little faster, Big Sister Wang. Others have already lined up."

"My feet hurt."

"Unbind them quickly! In this revolutionary time you shouldn't bind your feet!"

"I have no choice. They were bound when I was young."

Ever since the March Eighth Woman's Day celebration, most of these women knew that they were as human as men.* But they were pitiful— pairs of feet bound like red peppers. They leaned east and slanted west when they walked. Every time they participated in the mass meetings they would say, painfully: "My feet hurt, can't move!"

---

*International Women's Day, proclaimed at the International Conference of Women in Helsinki in 1910, was celebrated worldwide.—trans.

"You must walk even if you can't move—this is work we must be part of."

These were their own words, and what powerful words!

During the bright-red May our throats were hoarse from shouting, our feet had blisters from walking, and we slept only five hours each night. Our footprints were left in factories, huts, schools, and crossroads, at Hanyang Gate and at Jianghanguan harbor.

Ah! May, bright red, dyed with the blood of revolutionaries—I will keep you in my heart forever. But how many of the people who fiercely commemorated you in 1927 would later become heroes themselves?

SUDDENLY WE RECEIVED an order that the female company must select twenty students to form a propaganda group to accompany the army on its Northern Expedition. The first destination: Henan.*

"Reporting to company commander! I must join the Northern Expedition!"

"Reporting to company commander! I am a northerner, the perfect person for propagandizing northerners!"

"Reporting to company commander! My body is absolutely fit, able, and ready to fight a victorious war—I want to join the Northern Expedition!"

Commander Yang's room was like a beehive swarming with the comings and goings of our schoolmates. Commander Yang spoke without haste: "Don't be so noisy. It is not a question of *who* will join the Northern Expedition but of *when* you will join. At this time I am selecting only twenty healthy specimens, people who can run fast and who are able to spread propaganda by writing or by speaking. The rest of you will be dispatched later."

Each person hoped that she would be among the chosen. I was very happy, for I was in excellent health, could run fast, and also could write essays. Why shouldn't I be chosen?

Sure enough, early the next morning, when Commander Yang announced the names of those who would be going to Henan, I was second on the list. But could it be that I heard him wrong? Surely there could not

---

*The border of Henan Province is about one hundred miles northwest of Wuhan.—trans.

be two with the same name in the female company. I was crazy with happiness. After we were dismissed I went immediately to pack my bag and to write a letter to my third brother, but I had no idea my brother would actually come to see me two days later, the very next morning after he received it.

"Third Brother! What are you doing here?" I was surprised and delighted.

"Last evening I received your letter telling me you have been dispatched. You wrote with such sadness and such strength that I gave it to the printer to set it up in type, and at the same time I called a ricksha to take me to the East Station. I caught the special express at eight-thirty . . . and here I am."

His voice trembled a little, tears swimming in his eyes. I feared that I might be influenced, so I quickly focused my eyes on the slogan on the wall, which read, "Revolutionaries do not shed tears, only blood!"

"Maybe our second brother has already gone to Henan, and if so I will surely see him there. You come too, Third Brother. How wonderful it would be for us to meet at the front line." I glanced at him and forced a smile.

"I don't dare to tell our family that you have been dispatched. If Father and Mother heard about it, I can't imagine how sad they would be."

Honestly, I don't know why my heart was as hard as a rock at that moment. I shed not a tear, and felt only joy and excitement.

"Can you ask for leave and go out to drink a glass of wine with me?"

"No. The rules become more strict when it is near departure time. If you had not seen the commander and explained how you had rushed here all the way from Changsha, I doubt you could have seen me."

"Then I must leave immediately and take the train back to Changsha."

"Yes. And after I return and the war is over, we will drink as much as we like."

WAITING AND MORE WAITING. Our departure date had not been set, and just when the twenty of us were anxious almost to the point of tears, an emergency order came through: the enemy had reached Tingsha Bridge and now the entire company must prepare to fight before enemy troops began advancing on Wuchang. That evening the commanding officer called together all the male and female students and gave us our orders. He organized us into a central independent division and said we were to set out early the next day. Everyone would go except thirty or more female students who would be left behind to take care of propaganda and ambulance duties.

By five o'clock the following morning we were neatly packed and ready to move out. The scene at our gate was like a river overflowing, a swirling flood of people who had come to say farewell and people who had come to watch the commotion. Next to an officer who wore a slanted leather belt stood several old ladies who were crying and bending at their waists as they begged him:

"My child cannot go to fight the war—she's the only one I have."

"My daughter cannot go. What if something happens to her? I would not be able to live!"

Sounds of weeping, laughing, shouting, bugles blaring.

"Granny, don't be sad. We will fight to victory."

"Granny, don't worry about your daughter. We are all children with parents."

"Forward march!"

The entire regiment began to move forward to the stirring music of crowds cheering, people shouting slogans, our soldiers singing, the sound of bugles.

"Slaughter the enemy, return in triumph!"

The voices of the people rang in our ears like battle drums.

"Slaughter the enemy, return in triumph!"

Crazy with happiness, we echoed the shouts of the crowd. With swelling spirits we headed to the front. . . .*

THE MALE COMPANY had left a day ahead of us and was already opening fire at Tingsha Bridge. Our train stopped. I stuck out my head to look. Sud-

---

*The regiment did not go northwest to Henan Province as originally planned, but instead went to a region about sixty miles south of Wuhan. Among the places Xie Bingying mentions in connection with this "western expedition" are Fengkou, Jiayu, and Xianning. These three towns lie in a straight line running west to east, with Fengkou to the west, Jiayu about thirty-seven miles farther east, and Xianning about twenty-two miles east of Jiayu.—trans.

denly I saw several injured comrades bathed in blood and writhing in pain. Their excruciating cries for help made my heart shudder. Two people were dead, one with his whole head dyed red and the substance of his brain spilling out. The other's eyes were still half open, his arms broken. I asked the lieutenant to let us off so we could save our injured comrades and bury the dead.

"Impossible. The train will be moving soon and the work ahead is more urgent than this. An ambulance corps must be on its way." The lieutenant spoke sternly. I was filled with grief. I began to understand the cruelty of war.

WE HAD NOT HAD a good meal for three days. Each day we ate at six in the morning and did not eat again until after eight or nine in the evening. But not until we began to march did we realize that a soldier's life is about the most bitter and pathetic life that a human can lead. Sometimes our coarse rice was mixed with husks; eating it was like chewing sand and we couldn't swallow it. The accompanying dish was unspeakable. On the march we carried, for convenience, only a pot of moldy and smelly beans sprinkled with so much salt that we couldn't put them in our mouths. Yet it was curious. When we were hungry, we thought that this coarse hard rice and these stinking beans tasted even better than chicken or fish or meat: they crept into our mouths like dragon pearl rice and slipped down our throats.

June was a sultry month. Our sweat dripped like rain and our clothes were as wet as if they had been soaked in water. We felt very uncomfortable in these clothes, especially when we marched. Our feet burned as if we were walking on a hot stove. The skin on our faces began to peel, layer by layer. Cries of "Hot, hot!" came from all directions. Yet no one complained and no one wished to turn back or desert the company. All were willing to endure the distress and difficulties of the moment. We found our happiness in our struggle for victory.

Our male comrades swam and took baths in the ponds. Sometimes we used pond water not only for washing our faces and our clothes but for drinking.

In the midst of this intensely interesting life I began to write my *War Diary*. Using my knees as a desk, I wrote every day during the few minutes when we rested from marching, or I would give up sleep and write beneath the bean-size flame of an oil lamp. I mailed my writing to the editor of the *Central Daily News* supplement, Mr. Sun Fuyuan. Then came the unlucky day that I left my blanket, bundle, water bottle, and rice box on the grass when I went to the toilet next to the railroad tracks. When I came out to get on the train, I found that all my belongings had flown away without wings. At first I thought they must have been taken by a fellow student, but I checked with everyone on the train and no one had seen them. Bad news. I was finished. The diary that I had labored to write (and that I had not read even once) had disappeared, leaving no shadow behind. The shock of this loss, the fatigue of our march (every day we marched an average of thirty miles, sometimes forty), and the frantic work schedule made it impossible for me to continue writing my diary. I wrote only letters and random thoughts. Even now I can clearly recall—as I will forever—each tiny detail of my life in those days. Impressions of each place are vividly etched and still fresh in my mind. Yet it is curious that whenever I begin to write, I feel as if my brain has dried up: the tip of my pen cannot write down my life from that period. A puzzle. Truly an inexplicable puzzle.

IT MUST HAVE BEEN about the tenth day after we had been dispatched to the front that I noticed a schoolmate smiling as he read out loud from the English edition of the *Central Daily News,* speaking in a very clear voice.

As I walked near him I asked, "What fine article is making you so happy?"

"I'm reading your masterpiece, with great respect—it is quite interesting."

"Oh, sure. You know my English is poor, so you decide to ridicule me. You really are despicable." I turned away, angry.

But he impolitely pulled me back by the arm, pointing to the title: MAILED FROM JIAYU. "If *you* didn't write this article, who did? Obviously, you are the author. Even without knowing English, you can surely recognize your own name, can't you? The truth is, it was translated by Mr. Lin

Yutang and this is already the fourth article. I was just thinking about looking for the three earlier ones."

I didn't believe him until I saw the article with my own eyes. My schoolmates teased me and wanted me to take them out to dinner to celebrate, saying my work would be read overseas. But I really felt no happiness, only shame. For what I had written was very casual and had required no intelligence. What possible value could there be in translating it? This I could not understand, but I didn't have the courage to write to Mr. Lin and ask why he had bothered.

It was evening. Several schoolmates and I were crowded in a large bed. They had gone to sleep already, but I was still writing beneath the tiny flame of the vegetable-oil lamp.

My essay was translated into English? But no, I just don't believe it. And yet . . . it was my name. Could this be a dream?

MIXED IN WITH US as part of our troop was a group of farmers. One day these farmers captured three local landowners who had been oppressing the poor. They tied the men up with thick ropes, locked them in a large and dark detention room, and then went almost crazy with joy.

A fourteen- or fifteen-year-old boy pointed his finger at the prisoners. "Hah! You actually lived to see this day!" If he had reached farther through the door—which was made of round wooden posts—he would have touched the face of a white-bearded old man of sixty or so.

The three prisoners were sweating, panting. Their eyes still flashed anger, yet these men had lost their customary pompousness. From the eyes of the white-bearded old man flowed two streams of tears. His hands were tied with a cord. He kept shaking his head. These three had been captured that same day at Chenghuang Temple, which was fourteen miles away.

"Why are you crying? For your mother? Do you mean to say no one has sympathy for you?" These words came out of the crowd and seemed to have been spoken by a little soldier.

"Ha-ha! That old villain was also caught—very satisfying, very satisfying!"

"Officer! They are the ones who have repressed us the most. You should shoot them instantly."

"You should capture their wives and children. Yeah! Their women are terrible."

"Yeah! Yesterday every life in this village was in their hands, but today their lives are in ours. Ha!"

People poured in like a tidal wave to see these old prisoners. Sounds of victorious laughter mingled with a confusion of other noises. The proud faces of farmers and their wives—and even of young children—were beaming with victory. They all stretched their necks to look into the dark detention room. They jammed themselves in front of the door as if fearing that the prisoners would escape between the cracks.

"Comrades! Please leave—we are going to eat," said a brave little bugle soldier, jumping forward as he spoke to the crowd. He held in his hand a bugle draped with a large red silk cloth, and he put the bugle to his mouth as if he were about to blow.

Now a burly young farmer forced his way to the front. "Comrades, you all go to eat. We are here to keep guard."

A gong sounded outside: *dangg-dangg-dangg.*

"What is that?"

"A meeting for the people."

The crowd receded like a wave. As they hurried away, several people turned and cautioned us repeatedly, "Comrades, don't let them escape. Those three are truly contemptible bastards."

That evening I was on guard duty. I was not in this regiment, but I was substituting for a fellow student who had gone to a meeting. I was very happy about this assignment—though normally I was quite fearful of night guard duty. On a moonless night the blackness and loneliness can be scary: you stand there by yourself, holding your gun, wondering if there might be ghosts about. Tonight, however, my courage was up. My spirits were as buoyant as if I had captured the three prisoners all by myself. I felt indescribably happy. I walked to and fro in front of the cell door, carrying my gun on my back. The oldest man—the one with the white beard and mournful face—began to beg: "Officer, let me go. I am an innocent man. They have arrested me on a false charge."

Another prisoner even went so far as to kneel down and kowtow to me repeatedly. He was a short man in his forties, thin as a stick, as if he were mere bones wrapped in skin. "Officer, pity me! I have a family of more than twenty, old and young, and they all depend on me to survive. I am no oppressor of the poor, no part of the landowning gentry. Spare me, Officer—save me!" Tears flowed in two streams from his bulging eyes.

The other man was a nearsighted, opium-smoking ghost with black-stained teeth. He too knelt down and bowed and kowtowed incessantly.

But I pretended not to see, turning my face away. I walked back and forth, leisurely.

"What *officer* are you talking about? I am only a guard. Be quiet. Why all this raucous racket so late at night?"

I had never scolded anyone so loudly in my life. But today I was a guard who was in charge of prisoners—ha! I had to show my authority. Unfortunately, my voice was really not loud enough. They knew I was a female soldier, and they persisted in begging, for they thought a woman's heart would be soft.

I became more fierce and violent. With every phrase I hit the ground with the butt of my gun: "Save you? Hah! Don't daydream. Do you know how many people have died because of you? You exploit and oppress farmers. Count how many terrible things you have done in your life."

Still, they would not stop kowtowing and begging: "Guard officer! I am an upright man. I have never committed any crime. You go and check it out in the village."

"There is no need for me to check. You were arrested by the people from your own village. Look. We have just arrived here. How would we know if you are a criminal?"

"I had a run-in with Wang Sanmazi once, that's all. And this must be his private revenge. Officer! Save me!" This was spoken by the short one.

"The revolutionary army does not allow private revenge. Today you were arrested by nine hundred people, and they all publicly identified you as local thugs who oppress people, who are criminals. Would this be private revenge? Blind talk!"

"Aach! My joints will break from pain. Officer, please be merciful and loosen the rope." The opium ghost howled loudly, as if an injustice had been done to him.

"Be quiet, you bastard. If you cause any more disturbance, you will be dragged away and shot tonight."

If I had not come down hard on them like that, who knows when the grumbling would have stopped?

Though they did not dare continue their loud protests, they kept on whining and talking, and this annoyed me considerably. At twelve o'clock the company officer came over to investigate. For an instant—when he shined his flashlight into the room—he was startled: "Ho! Where did the old beard go?"

"By the door."

"Ah—you must watch diligently. Don't doze off. If they run away, it will be your head."

"Yes, Officer," I said, and I promptly stood at attention and saluted.

But already he had hurried off.

The moon hung like a jade plate in the center of the sky. The steaming heat of summer had dissipated completely; cool breeze blew in from the small courtyard. Outside, people were walking to and fro. In the next room four or five female soldiers were discussing what had happened today at the women's assembly:

"Truly a bastard—he said his wife should not have attended the meeting for women, so when she returned home he used a knife to cut off her ears and slash her eyes."

"How do you know?"

"Her neighbor came to the barracks to report the incident. The battalion commander then dispatched eight of us to arrest the criminal. Who would have guessed he could escape so quickly? There was no sign of him when we got there."

"He must have been hiding under the floor, or in the corner of a room, or in the cow corral. You didn't find him because only a few of you were looking." This was Shuzhao speaking.

Jizong, captain of the "miscellaneous regiment," jumped up. "Listen to *you*! Where *didn't* we search? We even used a stick to drag the toilet pit."

"Ha-ha—do you really think he would hide in the toilet like a maggot in shit?" I joined in and started to chat with them. For a moment I had forgotten my duty.

After a big laugh they all left to go to another meeting. During this time of military emergency we did not distinguish night from day, just kept working.

At last I sat down, wearily. According to military rules, sitting down was absolutely forbidden. But my legs were sore from standing. Four hours had passed and everyone was so busy that no one had come to relieve me. Even so, I dared not be careless, for my duty was to guard the enemy. As I sat on the cold rock I felt infinite pleasure. But my eyes suffered: I had to watch the gate to see if an officer was approaching on night patrol or if a colleague was coming to relieve me. And at the same time, I had to watch the three old reprobates to be certain they didn't untie their ropes and cause trouble. The cell door was not very sturdy. Had the prisoners been strong men, they might already have broken out.

"Officer, my mouth is terribly dry, give me a little water to drink."

It was the old beard causing trouble again.

"Wait until the sky is light. Then you will get something to eat."

"Can't wait until daylight, Officer. Do a good deed and give us a little water to drink."

"Even if you plan to cut off our heads, you ought to turn us into ghosts with full stomachs."

It had not been obvious to me until now that this opium ghost could be so violent.

"I am not going to give you any water, so what will you do about it? Have you reached the point that you are willing to reveal the sort of arrogant bastards you really are?"

The old beard and the dwarf quickly apologized to me. But I, knowing that they would be killed tomorrow, poured a cup of tea and held it to the old beard's mouth. The opium ghost began struggling to loosen the rope in order to hold the cup himself. I charged at him with my bayonet. Fearful, he politely sat down.

The morning sun rose and now the vast field was crowded with men and women, our comrades among them. Farmer representatives from different villages sat on the chairman's platform. One of them spoke excitedly and movingly about the crimes that the three prisoners had committed, and each time he described a crime, a loud response came from below the platform:

"Right, right! He was oppressing us just like that, and also—"

"Execution! Execution! Quickly! Quickly!"

"Let me open fire!"

"Everyone gets a slash with the knife!"

"Drag them onto the platform! Let us see the execution!"

When the crimes had been proclaimed, the crowd of more than three thousand could wait no longer. Holding their large rough fists high in the air, they pushed and shoved and shouted.

"The revolutionary army is dedicated to liberating the hardworking farmers and laborers and to giving them their rewards," the chairman told the crowd. "These two country criminals, Wang Fucai and Guo Shoukang, together with the oppressive landowner, Wang Xingxiang, were captured and tied up by you farmers, and you personally brought them here to this army division. At the meeting today representatives from each village proclaimed the prisoners' twelve serious crimes of oppression against farmers. In addition, more than three thousand people in the audience have raised their hands to support a sentence of death by firing squad. Since this is the will of the farmers . . . of course, we will comply. Now bring them up to the platform to be shot."

"YES!" The crowd shouted.

The chairman's announcement was soon followed by sounds of *pop-pop-pop*: the three hated criminals died instantly in a rush of fresh blood.

Waves of laughter and applause and shouting flooded the field where the three corpses lay.

AT EIGHT O'CLOCK in the evening we suddenly received orders from the division that the third company was to advance to Qingshanao, more than fourteen miles from Fengkou. We were to go there and protect the city. Intelligence reports said that a small number of injured rebels were hiding in the mountains about halfway along the route of our march and that these rebels might open fire on our army.

"This is the first time since we came to the front that you will be marching at night. A few of you, who have been used to life at school, may be timid and feel unable to take on this kind of hardship. But now you are warriors, willing to sacrifice your lives, so naturally you should not be afraid to suffer. We will be marching at night, first in order to avoid the enemy's attention, second because we have received an emergency order requiring us to reach our destination before midnight. I have heard that this mountain path is not easily passable. You cannot use flashlights. You must walk carefully. Don't be nervous or afraid. And don't make a sound. Even if you fall, just quietly get up. Everyone must keep a hand on his or her gun, to prevent it from hitting against the water bottle and the food tin and making *ding-tong ding-tong* noises. Remember, everyone must follow the rule of absolute silence. You cannot open your mouths to speak, and you cannot walk with heavy steps. Your footsteps must be as light as a mouse's—"

When Commander Yang reached this point of his speech, we all broke out laughing.

"What? You are already laughing before you have taken a single step? What nonsense! If anyone laughs later on, while we are marching, it will mean he or she is purposely causing a disturbance to let the enemy know of our presence, and for this the punishment will be severe."

Our smiles did not fade, just floated alongside our mouths—though none of us dared laugh out loud.

"Commander Yang is a born soldier after all. If he had said that our footsteps must be as light as a swallow's, think how rich with poetry his words would have been." This I whispered into Guanghui's ear after we were dismissed, and it made her laugh until she cried.

Like a long snake, our troop began to move. At first we could hear the noise of the water bottles hitting the food tins. But later, after several soft reminders by the lieutenant, we heard not even half a sound—except for someone who was wearing new straw shoes that made a sharp *tsi-tsi-tsi* noise as he walked. Lieutenant Liu stopped.

"Who walks so noisily?"

"Reporting to the lieutenant! It's no use. I am wearing a pair of new straw shoes, bought just this morning. That's what is making this rhythmic sound."

This was spoken by Liu Zhuanwan, who seemed inclined to write an essay on the subject.

"Don't be chattering on. If they make noise again, you will have to take them off and walk barefoot."

Liu was afraid to go barefoot because thorns might stick in his flesh; he walked as lightly as a mouse.

The night was so dark that we couldn't see our outstretched fingers, couldn't recognize the person in front of us. Sky and earth were one black mass. We couldn't possibly distinguish east, west, south, or north. We stepped very carefully, as if treading on thin ice. Suddenly came a sound—

poo-tunk! Someone in front had fallen into the water. Our file stopped temporarily, causing the *DING-TONG ding-tong ding-tong* sound again.

"Walk! Walk! Those in front walk quickly!"

Again it was the voice of Lieutenant Liu.

"My body is completely covered in mud. I can't open my eyes."

Whoever had just climbed out of the water said this, sounding pathetic.

"Keep walking, even if you can't open them."

Immediately word traveled through the entire company that someone had fallen into the water. We all cautioned one another: "Walk carefully; don't fall."

The road was extraordinarily difficult. Sometimes as we climbed upward we could hear water rushing far below us, loud as a waterfall. We could not see into the depths of the giant chasm, but we could tell from the distant sound of the water that this was a dangerous spot.

"Be careful, you in the back. There is a deep pool here. Everyone walk slowly. It's no fun to fall." This voice came from up front.

When we heard "deep pool" we all became concerned. I worried that if I fell down, I wouldn't be able to get up and the troop would leave me scrabbling in mud. Then I would certainly be desperate. Even if I climbed out, I wouldn't be able to tell directions—and if I took the wrong road, what then? If the enemy comes out now, I thought, we won't be ready to fight. Surely they are hiding deep in the mountains, whereas we have a cliff to our left and an abyss to our right—so if a fight breaks out, I can't imagine how many of us will fall *poo-tunk, poo-tunk* into the water, to become shrimps and frogs.

Someone bravely spoke up and said, "Reporting to the lieutenant. It is too dangerous up ahead. Allow us to use flashlights."

"You cannot use flashlights. This is a very dangerous place. Injured enemy soldiers may be lying in ambush. Walk slower and stay calm."

The atmosphere was tense. Yet our curiosity was up. This was our first time on a night march. Perhaps that is why we actually hoped the enemy soldiers would emerge from deep in the mountains so we could welcome them with an attack. I began imagining how we would see nothing at all in this boundless black night except the red lights of exploding bombs, and would hear nothing but the *pee-pa! pee-pa!* of the guns. Surely, a night scene like that would be beautiful, accompanied by such strong music.

I also thought that at night our courage would swell, our fighting spirit would grow more fierce, since in the dark we would not be able to see the number of the enemy or the mingled blood and flesh of the corpses. The solemnity and stillness of the night was nerve-wracking, yet my energy shot up 100 percent whenever I thought of how we were fighting for truth, for freedom, for our forefathers, for our brothers and sisters. At the same time, I was saddened when I considered how in the dark we would not be able to tell an enemy from our own comrade and would certainly kill many people by mistake.

The deep pool was now behind us. We walked on a little path. To the right and left of us rose tall mountains, enclosing us like windbreaks.

Pa! Pa! Pa!

We heard a few indistinct gunshots. Everyone shivered.

"Stop!" ordered the lieutenant. "Listen. Are those gunshots? If the enemy is ahead, our three rear files must fall back in reserve and the front files must prepare to open fire. But do not fire wildly."

Everyone became excited and nervous as the lieutenant continued speaking: "Forget fear. The enemy troops are injured, unable to sustain even a single attack. When the time comes to fight, be composed, be courageous, be ready to sacrifice."

Within three or four minutes the crisis had passed and all was calm once again. Still, I was eager to rush immediately to the front of the column, for I imagined that the enemy might lie waiting there. Our troops walked terribly slowly. I grew impatient. I crowded my way forward, passing close to the ears of those ahead, one after the other.

The class captain reprimanded me: "Why crowd forward like this? You are not allowed to disturb the order."

I answered, "I want to get to the very front of the line, to charge with my bayonet."

Poo-tunk! My right foot suddenly plunged into water, but luckily my left foot stayed on firm ground and I avoided taking a tumble.

"Hey! Who fell this time?" All were concerned.

"Me." Ashamed, I ran to catch up.

"She talks about charging with a bayonet but she can't even walk without falling. Oh, ooooooh."

One fellow mocked me, drawing out his final sigh to such a length that everyone laughed. Even I couldn't hold back my laughter.

Guanghui couldn't keep up with me. She had long since fallen behind. Her feet, like mine, had been bound, and hers were even a half-inch shorter than mine. Pitiful creature. At age five she had already become a sacrifice for her mother.

Night marching proved quite comfortable. We had to grope our way like blind people, since there was no moonlight or starlight. Yet the clear breeze blew a fragrance of flowers across our faces, and the fragrance penetrated our hearts with the sweetness of ice cream and made us all feel unspeakably happy. The light breeze rushing over the tips of the trees made a clear soughing sound that was absolutely the world's most beautiful music— lovely music that made one drunk.

Everyone strode along silently, each carrying a soul that sought light and revolution. We had walked for three or four hours without stopping to rest, yet no one spoke of weariness. Full of energy, we all hurried to keep up with the troops ahead.

On the sides of the far mountains we suddenly discerned a few red lights, like stars in the sky. Our destination was fast approaching.

> "Onward toward the dawn
> ahead, oh, Comrades, struggle!"

I was the first to open my mouth in song, and then everyone joined in. A swell of singing swept through the depths of the still, dark night.

IT ALL TURNED OUT entirely as we had hoped. The battle lasted a month and four days, and then suddenly the war was over—for the moment—and we were returning in triumph. On this western expedition we had lost more than seventy students and more than a hundred comrades from the education corps. But we had gained several thousand guns, and we had established the foundation for revolution by planting in the mind of every common citizen a belief that could never be shaken. This was our biggest victory: we had taken from the warlords the allegiance of thousands of common people who had met us and who now believed and trusted in us. We had scattered everywhere the seeds of revolution. Having won this victory, we returned from the front.

ONLY A FEW shining stars hung in the moonless sky. It was the seventh evening after we had gotten back from the front line. I was sitting at Miss Lu's. She was head nurse for the female company. I was just telling her about our happy and interesting life during the march when suddenly we heard the bugler blow the call for assembly. In three minutes flat the entire school fell into line, reported, and counted off, just as always.

Everyone's eyes fastened on the five male and female officers who stood with lowered heads on the platform in front of us. We had no notion what they were thinking.

Company Commander Yang began to speak: "Fellow students!"

Strange. All of a sudden his voice seemed so different. Why? It seemed to be trembling. I feared some misfortune had occurred. Sure enough, he was announcing our fate, announcing our death sentence.

"First, please be calm, have courage."

What? Are we again setting out for the front? What is there to be afraid of? Such were my thoughts.

"I have some very unfortunate news. Please try not to be depressed when you hear it. It is common for revolutionaries to suffer obstacles and impediments. We must welcome the challenges and absolutely refuse to lose heart."

What is he trying to say?

"Because the opposition's power is too great, to preserve our revolutionary spirit . . . there is no way to avoid temporarily disbanding."

This was like a thunder clap in a clear sky or a bomb in the still of night. Stupefied, we scarcely dared listen to any more. But Commander Yang continued speaking, and his voice rang even louder and became more somber:

"Of course, this is certainly not a matter of fear or of giving up our resistance. Whatever happens, we must struggle until the end. Those of you who are healthy and able to run, go follow the Eleventh Army as they set forth. All the rest, return to your families and put up with this temporary disappointment. In the not-too-distant future we perhaps will live happier and freer lives than now.

"Everyone will now receive ten yuan of disbandment money. Quickly, take it and have some clothes made—you can no longer wear your military uniforms."

Why disband us? Our hopes, our beliefs—are they so quickly destroyed?

After Commander Yang had finished his report, each of the other officers gave a grave speech. Their words seared our brains.

"If only your convictions are constant, if always you think of sacrificing for the revolution, then it is all right to become concubines to a warlord, if you have no way to make a living at the moment. But never get so drunk on material pleasures that you forget your own duty: one day you must kill that same hateful warlord. Do this and you will never regret that you have been a warrior, baptized by revolution and trained in military and political tactics, a brave and ambitious and idealistic female."

These words pierced our hearts like a bright, sharp knife. Many people were crying. And what of our tomorrow? We never thought that our promising tomorrow would prove to be hell. Who would want to be buried in a feudal family? Who?

We did not sleep that night. We sat in a circle on the exercise field and shouted slogans, sang songs, and gave speeches until the sky turned light. The next day the female students from Wuhan returned home, one by one. Flowery and colorful dresses replaced severe and dignified military uniforms. I could not stay in Wuhan, for my feet were injured. I had to return to Changsha with Shurong and Xiang.

Shurong, Xiang, Shanshan, and I all bought the same white silk, and each of us made a long Western-style collarless gown. I say "Western style," but our dresses were not really like the stylish gowns worn by Western ladies. Ours had no buttons, and each had a peach-shaped collar. We put the dresses on by slipping them over our heads.

All of us had hair that was very short, especially Shurong. Her head was shaved almost like a potato. So no matter how expert we were in applying makeup, people could tell at a glance that until recently we had been female soldiers who had been walking around carrying guns and sticks. Sun had dried and darkened our skin. Months of gripping gun butts had calloused our right palms. These were two other signs by which people recognized us.

Two hot tears fell as I remarked, "After we take off our military uniforms, when will we wear them again?"

Shurong could not help but begin to cry too.

The four of us sat as silent as puppets, staring at our new clothes lying on the bed. None of us wanted to take off our gray military uniform, especially the shiny, slippery, soft leather belt. We remembered how it was when we had put that belt on for the first time, cinching it stiffly around the waist. We had thought it very uncomfortable and troublesome, and whenever we were dismissed the first thing we did was loosen it so we could bend and stretch luxuriously. Sometimes we forgot to put it on when we went to exercise, and for this the lieutenant had bawled us out and punished us by making us stand at attention. But slowly we had grown used to that belt. In the end we seldom allowed our belts to be off our bodies for even fifteen minutes, except when we were sleeping. I came to treat my belt and my gun like my lovers. I needed the belt to tightly bind me, especially in winter, when it kept out the cold wind and kept my body warm. As for the gun, it was more precious than life. I needed it to destroy the old and create a new society.

But now nothing was left. The gun was gone and we couldn't even keep the leather belt.

Finally came the afternoon when we had to leave Wuchang. We unwillingly changed out of our military uniforms and into our new dresses. They were very much like simple dance dresses. We then went to a very small photo shop and had a picture taken as a souvenir. Because our heads were not fit for public view, we also went to a department store and each of us bought a foreign hat of woven straw.

The hour arrived to board the train. Only Hong came along with us.* What a sad farewell! A month earlier our departure for Exi had been grand and awe inspiring. But this time as we left Wuchang the day was thick with clouds, the wind howling and gusting, and every pedestrian's face seemed as gloomy and overcast as the sky. Freezing weather. Cold anger filled our hearts. We were ruled and beguiled by a strong belief that someday a new China would dawn. If it hadn't been for this hope, who of us would want to continue living such a miserable life? Wouldn't the iron tracks be a fine burial ground?

At each station the military police came on board as soon as the train stopped, and the officers questioned each passenger, asking everyone where he or she came from, inspecting each person and each piece of lug-

---

*Hong appears throughout Xie Bingying's narrative. He was her comrade in the military and her second brother's best friend. At some point they had a love affair.—trans.

gage. Our skin and clothes made the police take special notice of us.* Several times they almost discovered our identities. Fortunately, we were helped by a Mr. Li, who happened to be from Shurong's hometown and who was an assistant officer in a military unit. Whenever the police came aboard, Mr. Li told them we were his relatives and said that we had been studying at a missionary school in Hankou and now were returning home for the summer recess.

When we arrived in Changsha we needed a place to stay, but going to a hotel was out of the question since the four of us had less than six yuan in our pockets. Anyway, we couldn't find anyone to vouch for us. So I boldly took my three companions to see Lan, a girl from my county who had been my schoolmate at Datong Girls School. She and I had been very close friends. I thought she would be the one person who could not refuse to help us. Yet as soon as we entered her door, poor Lan began trembling and whispered in my ear, "Why are you returning now? This is a fearful world. More people are killed than chickens and ducks. My family cannot keep you. Five families must act as guarantors, no matter who the guest is. Do you understand? You must be vouched for by five families. Every day the military police come to inspect several times, not to mention that you just came from Wuhan . . . !"

What could we do? In everyone's eyes we had become outcasts. To be fair, though, we ought to have forgiven Lan for not daring to keep us in her house. No doubt she had problems of her own.

Shurong and Shanshan went home the next day. Because my feet were hurting terribly, I had to borrow five yuan from Lan to stay at the public hospital. I used the name Xie Tian to register as a patient. A very gentle and considerate nurse named Chen looked after me day and night, and comforted me in my loneliness. A week passed and I still had not recovered. But at least I had received comfort for my spirit.

---

*The Left-leaning Guomindang leaders in Wuhan were under pressure from Chiang Kai-shek, from their supporters in the Soviet Union, and from local warlords ostensibly allied with the Guomindang. As a result, they constantly shifted policy. In the summer of 1927 they acquiesced in the dismantling of labor organizations, peasant organizations, and the Central Military and Political School, and in the ruthless persecution of labor leaders, peasant leaders, and young women whose tanned skin and short hair (cut in what was considered to be the Russian style) gave them away as recent soldiers who might—or might not—be Communists.—trans.

Soon the borrowed money was spent. Things began to look pretty grim. I had no choice but to return home with Xiang. I knew this would be a disaster, whatever few advantages it might bring. But I wanted to end my marriage contract so I decided I *had* to go home, in any case.

It was exactly one o'clock in the morning when we reached Lantian.* I called for someone to open the gate of the Yu Tongheng shop. The people in the shop thought I was a ghost. They couldn't believe I was still alive, for a half-month earlier they had heard news that I was killed at the front line. Now, suddenly, I was standing before them.

No wonder they were suspicious and startled.

---

*Lantian is a town near her home village of Xietuoshan.—trans.

PART 4 Prison

TWO SMALL, SKINNY SEDAN-CHAIR BEARERS CARRIED ME, STEP BY STEP, closer to the village that I had left two years before. My heart grew heavier and heavier with every step.

Sitting in the sedan chair behind me, Xiang called, "Aunt Ming, we'll be there soon!"

"Yes."

Xiang was my schoolmate in grade school, middle school, and military school. According to the genealogy, she was one generation behind me, and so she always called me Aunt Ming.

We passed a teahouse and then suddenly we were on a small road, and less than three hundred yards later we arrived at a large new house—my home.

I quickly lowered my head to my chest, fearing I might be recognized. As I glanced at the new house I heard an anguished voice whisper in my ear, "This is a prison to seal you up." And yet I was not afraid. I had returned home determined to struggle against any adversity. This prison might be strongly built, but I believed I had the strength to break free of it.

So we had arrived home. My sister, sister-in-law, mother, and many children came to welcome us. Their faces were piled with smiles and they held my hands tightly. The children kept tugging at my clothes and asking, "Do you still recognize me, Aunt?"

My old mother, with her head of white hair, was so happy that she cried. "Child, you have become thin! It must have been a terribly hard life for you outside." She used her sleeves to wipe away her tears.

My sister and sister-in-law also cried until their eyes were red, and my three-year-old niece, Yunbao, pulled at my hand and asked, "Aunt, did you bring me a foreign doll?"

As I entered the gate, I saw many red and green wooden household articles in the reception hall, sparkling in the golden light. I knew this was part of the dowry prepared for me. I sighed for my poor mother, who had wasted all this money.

After lunch they led me around to see the new house. It was a building constructed in the old style, yet the rooms were large with plenty of light— not to mention that the air in the house was wonderfully fresh, redolent of the green hills and sweet waters of our village. According to Mother, the original plan had been to build two main buildings and two side buildings, but they found they had only enough money to build the main house, which had cost more than three thousand yuan. The upstairs windows had been set too high, making the light there quite dim, so the second floor was ill suited for living. The bricks, stones, and floors could not have been stronger. Perhaps they would last a hundred years. Yet I felt no attraction to this spacious and well-built house. I would not have wished to live in it even if it had been as splendid and beautiful as a Roman cathedral. I had absolutely no intention of growing old and dying in this village.

"Daughter, you see how careworn your mother is because of you? For more than two months I have not been able to sleep because I have been worrying over having these wooden household articles painted, and then when the wind blew I feared that dust would land on the gilt-pattern paper, so I often got up in the middle of the night to cover everything with oil paper, and during the day I feared that the children would dirty them, or that sparrows would fly in and scatter droppings on the top of them, so every day I must have looked at them at least dozens of times—and each day I had to oversee the workers since otherwise they'd likely have taken two years to finish—but now more than thirty pieces of wooden household articles are completed, and also the bedcovers and the nets are all prepared, and we have only been waiting for you to return and sew your clothes." Mother spoke it all in a single breath.

I didn't answer her, just paced with my head down.

Thinking this was the sign of a young girl's bashfulness, she became even more breathless with delight, saying, "This time it is really the Buddha who urged you to return—ever since I learned that you had 'gone for a soldier,' I have lived a life of washing my face every day with tears, fearing the dangers you would encounter, and day and night I burned incense for you, and asked about your fortune, and made promises to the Buddha, and I fainted three times from anxiety when I first heard the news that you had gone to fight in the war, and once I passed out for more than two hours, and the Xiao family has been very concerned about you also, and they often send somebody over to ask news about you, and all their neighbors have been worried that their son might not have the good luck to have you, so I thank the heavens, the earth, and the Buddha that you have returned safely, and that now all is well!"

My head was full of words, but I didn't know where to begin. I thought I had better wait until Father returned before I brought up the matter of dissolving the marriage contract. Mother was so stubborn that I knew if I talked to her first, it would be a mistake. So I endured two days of living as a mute.

Who would have guessed that village news travels even faster than news on the wireless? Already the Xiao family knew I had returned. My fiancé's uncle Zhulin wrote a letter asking my family to find a date for his family to welcome their new relative. My big brother promptly brought the letter to me and asked, "How shall I reply to him?"

"Tell him we must wait for our father to return," I said.

He did as I suggested.

But how would I solve the big problem? The Xiao family knew I was back. This meant that the wedding day could not be far off. If I did not quickly cancel the marriage contract, it would be too late. Fortunately, Father came back from his friend's house that evening. No sooner had he read the letter from Zhulin than he came looking for me. He asked me what I thought would be the best date for the wedding.

"I returned home precisely to take care of this matter, Papa. I think you must still remember quite clearly the last letter I sent you. Xiao Ming and I simply cannot be united in marriage. He and I have never spoken a single word of love, and we feel no affection for each other whatever. His thinking and his interests are altogether unlike mine. His personality, his abilities . . . I am totally mystified. How could we come together as husband and wife?"

"What? Not marry? Are you thinking of dissolving the contract?" Father had barely opened his mouth when suddenly he slapped the table and began to berate me. Mother joined in, scolding me angrily and unceasingly, "Brute! Brute!"

But I had already decided to endure all. I answered, quite calmly, "Yes, I came back this time only to dissolve the marriage contract with Xiao Ming."

"Ha! You are thinking about dissolving the marriage contract?" cried Mother, growing angrier and angrier. "That you could never do, unless you had *never* come home. Now that you are here, do you still imagine you can break free? Even if you had powers greater than heaven's, you could not escape the grip of my hand." She made a gesture as if to hit me.

Father had already left in anger.

I realized it was impossible to continue our discussion at that moment. I retreated to my bedroom and wrote them a letter of more than five thousand words, explaining why I wanted to dissolve the marriage contract. The next day Father read the letter. To my surprise, he was unswayed by what I had written. In fact, he began to reprimand me in the severest terms: "Having read your letter, I see your reasons for wanting to dissolve the marriage contract. The two main ones are, first, that you do not love each other and, second, that your ideals are not the same. Now, I will answer you. Number one, love can exist only between husband and wife. Love begins *after* two people are married, certainly not before. At this moment you are not yet married to him, so of course there is no love. Number two, the word *ideal* can be used only between revolutionary comrades, not between husbands and wives. Let me ask you this—after you go with him and become his wife, is it not true that you will build a beautiful and perfect family where 'husband sings while wife follows,' that you will propagate and continue our ancestry with a new generation, and that you will manage your household duties and be a model of the virtuous wife and kind mother? You are not going with him to start a revolution, so why must your ideals be the same?"

"Papa, the idea that love comes only after marriage is merely your philosophy on the subject, and it is a strange philosophy, one that exists only in a feudal society. Times are different now. A man and a woman must experience emotional progress. Only then can they reach the goal called marriage. They begin by getting acquainted and becoming friends. If they have affection for each other as friends, they enter the romantic stage. When their love has reached the highest point, these two people will unite and become companions forever: husband and wife. As for having the same ideals, this is even more important for a husband and wife than for others. When two people have different ideals, they cannot connect. In that case, what would happen to a husband and wife who are trying to create lifelong happiness and bliss? If their ideals are not the same, each would go his or her own way, and instantly their love would be shattered. For the new generation, especially, marriage is not like it was in the feudal period, when its sole purpose was to allow people to organize a home. Marriage in the present generation is directly related to the reorganizing of society. After two people have united, they do not look for merely their own happiness. More important, they work together to serve the society and work hard to create a new society. They are not just spouses but also friends and faithful companions, offering each other mutual love. Xiao Ming's ideals are the opposite of mine, so he lacks the basic requirement for marrying me."

"Hah! Ideals? What does a woman want with such dangerous revolutionary ideals? You have had several years of teacher training. Once you are married, we will permit you to become a grade-school teacher in the village. I certainly don't think your husband will stop you."

"Stop debating with her, instantly!" Mother's words quickly followed Father's, and now she loudly bawled: "This thing is inhuman! Parents are as big as the sky! How dare you contradict us? We sent you to study because we hoped you would understand duty, courtesy, devotion, trust, politeness, righteousness, modesty, and shame. Who could have guessed that you would turn into a brute? You do not even want your own parents. The marriage contract was arranged by your parents when you were being nursed. To oppose the marriage contract is to oppose your parents. If you go forward with this shabby, shameful annulment, ruining your parents' reputation and shaming your ancestors, then I must . . . 'Water whirls in the Dongting Lake, good husbands and wives are beckoned by fate.' No matter what kind of person he is, if you are matched with him, you must marry him—especially since the Xiao family has both reputation and wealth. Xiao Ming is a good person. He is not blind or crippled. You must know that 'the match which lies a thousand miles apart is carried by a thread,' that husbands and wives have been matched in their previous lives. How can you oppose it?"

Hearing these words, I did not react, not even with a cold laugh. I had always anticipated that Mother would say these exact words.

"In this day and age we cannot force you to 'marry a chicken and follow the chicken; marry a dog and follow the dog,'" said Father. "But you certainly can marry a person like Xiao Ming. Read the letters he wrote to your third brother. They are fluent and to the point."

Father's words almost made me laugh out loud. His last sentence was most amusing. Xiao Ming couldn't even write a letter that made sense. I remembered how when we were both in grade school our Chinese language teacher, Mr. Xie, had asked me, "How is it that you and your fiancé are so different? Your marks make you number one in the school, but I am afraid he is number one in reverse." Later I received several letters from Xiao Ming, and I realized that his knowledge and intelligence were exactly as Mr. Xie had said. How could I join myself to a person who was so simple-minded and had no ideals?

Mother was berating me again. She said she could not imagine that, after sending me to study for so many years, I would disappoint them like this when I returned. From now on, she said, she would refuse to send the daughters of my oldest and youngest brothers to school.

When I heard this I became concerned for the children, who were now only in fourth grade. I knew from past experience that Mother would surely prevent them from studying any further. She would use this episode as an excuse and would deny them a chance to go to school. Oh, unlucky children! Is it I, or society, who has consigned you to this fate?

While I was deep in thought, I suddenly heard my father cursing again: "What kind of devil's den is a school? All those who enter it become bewitched. When they return home, they all make an outcry and beg to break off their marriage contracts. If parents have arranged a marriage, whether good or bad, they will not acknowledge it."

"But of course," I said. "How would parents know what kind of wife or husband the son or daughter needs? Marriage is of the greatest importance. It lasts a lifetime. Naturally, one must choose for oneself, in order to get a good partner." I knew these words would cause my parents to go berserk. Yet if I didn't say them, my brain would explode.

"Stop disgracing yourself, stop it instantly," cried Mother. "How can a girl choose her own husband? The Xiao family has a very good reputation. His third uncle was a member of the parliament in the province and has a reputation in the county. Your in-laws have sent us many gifts. Two years ago your fiancé came personally to visit me on my birthday. If you do this disgraceful deed, how can we face them? The common saying goes, 'A good horse does not eat the grass behind him, a good woman does not marry two husbands.' Do you still remember the story from *Biographies of Chaste Women*?"

"Hah!" interrupted Father. Mother had not finished, but he couldn't wait to continue. "Is it likely she has read *Biographies of Chaste Women*? She reads only novels about free love, and magazines and newspapers that tell about young girls committing suicide because they are not free to marry as they please, and that tell of young men breaking up with their families because they oppose old traditions. She has been influenced by these novels and newspapers, and now she has come back to oppose her parents, to oppose traditions."

"Laughable! Does she dare to oppose traditions?" Mother was becoming more and more pompous: "They were established by saints several thousand years ago. . . ." (Mother did not know how to speak the rest of her thought, so I have used dots.) "No one dares to oppose them. You mean to say that you, a girl, dare to oppose traditions? Aye! You should think about how the tablet that honors chastity was erected. Even a twelve-year-old girl knew enough to stay chaste, but you people who talk about freedom will probably marry twenty-four times in twelve months and still have no husband to celebrate the new year."

"Hmm." I made a light grunt, for I did not care to argue even half a sentence with Mother. I knew better. It was absolutely useless to reason with her. The only way to deal with her was to fight her to the death. I swore I would not give up until the marriage contract was dissolved.

"Though poverty and wealth are decided in heaven, personal effort still counts," said Mother. "The Xiao family has great wealth, and you too are able to earn money. The two of you will establish a family and occupations, and slowly you will become wealthy owners of a farm and land. What happiness you will enjoy!"

Oh, the more Mother spoke, the more muddled she became. These words were heartbreaking. She insulted me, belittled my character. She just did not understand her own daughter's views or character or individuality, or her ambitions. She thought I was a commonplace woman who disliked the poor and loved the rich. So she went out of her way to talk about getting rich.

"Don't speak such words, which have nothing to do with me," I said angrily. "I would be willing to marry a poor fellow who loves me. I certainly will not marry someone with money."

"If you don't marry him, what is your plan?" Mother slapped the table hard. Naturally, this did not scare me. But I was worried that she had hurt her hand.

Father answered for me: "She plans to dissolve the marriage contract." (I was very grateful to him at this moment.)

"What will she do if we do not dissolve the marriage contract?"

"Her letter says that if it is not dissolved, she will kill herself."

"Good, let her die. I nurtured her in vain. I even sent her to study for these many years. Perhaps in my previous life I owed her a debt, and now . . . she . . . she—" Mother suddenly burst out crying. Her teardrops, nose drips, and spit all ran together. She recklessly hit her head against the wall, continuously. Father was afraid that she would get hurt. Immediately he ran over and held her tightly. When they heard our mother crying, my sister and sister-in-law rushed over. While they all were entangled in turmoil, hand and foot, I secretly slipped away and went to walk in the fields.

The sun shone warmly, yet my heart was cold.

Far away, a man wearing a long white gown walked toward me. I took a closer look: it was my big brother.

He asked what I was thinking about, walking all alone. So I told him all the details of the farce we had been enacting. My brother hesitated a long time and then wrinkled his brows. He said, in a discouraged tone, "You shouldn't have come back. Now that you are home, how can you escape? I think—"

"What are you thinking? Do you actually want me to sacrifice myself and marry Xiao Ming?"

"Uh . . . that is my thought."

"No, I absolutely cannot marry him. I will struggle to the end."

"Mother is far more fierce and frightening than any autocratic emperor in history, whether ancient or modern, in or out of China. Do you mean to say you don't realize that? I failed to ask for her consent when I took your sister-in-law to Yiyang, and when I returned Mother said that I had committed the crime of 'disobeying parents to please the wife.' She punished me by making me kneel for two hours while balancing a large basin of water on my head. I will never forget that incident. As for the marriages of your other brothers and your sister, they are all extremely unfortunate and cause much pain, but no one dares to mention divorce. You are braver than we are, but I am afraid that even you can only fight the war outside—you cannot make a revolution at home." As my big brother spoke this last sentence, he started to laugh.

But I spoke seriously, saying, "Big Brother, don't ridicule me and don't underestimate my power. To tell you the truth, I knew long ago that if I came home, I would be imprisoned. But if I don't dissolve the marriage contract, I will never be able to marry another person. The Xiao family could find me at any time and use the marriage contract to cause trouble. To avoid this—and also because I want to formally declare war on feudal society—I will stand firm to the end. I certainly don't intend to stop until I have reached my goal. I would rather sacrifice my life to oppose ancient traditions and overthrow feudal rules, than to submit to the old society's immoral power. . . ."

"I must go back," said my big brother, looking pitiful as he glanced east and west to see if anyone had spotted us. "If Mother should find out that we have been talking here, she will think we have arranged this meeting."

"OK, you go on back. I don't want to get you involved. You or anyone else."

"Yes, all right. Good luck in your struggle as a lone soldier."

He walked away, wearing a smile of ridicule.

I lingered alone among the dikes in the fields for a long while before at last I returned home. I didn't eat dinner on that day. I didn't dare look upon my parents' faces, which were as cold as iron and seemingly prepared to devour a human being. Right after twilight I went to bed.

Knowing I was very upset, my sister and sisters-in-law came to my bedroom to comfort me. They dared not speak too much or too loudly, for Mother was in the next room and could clearly hear our every move. For fear she would hear them, they each leaned down to my ear and spoke in a tiny voice. They begged me not to grieve too much.

My sister invited my aunt to come see me. She was Mother's second youngest sister, the one who now lived in our old house. Her husband, a doorman at the county office of the department of education, earned a monthly salary of six yuan. Their two sons had been military men, and the younger was still a lieutenant in the military. The older son, who was fond of prostitutes and gambling, had once served as an assistant to the regimental commander but was drummed out of the service for not observing military regulations. Now no one knew where he had drifted to. Originally, this aunt had also had a younger son and a daughter, but those two children had died of illness two years before. Their deaths had made her cry until she went blind. She had absolute faith in the notion that Fate decides and that everything in this life has been arranged in a previous life. She was a true Buddhist; each day she chanted prayers and ate vegetarian food. She was even more superstitious than Mother, but not so bigoted. For instance, she allowed her son to marry a woman from the outside. Also, she often urged Mother to reform, saying to her, "Now the world has changed— don't treat your children too harshly. They are educated people. They want to have important careers. Don't hold them back."

Mother did not accept her sister's honest advice. Instead, she reprimanded her sister, accusing her of having neither the ability nor the good sense to be a parent: "No matter how the world has changed, parents are still parents. If children born to me do not obey me, how can I rule other people?"

When my aunt heard Mother assert that "parents are as big as the sky," she was silenced. She could only lower her head and answer, "Yes, yes."

I pitied my aunt when she came into my room. For a long time after she sat down, she didn't dare open her mouth. She waited until Mother began talking with the foreman. Only then did she dare speak to me, in a faint voice, saying, "Minggang, you have just returned, don't quarrel with your mother. Her temper has always been very short—go along with her for a bit. Marriage is destined in the previous life. Even though your future husband may not be as smart as you, it won't hurt you to submit a little. Then in days to come everyone will call you virtuous, and your name will be passed down through the generations—how imposing that will be!"

"Aunt, please don't say any more. None of you understands my pain. I don't wish for you to come and comfort me. Please don't pay any attention to me from now on." I begged her, and my tears rolled down. My aunt was full of pity for me, and she accompanied me in crying. My sister also wept.

From that day on I lived my life as if I were in prison.

·ૠ·

LONG AND GLOOMY NIGHTS of loneliness and silence.

After eight o'clock each evening our village turned quiet as death. Yet on one particular day the people of my family were very late in going to bed. Perhaps they were discussing my problem; they talked softly till after midnight. Finally, they stopped.

Moon climbed to the middle of the sky. Pale moonlight shone on the netting over my bed. A mosquito buzzed. Had it not been for this weak sound, breaking the profound silence of the night, I might have suspected that I was lying in a solitary, soundless grave.

Tossing and turning, I considered my problem. Certainly it was not one that could be resolved peacefully. Already my parents had taken up their position as my enemies. They would not give way or give up their authority as parents, nor would I yield to them. Mother would insist on carrying through the law of the feudal society, namely, that if the father wants the child to die, then it must die. But I happened to be a rebel who opposed feudal society. With mother and daughter two eras apart in their ideals, how could they avoid clashing? No question about it, only by risking my life in a struggle with my family could I finally prevail and gain my freedom.

But how difficult the situation is! Other than Xiang, no one in our village understands me. Though my sister and the others cry with me, my sister does not understand why I must dissolve the marriage contract, and she wonders why I cannot simply put up with the suffering, like she does. She wonders why a girl must go away to study and why a girl must marry only the one she loves. My sister's tears show that she loves me very much, feels sorry for me, fears the unexpected dangers I face. When I was little and wanted to go to school, I tried to commit suicide by refusing to eat, and after that incident my sister understood my resolute character. She knew that whenever I undertook to do something, I would never stop until I achieved my goal. In these ways she understands me better than my sister-in-law or my aunt, but what good is it when she cannot help me get out of here? She cries with me all day, but what use is crying?

And as for Xiang? Though she lives quite close by, she cannot come to see me. Her family is as autocratic as mine. Because she has refused to marry a man who whores and gambles, they now keep her in a soft prison, like me. Even if by some fluke she managed to visit me, she and I still could not discuss anything, for my mother would be close by, spying on us. . . .

And my big brother? His fear of Mother turns him into such a pathetic weakling. Though his brain is slightly more modern than Mother's, his aspiration to become an official and earn big money makes him the perfect model of officialdom. It is true that he speaks sympathetic words to me. But who can guarantee that he does not disparage me behind my back? No, a person who does not think as I do certainly will not want to help me.

And my youngest brother is in Changsha: distant water cannot save one from nearby fire. Even if he should write and speak on my behalf, how could my parents—deeply rooted, as they are, in their feudal ideas—accept his suggestions?

Or my second brother? He really loves me the most, and he is the one who can give me the most help, but we haven't communicated for several months, and I don't know where he is.

Big Brother speaks true . . . I am a lone and struggling soldier. Yes, and with no one to help me, I sometimes fear I can only fail.

Suicide is probably the best solution: a single moment of pain, then a lifetime of anguish is relieved. And, anyway, what is the point of life? Sooner or later comes death. Whatever one achieves, however many distinguished services one performs, when the last breath ceases, it all turns to nothing. All illusions are then wafted into nothingness. Rather than offer this vigorous life of mine to be butchered by others, let me sacrifice myself. I might as well die by my own hand, to my own satisfaction. My life is mine and I have the right to do with it as I please. Death, my final peace, will be also my final victory.

I thought and puzzled, writhing amid my own thoughts till I seemed to be twisting and wringing my own guts. Death seemed about the only way out. Yesterday I had thought that Father might pity me, might be moved by the letter I had written to him, for each word in it had cost me a tear. But today proved that Father and Mother were on the same side of the battle line. His strong, stiff, cold, and cruel manners were no longer those of the loving father who once had wrapped me in his leather coat and held me while I slept. I understood completely—in a single instant—what sort of thing affection really is: it changes as soon as thoughts conflict, and then children do not recognize their parents as parents, parents do not acknowledge their children as children. Each person struggles for his or her own way, his or her own ideal. This thing called affection is terrifying.

Better for a person rich in emotions not to understand the truth about emotions. Now I do understand, and so I have thrown out the philosophy that a mother's love is above all things . . . and my heart is almost breaking from pain. Mother, who once loved me the most, does not spare me or pity me now. What is there left for me to desire?

Slowly the moon grew pale, sank low. I could hear the faraway sound of a dog barking. Our cock was beginning to crow. Suddenly the room became frighteningly dark, and I knew that this was a sign that dawn would be breaking. Father and Mother were beginning to talk. Their voices were so low that no matter how closely I listened, I couldn't hear even half a sentence.

Death? Is it true that this is the only road to follow? Why not think of your own future? You have often blamed those who commit suicide for lacking courage, for being too weak and too useless. To search for life is the instinct of all living creatures. So how can a person filled with the spirit of all things, who has the intelligence to create all things, be seeking death instead of striving for life? Suppose it is true that you are utterly insignificant. Then killing yourself will have not the least effect on the society—certainly it will be no loss to society. But can you face your country? Or face your parents, who have fed and clothed you and who gave you an education? Think: you have been baptized by revolution. You have the mission to change society. You have been to the front line and worked under fire to kill enemies and save comrades, and you once swore to struggle for the liberation of millions of workers of the world who have been repressed. You are not a weak and old-fashioned female who lacks abilities. Rather, you are a modern woman, resolute, courageous, strong willed. You are a warrior who opposes all feudal rules . . . now, have you really forgotten your duties? Death would show your failure and tradition's victory. The feudal society is an evil that murders without shedding blood. Every day it opens its bloody mouth to devour those youths who lack the courage to struggle. Are you willing to be swallowed by it? Also, consider a little further—suicide is a stupid act. When you are dead, the old society will have one less rebel. Even if you haven't the courage to carry a gun and rush onto the battlefield to attack and kill enemies, you should do a little work to benefit the human race.

All night, Life and Death struggled in my brain. And finally Life won.

Even so, the following night I couldn't sleep. I watched the moon struggle out of the dark clouds . . . and shrink away again into blackness.

I thought of what my big brother had said that same day, that he was going tomorrow to the main town of our county. I wondered if perhaps he could help me a little. Under silvery moonlight I secretly got up and wrote him a letter, asking him to rescue me.

The following day my big brother read my letter but said nothing. He just kept shaking his head, showing that he could not help. Again I cried. The two of us sat silently and faced each other for a few minutes. Then he quietly left this narrow prison.

My life of lost sleep now began.

Deep night. I opened my window to let in the breeze. The moon had already passed over the top of my mosquito net. Because of the humidity, my swollen and infected feet had been extremely painful ever since I had returned from the front. I groaned and cried all night, but Mother did not call out to me even once. Now I was truly an abandoned child. No longer would I be stroked by my loving mother, no longer comforted by her. Never would I be able to kiss her, to lie in her warm bosom. Never would I hear cries of "Sweetheart, Precious!"

I remembered how when I was sick in times past she had kept me company all night and nursed me diligently. But now? She would not come to ask about me even if I were dying in bed. Heavens, what was happening?

Moonlight shone on my teardrops as they fell on the pillow.

Bright teardrops, leap into my mother's heart. Moon, take my sad and skinny image and shine it into my mother's eyes. Why has she become so cold, so cruel?

I cried the entire night, yet heard not a whisper from my mother. Was she purposely ignoring me? Mama—are you really unable to give me your true love, just one more time?

✣

AFTER MY BIG BROTHER left, I awaited his letters every day. Five days went by. Ten days. A month. Still no word. I thought: only I can save myself; I can't ask for help from others.

Now all books and letters mailed to me had to pass Father's inspection. Things I mailed out were inspected even more thoroughly than if I had been in a real prison. I had given my big brother a letter to mail to Mr. Sun Fuyuan, and fortunately my brother had hidden it beneath his hat. Otherwise, that letter would certainly have been checked and confiscated.

How could I put up with such a life of total bondage?

Xiang's younger sister, Qingqing, was a smart and lively twelve-year-old who often did favors for Xiang and me, and for all her help we would never forget her. She was our green-clothed messenger. Many times my mother scolded her, calling her a spy. Yet Qingqing continued carrying our letters secretly, passing our words back and forth. Each time she came to visit me, she was forced to suffer a long interrogation and search before my mother would allow her to enter my room.

I was like a prisoner, period. Pathetic. I was locked day and night in a small room. During the daylight hours only a ray of sunlight and I were companions; at night the moon shone on my tears and was my only friend. No visitors from outside could see me. I had become a prisoner without having committed a crime.

One day Mother suddenly called me out of my cell, for Qingqing had come again. As soon as I saw Qingqing my spirit was lifted and I felt unspeakable joy and gratitude, as if I beheld a savior who would rescue me.

"Is your sister well?" I asked.

"Of course—she is better off than *you*."

Just as Mother was about to launch some thunder, Qingqing used her eyes to point at the ground. At the same time she moved her foot to reveal a ball of paper all blackened by her stepping on it.

How to get it in my hand?

As I was anxiously pondering what to do, someone arrived at the house and Mother left to talk with the visitor. I quickly grabbed the paper ball and returned to my room to read it. On the slip were these simple words: "I can no longer endure this kind of life. Let's plan to escape."

Luckily, Mother didn't notice this slip of paper, or she would have turned the sky upside down to crush our escape plan. A dangerous moment.

Father now ignored me, treated me with the same looks that he would treat an enemy. Clearly, he knew the pain in my heart. Yet he didn't speak so much as a single sentence to me. Each day he just played with his grandchildren and smiled. It seemed to me that he had changed his disposition utterly and deliberately. Mother had changed even more drastically. Each day she put on her wanting-to-eat-people face and spared me not a single glance. But when female guests arrived, she would entertain them with smiles and brag about how I obeyed her and would tell them I was quietly preparing my trousseau at home.

"Your young lady has had such good family training that she is surely different. Even after studying away from home all these years, she has not turned into a 'free' person.* Truly this is your venerable self's good fortune." Many times I heard people flatter my mother in this manner, and it made my flesh creep. Mother even proudly bragged about her awe-inspiring reputation, saying, "Other women change into bad women as soon as they leave home, but my daughter didn't dare. Even if she had become a female emperor outside, she would still obey her parents' orders."

Again, she brought up the philosophy of parents being as big as the sky. I felt sorry for her, knowing that soon her authority would be overthrown by me alone. If Mother had guessed what lay ahead, perhaps she would not have locked me up and kept me so closely watched.

My two legs were swollen like round pillars. I put plaster medicine on them, but they did not get better. Doctors were not to be found in the village. I regretted having returned so soon, but I never regretted having gone off to be a soldier. I had contracted my illness during the march when we camped at night in the fields. Damp air had made my legs swell, and the

---

*Our village referred to free-choice marriage in the outside world as *free.*

abscesses had burst. If I had not been hindered by such painful feet, I would have already escaped.

⚜

ONE DAY I received news that infuriated me and pushed me almost to the point of committing suicide: my cousin told me that every letter I had mailed to my friends had fallen into Father's hands.

"My God—am I not even as good as real prisoners? *They* at least have the right to communicate by letter. And yet I do not?"

Sobbing, I fainted on my sister's bed. Then she flew into a fluster, thinking this must be a medical emergency. How pathetic I was—secretly getting up to write to my friends to beg for rescue, yet not even a single letter had reached their hands. The more I thought about it, the more miserable I felt. Sister's pillow was wet from my crying.

"Don't cry, Sister. Even if you break your heart with weeping, our parents will not return the letters to you."

Sister's words awoke me to the truth, and I stopped crying. Since my parents treated me with force, I would answer with defiance. Already I had an escape plan in mind. But when to act? And by what route? Those were the questions. Xiang was locked up and couldn't see me, yet we had to make our move at the same time if we were to escape together. How could we pull it off?

For a full month I had received no letters, not even a newspaper. I realized that all my letters must have been confiscated by Father. One day when everyone was out of the house, I found a way to open the door that connected to Mother's bedroom. Under Father's pillow I discovered a registered letter from Mr. Sun. In it Mr. Sun mentioned that he had already sent me twenty yuan to pay the fare to escape to Hankou. Of course, I had never seen the money. I looked at the envelope closely and saw that it had been forwarded from the major town in our county. I could hardly believe that all this was happening to me. I was stunned that I had fallen into such desperate straits.

I spent my life sleeping all day. No books to read, no papers to look at. I didn't bother writing any more letters. Apart from some coarse sheets of toilet paper, I had nothing to write on but my precious treasure, my diary. This I had hidden under the straw mat. Late every night or before the sky was light, I would quietly light the lamp and lie in bed and write about my distressing life. When I finished writing I would put the diary back into its hiding place. Mother didn't realize that I had this big secret. I dared not think what would happen if she should discover it.

Was this the life of a human being? I couldn't tolerate it any longer. I wondered whether perhaps another letter had come from someone wishing to help me escape, for my parents seemed to be even more vigilant. One day at twilight I decided to write a short letter to Mr. Sun—I would ask Qingqing to find a way to have someone mail it. I couldn't write in my room, because Mother now sat in my room all day and did her chores. I could only take a pencil and go into the toilet to write, and this I did. But just as I had laid the toilet paper on my legs to begin my letter, the lavatory door opened suddenly and a head appeared. It was Mother.

"What? You are so clever as to hide here and write letters? Quickly, give it to me!" She walked over to grab the paper out of my hands, but I promptly threw both paper and pencil into the toilet pit. At the same time I angrily answered, "Is it necessary for you to watch me defecate?"

"Yes! So what will you do about it?"

After this Mother treated me even more like a prisoner. I treated her like a cruel warden. Often we did not speak to each other for four or five days at a time.

WHEN MOTHER SAW that my legs were not completely well, she said it must be because we had not yet fulfilled her promise to repay Blood Basin Incense—a promise that she had made when I was born. She decided we should leave on August 28 and travel to Heng Mountain to burn incense. I took a bath on the evening of the twenty-seventh, changed into clean underclothes, and very early the next morning I arose and put on a bright red shirt and pants that Mother had made especially for this occasion. I wore a green belt and my head was covered with a red scarf. When I looked into a mirror, I was astounded to see I had turned into a red demon.

Ever since I was small I had resisted meaningless superstitions, so why today, like a little lamb, was I letting Mother manipulate me? There were reasons.

First, every day locked in that room I got so bored I could barely breathe. I thought that a long journey would naturally dispel the accumulated boredom in my brain—particularly since Heng Mountain was one of the famous Five Peaks, a place long recommended by travelers for its mysterious and secluded scenery. This would be my chance to see it. Also, perhaps partway through my journey I would be able to run away—and then I'd truly thank sky and earth.

The road from my home to Heng Mountain was more than 180 miles. The round trip would take ten days in a sedan chair, if we did not dally. From the day we left until the evening we returned home, our entire family would have to eat vegetarian food. In addition, before each meal my mother and I would be required to run to the so-called Three Heaven Gate and kowtow, and Mother would inquire by divination—this was even more laughable—whether the Buddha would allow us to eat. If he would, then we could get up from where we touched our heads to the earth and eat our meal. If not, we would need to repent all our sins so the divination signs would be reversed and we could finally get up. It was a pitiful performance, yet Mother claimed that her devout heart could move sky and earth.

Most disagreeable of all was that we had to sing the Incense Worship Song, a song Mother sang and sang until it turned to mush. Whether she was sitting in the sedan chair or resting, or praying in the morning or praying in the evening, she kept singing that song from beginning to end, nonstop. I held the song in my hand, but I simply did not want to turn a single page of it.

Mother's sedan chair was always right behind mine, and at night we slept in the same bed, and the moment we entered our lodging she refused to let me take a single step outside, as if she feared I'd escape in an instant.

On the third evening we stayed in a spot rich with poetry, a place called Shijiawan, where a large yard was surrounded by a flowing creek, with green trees and long, slender bamboos growing in disorder. A young girl of seventeen or eighteen was out strolling. She noticed my red shirt and pants, and she walked near to have a closer look at me. I got up to let her have a seat. She smiled and asked, "Are you going to repay the Blood Basin Incense?"

"Yes."

"Have you gone to school?"

"No."

"You look like you have."

"Actually, no—I cannot read a single word."

She examined me minutely, head to toe, as if she were a fortune-teller—and this made the sedan carriers all break out laughing. Mother, who was preparing to pray to the gods, didn't pay any attention to our conversation. The young girl finished praying and began pressing her views on me, saying, "Two months ago we had a Women's Association here, to liberate women who are repressed. All who joined us had to unbind their feet, cut their hair, and not blindly worship Buddha."

Listening to her, I realized she was a woman who had new ideas, so I felt very happy and immediately started to talk with her. When Mother went to the toilet, I took the opportunity to walk to the home of this Miss Shi, and we chatted for half an hour. Her father, who was very free and open, did not believe in Buddha either. He offered me two salted eggs. I quickly accepted and ate them.

Then Mother came running to find me. As soon as she spotted me she began scolding me, not caring that I was in someone else's home. After we returned to our lodging she immediately told me to kneel down and repent. "The head lady here told me that this Miss Shi is not good to associate with. She is an officer of the Women's Association and she is—on top of everything else—always talking about freedom. Why were you speaking to her?"

I didn't answer, just stood quietly.

"You didn't drink their tea, did you? When paying respect to the gods, you must not taste even half a bite of other people's food, not even boiled water."

"No, I didn't drink their boiled water," I replied—but I was thinking, I not only drank their tea but I ate their salted eggs.

Mother said I should not have any contact with the outside world, and she finally forced me to kneel, for she wanted me to repent. She too knelt down. She began burning paper money. But I was tasting again the words of Miss Shi: "The Women's Association was disbanded two months ago. This could not be helped, but we won't lose heart, no matter what. There will be a day when we will take the lead, . . . if women don't join the revolution, they will forever remain unliberated."

After five days in a sedan chair every bone in my body was aching. Still, the wilderness scenery was intoxicatingly beautiful at twilight and dawn. As the red sun rose, a million rays of gold suddenly lit the earth and I felt all of life's force exploding. The world was a mass of fire and everyone was living inside the fire, inside the heat and the energy and the light. I was as happy as angels in heaven. I utterly forgot life's pains and worries. I knew only that the entire earth was filled with beauty, filled with the lively and stimulating air of dawn, filled with infinite hope and radiance.

We arrived at Heng Mountain. The town, although a district town, was not as festive as Changsha, yet it had a hall even more beautiful and splendid than a palace. The hall was jammed with crowds of people coming and going, everyone burning incense.* After we had burned our incense we started immediately for the top of Zhurong Peak, passing by many interesting places without visiting them—as if gazing at flowers while riding a horse. We left early in the morning and returned after twilight, for it was more than twenty-one miles from the foot of the mountain to the top and back. The road was steeper than a ladder and twisted like a Z, so riding up in a sedan chair was impossible. We had to walk. The sedan carriers and the man who carried incense paper hiked behind us, panting. On that day my spirits were light and my legs did not hurt as much as usual, especially when I was climbing, so I walked quite quickly. Mother could not keep up, yet her mouth kept moving, reciting the Incense Worship Song. Then, suddenly, I saw that she had stopped walking. Her entire body appeared to be trembling. I ran to her and begged her to sit down and rest for a while. She knelt and said, "Grandfather Divinity, please forgive her, she is a child without sense: she opens her mouth and the river runs. I beg the Divinity to be merciful, to save her."

"What? Why should I repent?" I asked sternly. "I didn't say anything wrong."

---

*Those who burned incense had to kneel and pray every five or ten steps. This was called incense praying. All people who did this wore the same clothes. They covered their heads with red scarves and wore green belts. But if their mothers were dead, they covered their heads with green scarves and wore white belts. Around the waist of each was tied a big red packet. In their hands each held an incense rack that was like a small bench with three lit sticks of incense on top of it.

"No matter how difficult it is to walk, you must not rest. For if only you think about the Divinity with a sincere heart, he will let the wind blow you upward."

"Good. Then you can wait for the wind to blow you."

Saying this was a mistake. Mother punished me by making me kneel for several minutes. Naturally, I had to repent again.

Along the way were many tea houses with thatched roofs. Inside they sold boiled water, sweet potatoes, and corn. I liked to sit in them to look at the scenery or to buy food.

We were fast approaching the Southern Heaven Gate when Mother suddenly had stomach pains. Unable to walk a single step farther, she ordered the carrier to call me. I was to kneel down and repent.

"Now? Why?"

"You must kneel. I can't walk. This must be because you have done wrong."

"What a joke. If I had done wrong, why doesn't the Divinity punish me?"

"Don't talk anymore. Quickly, kneel down!"

There was no way out. I had to obey her.

After she had rested for a while, she recovered from her exhaustion. Then she continued walking. But she was so stubborn that she insisted to the carriers, "Grandfather Divinity, truly, is the most clever of all. Nothing can fool him. If the child had not knelt and repented, my illness would never have disappeared so quickly."

I very much wanted to tell her that she was the Divinity, that she had caused her own stomachache and breathlessness by walking too fast, and that naturally she felt better after she had rested. But I was afraid of having to kneel again, so I said nothing.

After passing the Southern Heaven Gate, the Lion's Peak, and the Pine Remembrance Temple, we arrived at Divinity Celebration Temple. It was packed with men and women earnestly burning incense and casting divine lots. Some people, who were fasting and burning Hunger Incense, were so skinny that they looked as if their bones were covered with pieces of leather.* Those who were praying while burning incense sang in high-

---

*Those who burned the incense could not eat anything and could drink only a few mouthfuls of water each day. This was called Hunger Incense.

pitched voices, "First pray to Heavenly Father and Sun and Moon, second pray to Earth Palace and Heaven and Earth." The whole temple was filled with smoke and the mingling sounds of noisy gongs and drums and the clacking of wooden fish. Everybody knelt behind the priest and chanted prayers as if they had just seen the devil—and suddenly the whole place seemed to me like hell, and every skinny, yellow-faced, incense-burning guest seemed a demon messenger.

Just as I was gazing, almost mesmerized, my mother pulled me down and made me kneel. Grandfather Divinity (according to her) had refused my incense. We cast more than thirty lots while Mother forced me to kowtow and repent. But my mind was elsewhere. I was counting the kowtows of the woman next to me—she had already kowtowed sixty times and was still going for more.

I certainly thought that after we had burned our incense we would have some leisure to enjoy the scenery. I never imagined that Mother would not allow me to so much as linger. Just as we had hurried up the mountain, now we hurried down it.

Failed. My plan had utterly failed. I had had no time to enjoy the scenery, no chance to escape. What could I say? I could only follow her, downcast. My first impression of Heng Mountain had been but a blur. Apart from the lofty peak, the climb up, and the diversions of the road, I had experienced no sensations of beauty. Even so, I did see many strange sights—yes, some heartbreaking glimpses—and I did taste a sort of life that other people had not.

IN THE TWILIGHT of a rainy day my aunt secretly brought me a letter from my third brother. My heart began to pound even before I opened it. . . . I knew this was a sign of bad luck. Sure enough, on the sheet were drawn a few large words that said my second brother had died in Nanjing.

My god! Just a week ago I had received a letter from him. Could he really be dead? I don't know how I got through the next few days. I lost interest in living. I no longer had courage to struggle, I could think only of dying. I wished to go down to the Yellow Springs to find my second brother, who adored me.

There were five of us children, but I was closest to my second brother. When I was studying in grade school, he introduced me to modern novels and wrote me many interesting letters in the vernacular. When I passed the exam to enter the First Provincial Girls Teacher Training School, he did his utmost to lead me onto the path of literature. In those days he was teaching at the Jinshan Middle School in Shanxi Province. His salary was small, yet every year he mailed me at least twenty or thirty yuan to buy books. Later, when he returned to Changsha, he enthusiastically introduced me to many more famous Chinese and foreign classics, and any passages I did not understand he would always carefully explain to me. In the spring of 1926 his tuberculosis flared up, and he began spitting blood two or three times a day. After he finished his treatments at the Xiangya Hospital, he went to convalesce at Kuntao Pavilion and Daoxiang Temple, two places on Yuelu Hill.* For more than four months I gave up my studies to keep him company. At that time he could not eat solid food. During the day I took his pulse and his temperature, and I heated milk and cooked chicken broth for him. At night I sat at the head of his bed and told him interesting stories from school and softly sang lullabies from our childhood to lull him to sleep. When I went across the river to shop for him, he would sometimes become anxious after not seeing me for three hours, and when I returned he would cry while holding my hand, saying, "Good Sister, do not leave me again. I would rather not eat, I only want you to be by my side all day long."

My third brother was teaching at the Yuyun Middle School at that time, and he could come to visit us only on Sundays. Apart from a child who cooked for me, it was only the pair of us, brother and sister, who relied on each other and lived on that quiet hill.

I remember a night in early summer when the moonlight was splashing the earth like mercury, breeze whistling softly through the trees, little bugs crying *chi-chi* in the grass. The entire Yuelu Hill seemed like a beautiful goddess bathing in moonbeams. The graveyard watchman, Zhusan, and the cook, Xiaodong, had long since gone to sleep. My brother begged me to hold him up, to help him outside to see the moonlight. I tried to stop him

---

*Yuelu Hill is in Changsha on the west bank of the Xiang River. Along the paths of the hill are various temples, pavilions, and other scenic spots.—trans.

from going, for I feared his blood vessels would break if he moved. But he insisted. I arranged the lounge chair and then helped him outside. As soon as his feet had stepped beyond the door he loudly shouted, "Yah! How beautiful! How beautiful!

> The moonlight is like water.
> And the water like the sky."

I laughed with joy because of his happiness.

And when he had spoken that last line, he too began to laugh. "Sister, you see how pitiful I am from having been ill. I can't even compose an ordinary poem."

I helped him lie down. The gentle breeze had blown away the remaining heat of the day and had blown away my brother's delirium. He was extremely happy. Slowly, he told me of a scene long ago, when he had watched the moon at the Yantai seashore.

"You cannot even imagine the greatness of the sea and the beautiful colors of night by the seashore. If my illness is completely cured this summer, I must take you to Yantai or Qingdao."

Because he was well treated and well cared for, his health grew better day by day. But then another misfortune landed on him: he fell in love with my friend, Miss Shu Ruiyu. Those two poured out their hearts at first sight, and not long afterward the heat of love reached a boiling point. But within three months Ruiyu quite unexpectedly dropped my brother and went back to her old lover. After this shock he immediately left Changsha and went to Wuchang. In Wuchang he lived a very hard life. His bedroom furnishings consisted of an army cot, a military blanket, and a few books that he used as a pillow.

I also remembered the days when I was in the military school, and every week he would come to visit me and a few of my friends. He would always bring us candy and smoked fish and fragrant pieces of beef jerky.

"Brother, bring more next time; otherwise, I'll not so much as look upon your face."

I was just teasing him, but he was really afraid I would refuse to see him, so on his next visit he actually brought along six large bags of peanuts, melon seeds, candy, dried shrimp—all the snacks I liked to eat. Carefully, he opened all the packages and set them out on the table in the visitors' lounge. But suddenly, just when we were in the midst of eating them with great delight, we heard a whistle blow. So we all hurried away to assemble, leaving the treats behind. My brother had to rush away, for he saw that the visiting hour was over. My friends and I drilled for two hours and then returned to the lounge, but the peanuts and melon seeds had all vanished without a trace. I thought perhaps my brother was playing a trick and had taken them back with him. Later I found out that they had been confiscated by the officer in charge for the week; he claimed that things with shells were dirty.

In June my brother was sent out to Henan Province. He did not tell me when he was leaving. He only sent a very tragic and moving letter en route; the last two sentences were these: "Dear Sister, I have left, don't be sad. We will shake hands at the front in the not-too-distant future."

A few days later I too was sent to the front, but to Exi. From then on, he and I were in different corners of the earth, our voices and letters cut off from each other. When I returned home I wrote to several friends, asking his whereabouts. But they all said they didn't know where he was. Then, suddenly, just as I was becoming extremely worried, I received a letter from him. In it he told me that he was spitting more and more blood. I mailed my reply. Not long afterward the tragic news suddenly arrived.

I cannot write more. In my life history the death of my second brother is the saddest page. Countless bloody marks were drawn deep in my heart. I called, "Second Brother!" all day long, as if I had lost my soul. Sometimes I cried and sometimes I laughed.

They all said I was mad.

I knew that my brother's death had been hastened by this feudal society, and I wanted revenge. I wished to fight this society-of-a-thousand-wrongs until its flowers dropped and water washed it all away.

Night fell. I blew the lamps dark. Silently, I sat and waited for his soul to return.

One night, two nights, ten nights—they passed amid my tears and sighs. The house stood silent. I did not see his shadow return.

I spat blood, what bright red blood! I wished I could end like my brother. I wished to become a little bird and fly with my brother to Qingdao, to Yantai, to the Himalaya Mountains, to the most beautiful forest, to the loneliest island on earth. We would fly to the ends of the seas, to the highest point in the sky, through a wide and boundless world that would let us soar, let us flee. . . .

Everyone was terribly sad when they heard the news of his death. Father almost died of a broken heart. Mother fainted twice and cried every day. Yet no sooner had she dried her tears than she again began preparing my dowry. I thought perhaps she would have learned a lesson from what had happened to my brother. I thought perhaps she would lighten her pressure on me, maybe even allow me to dissolve the marriage contract. On the contrary, she stubbornly held her ground and insisted on carrying out her plans.

Ah, dear Mother, you true believer in feudal philosophy. Was it not enough to have caused one death?

NOW CAME AN excellent opportunity—Xiang and I found an excuse to meet. We would take incense to Chaoyang Buddhist Convent to worship the Goddess of Mercy on September 19, traditionally the third birthday of the goddess. Starting at seven o'clock in the morning on that day large groups of women brought incense and paper money to worship her. Mother was devoted to the Goddess of Mercy, so if I earnestly said that I wished to go and burn incense, she would certainly allow it. She was confident that I could never escape her grip, however crafty I might be—though she was clever enough to foresee that I might use this occasion to discuss secret plans with Xiang.

We carried baskets filled with stick incense, wood incense, and paper ingots. On the wood incense I wrote the words "Girl believer Xie Minggang prays for Goddess of Mercy's protection." We knelt and kowtowed four times. Hurriedly we burned our incense. But just as we were about to slip away and run to the mountaintop to discuss our plans for escape, we were unexpectedly stopped by some worshippers who asked us to write words on the wood incense for them. We did so, then slipped off.

In a mountain hollow amid many ancient cypresses we sat close, knee touching knee. Dry yellow leaves danced through the sky, following the autumn breeze. The locusts' somber wail sounded like sobbing. We sat in the silent desolation of a mountain forest.

"Xiang, I really did not imagine that coming home would mean such suffering. My life is actually worse than a prisoner's." I spoke only these two sentences before I choked up and could not continue.

Xiang did not cry easily. She sighed a long sigh and waited a long while before answering, "I too never thought your mother could be so cruel and stubborn. But because you came back, you will just have to put up with the situation. I mean, if it turns out that you just can't stand it, then we will escape."

I interrupted her. "You mean to say *you* can stand it?"

"Of course not. I can't bear it. But I also know that you are less tolerant than I. So, yes, I am thinking that today we should discuss a way of escape."

"I have already made up my mind to run far and fly high. Xiang, let us go soon. Don't bring anything. If only we escape the tiger's mouth, our lives will be much more satisfying than they are now—even if we must beg for food, even if we must become servants. Supposing no one hires us or that we can't get food to eat. Then I would still be willing to die of hunger in a strange land. Let's decide to do it. We only need to agree on a date, time, and place of our meeting. But to keep others from discovering our secret, let's not be seen together before we set out."

Just at this moment someone found us—sent by Mother. We hid the unspoken words that filled our chests and, disappointed, returned to our dark prisons.

Now that my plan was in motion I felt quite happy. Several times a day I visited with my sister and others, and now I began to tell them that I realized I had been wrong. I said that I now understood my mother's love for me and saw the errors in my past thinking. I said that I now believed completely and utterly that everything about a person has been arranged in a previous life. I said that from now on I would chant the Buddhist scripture and worship the Buddha every day, and that I would lead my life peacefully and contentedly. After all, my parents were big as the sky, and I must obey them absolutely.

On hearing these words, they at first all asked me, suspiciously, "You are an educated person—you mean you still believe in Buddha?"

"Of course. If it were not for the educated people who believe in Buddha, how could there be all those big books of Buddhist scriptures for you to chant from?"

They smiled and nodded at my reply.

Mother noticed that I had begun helping her pack the wedding trunks with clothes, threads, pieces of cloth, embroidery, and so on. So at last she actually began discussing matters with me.

"We will have clothes made according to your wishes. Ask the tailor to make them in whatever style you like, but don't make the skirts too short. The village people are not open minded. They will laugh and say you are wearing only the jacket and nothing below. For almost twenty years I have saved these silks and satins for you to make into lined garments. As for the red satin, there should be two sections of it left after you make your bedding, and when you have given birth to a baby, I will use them to make flower caps for my grandchild."

When I heard these words, I thought of saying to her, "Mother, don't dream." But because I wanted to carry out my plan, I bit my tongue and bashfully replied, "Ma, it would be best to make fewer clothes, in case the style should change. Let me take less cloth with me. After all, I will be returning to Mother's home several times a year. Couldn't we have new garments made each time I come?"

"Mother's house is where your placenta was buried. Of course you can return often. But you will be a new bride. If we don't sew up several trunks of garments, others will look upon us as unworthy. Many families actually sell their land in order to marry off their daughters. When your sister's mother-in-law married off her daughter, they had thirty-two sets of silk bedding and twenty-eight wool blankets. In addition, they drew up a contract that showed that four hundred loads of grain would be delivered. These people actually sold off their land just to show off. I don't agree with that kind of extravagance unless there is enough money so that no one ends up poverty stricken."

"Mother, you were very extravagant when you married off my sister. I was upset when I saw it. The money you save from your own hard work and from Father's hard work should be kept for your own use. You are both old. You should eat more nutritious food. I love to read—when I get married, I only wish Father would give me several trunks of books."

"Good sons don't want land; good daughters don't want dowry." Mother smiled happily. "Child, you really are an educated person who understands manners and righteousness."

When Father heard that I wanted him to give me books, he was so happy that his mustache stood on end. "Good! If you intend to concentrate on studying, I will definitely give you four trunks of books."

In the quiet night I thought of their sorrows. I cried, feeling sorry for them. Father loved my second brother and me the most, but now my brother was dead. As for me? I would make them even more brokenhearted than my brother had. They were like swallows busily carrying mud to make nests—"The swallow wastes its energy carrying mud, for after each fuzzy child is grown, it will fly away." The song that Mother had taught me long ago was now a sketch of her own life.

I REMEMBER IT very clearly: on October 18, Aunt Yiwu invited my parents and me to lunch, and although for half a year Mother had refused to let me go anywhere, on this occasion she actually agreed that I should accept the invitation. Mother had to stay home and prepare food for guests of her own who were coming that day, so she asked the wife of my youngest brother to go with me to the luncheon—not really to keep me company, as everyone pretended, but to spy on what I said and did. Father also attended the luncheon, but he did not sit at the same table with us. When I saw Xiang seated at my table (which had already been set with glasses and chopsticks), I almost wept for joy, and I cried out in surprise, "Oh! So you came too!"

She quickly stood up, giving me her seat. "Please sit—why didn't your mother come?"

The hostess had invited a bride as the guest of honor. The banquet consisted of three tables, and two-thirds of the guests were female. At my table everyone was unmarried other than my sister-in-law and the new bride, and we teased the bride incessantly. An old lady sitting at the next table said to her, "New Bride, do not be intimidated. These two young women will soon be married also, and you should generously inform them of the common knowledge all new brides should know."

All the other guests laugh aloud, and Xiang and I were quite embarrassed—our faces turned as red as a summer sunset.

This banquet was bountiful by village standards. Usually only six large dishes were provided, but on this day there were eight, and all were delicious. Everyone was happily eating, drinking, talking, and laughing. I squeezed Xiang's leg hard, our signal to start moving.

Before long there would be news that would stir up the entire village of Xietuoshan. Just as they all were toasting one another with wine and passing the food and bustling with great enthusiasm, I put my plan into action. I clutched my stomach and doubled up at the waist and contorted my face as if I were in pain. "*Aaahhh!* My stomach hurts!"

"Why is your stomach aching all of a sudden? It could not be that you have eaten bad food." All the people at my table put down their chopsticks and looked at me with alarm.

"Never mind, I caught a chill last night and just now I ate too much. My stomach is bloated. Sorry. I'll be back in a minute. . . ."

I left the table, saying I had to go to the toilet. Xiang went with me. The toilet smelled foul.

I said, earnestly, "Let's go. It is time."

Xiang replied softly, "Qingqing knows our secret, but no matter. She won't tell anybody. She even gave me one yuan—she stole it from our mother."

Suddenly Qingqing rushed in, eyes brimming bright with tears. "Sister, Aunt! When will you return?"

Xiang held her hands, as if unwilling to part from her. I too felt sad. Fortunately, good sense spurred me—we dared not linger another minute. "Qingqing, good child, don't be unhappy. We will write in a few days. Xiang, don't delay, we must move quickly."

So we hurried out of the toilet and slipped around the back and climbed up the slope to the top of the hill. Two vicious dogs barked and came running toward us. A middle-aged woman emerged from a shack and stared at us. I feared she might guess our secret, so I assumed an easy manner and strolled along casually, though in fact I felt terribly anxious, as if fire were singeing my brows. I kept thinking that the hostess would run after us, or that when Xiang's mother saw Qingqing crying she would realize we had escaped, and she would run to tell Mother. It surely seemed that someone was bound to come after us eventually.

"Xiang, let's go. That woman has gone back into her house."

We hurried ahead with great energy. Fearing pursuit, we constantly turned around to check behind us. Two miners who happened to know us gave us the stare, but I pretended not to see them. We walked calmly on.

Apprehension and anxiety filled every cell of our bodies. We feared meeting other people we knew, so we turned off the road and onto a very narrow path through the fields. Now our two pairs of legs were rolling forward like wheels. In the clear and watery field our fleeing, fast-running reflections played like a scene in a beautiful movie.

Sweat fell like raindrops from our foreheads. We both gasped for breath. We felt like camels exhausted from hauling a heavy load, yet dared not rest for even a second.

"Aunt Ming, what will we do if our families come after us?" Xiang—less brave than I—was already thinking of stopping, though we had come only halfway.

"If we move quickly, they won't catch up."

"No? But surely they'll send men to chase us, and men obviously run faster than we can."

"Right now they are all happily drinking wine and have no inkling that we have escaped. We will be safe if we hurry and get on a boat at Lantian."

Hills and rows of fields flew by alongside us.

"What happiness!" I said to myself. "I have left the dark prison. Forever farewell, my beautiful native village."

Before we knew it we had arrived at Fuying Pavilion, which was less than two miles from Lantian. When I saw that no one was after us, I felt like a prisoner who has escaped the guillotine. I was utterly beyond myself with happiness. I shouted out loud and leaped in the air. "Xiang, now it really is our world!"

"Don't be happy too soon. Wait until our boat has left—then there will be plenty of time to be happy."

Suddenly she squatted down by a little creek. She scooped up water with her hands and drank. I too was very thirsty, so I squatted down and drank with her.

"I'm out of energy—let's rest a while," Xiang begged.

"OK. Lantian is coming up anyway."

We sat on the path in the field and discussed the question of what to do next.

"We have only one yuan," said Xiang. "It is not enough for our boat fare." She always worried excessively. Before we had the first problem solved, she had already spotted the second one coming.

"Even if we don't have the fare to go all the way to Changsha, we can at least ride the boat a few miles. After that we can be like refugees—we'll beg our food from door to door, and so make our way to Changsha. When we get there, we will find work."

"Let's go, someone is coming." Xiang stood up quickly. Perhaps her nerves were on edge. She thought she heard hurrying footsteps behind us. I turned around and saw several ducks *quack-quack-quacking* and drinking water in the field.

"Let's go," I agreed. "It'll soon be noon, and we will likely run into many coal carriers we know on the streets in Lantian."

Then the two of us resumed running.

Though we had known this area since childhood, we knew only the main road, not the smaller paths, so we were forced to go directly into Lantian. Fortunately, we did not meet anyone we knew. At last we stopped hurrying and sighed in relief.

But heavens—was this a dream?

Just as we were discussing the fare with a boat owner, I saw my mother standing behind us. Two hard-breathing sedan-chair carriers were wiping sweat off their foreheads with their sleeves. Grinning, they watched us.

There is no hope, my heart cried out.

Mother had superhuman skills. She had spotted us two rebels in the restaurant in the midst of many people who were eating their noon meals. Her face showed not the slightest anger. On the contrary, she smilingly explained to the boat owner (and to the people watching us), "These two are future Ph.D.'s. They are so anxious to go away to study that they can't wait even one more day. But how can the boat leave when there is no rain? Mr. Boat Owner, do you think I am right?"

"The boat can leave, though the water is a bit low," the boat owner answered with a smile. He didn't know the story behind this little scene, and of course he hoped to do some business.

"The boat will certainly move slower when the water is low," Mother continued. "Rather than wasting time on the boat, they might as well stay at home a few more days."

"Young people are anxious," an elderly person said to Mother. "Have you, honorable old person, come to take them home?"

"Yes, I wish to keep them for a few more days. Boat Owner, sorry. When the Old Gentleman Sky provides rain, then we will come and do business with you."

A disappointed smile floated on the boat owner's face.

The people watching this commotion stared at us two fools and laughed. We didn't open our mouths. Since the moment I had discovered Mother's presence, I felt as if my feet were shackled in iron—or, rather, that I was shackled and my head was already being placed on the guillotine. At that moment I knew that Mother's earlier words had been absolutely correct: unless I changed into a mosquito and flew away, I would never again escape from her palm.

My first escape attempt had failed utterly. I lowered my head and followed Mother home. That night she berated me until sunrise, using all sorts of hateful and barbaric words to insult me. I was completely mute. I did not answer her with so much as a murmur.

Next morning the sky was not yet light when my third sister-in-law sneaked over to tell me what had happened the day before, after we had left for the toilet.

"We waited in good faith for you and Xiang to come back and eat. After more than half an hour there was still no sign of you. So I went to the toilet to check. You and your shadow had vanished. So I asked Xiang's mother where you were and she said she didn't know. Someone thought you had gone home. So without finishing eating my food, I hurried home to ask Mother. She said, in great surprise, 'She hasn't come back. She must have escaped. Quickly—call two strong sedan-chair carriers for me. I'm going after her.' Mother bawled me out for being useless and accused me of plotting with you. Unless I was a clay Buddha, she said, how could I *not* know when a person had vanished? She shouted and scolded as she jumped into the sedan chair. Of course, she completely forgot that she had guests for lunch."

At first, I had no inclination to listen to all this, but when my sister-in-law described Mother's anxious state, I almost laughed out loud. Though I hadn't succeeded in escaping, I had succeeded in letting them know my power.

News of our escape spread through Xietuoshan and Lantian. Whenever people met, morning or evening, they spoke of our escape as soon as they opened their mouths.

"Women daring to move so freely—really, is there no law and no limit?"

"Hah! No matter how the world has changed, a woman is still a woman. If she is told to live, then she will live. If she is told to die, then she will die.

What is all this talk about opposing feudal thinking and destroying feudal rules—how preposterous! Does a woman dare to speak of opposition and destruction? Really, such nonsense."

"Aye! Rebels! The world has changed. Even the yellow flower girls dare to escape. Utter madness."

All these outside opinions reached my ears. But I comforted myself with the thought that for the sake of the revolution I could endure insult and pain that others could not.

My life now became more confined and more painful than when I had first come home. After my escape attempt I officially became a prisoner. Mother burned all letters and magazines sent to me by my friends. Qing-qing didn't dare carry any more messages or news to me. Mother even forbade those who lived in the same house—my sister, sister-in-law, and aunt—to see me.

At night I looked out the small window, saw deep blue sky inlaid with a white jade moon. I heard startled dogs barking far away, and I suspected that perhaps they had been frightened by my wandering soul. I knew that not long from now I would be saying my final farewell to my native village.

I again thought of death. Life without freedom is just too painful. If I were locked in a large prison, I would be with many others and surely I would not be so depressed. We prisoners would talk about our experiences, our interests, our goals. But unfortunately I was now isolated. I kept my lips closed all day. I was utterly stifled, had no place to give vent to my feelings, no way to blow off steam. I had become a little lamb waiting to be slaughtered—the knife hanging around my own neck. Who could tell how many more hours or days I would be in this world? Death, yes. I would take that way out.

But are you really as weak as a little lamb, unable to resist? The first time was a failure. But couldn't you try a second time, a third time, countless times?

Reason prevailed.

DURING A DARK NIGHT of fine driving rain I made my second escape attempt.

That day Mother had become very tired from arranging my wedding trunks and she had gone to sleep quite early. As I listened to the *hoo-hoo* of her snoring I suddenly thought of breaking free. But how? I knew the door on the right was tightly locked. The door on the left (which led into Mother's room) had been fastened for the night. The window was nailed shut with thick boards, and beyond the window stood a barricade of bricks and stones piled more than ten feet high. To attempt to escape through the window would be utterly futile. I concluded that the best tactic was to call out softly, asking for the door to Mother's room to be opened because I was thirsty and needed some tea. Luckily, it was Father who came to open the door. He never imagined that I would be plotting anything on such a cold, rainy, and miserable night as this. He felt around, opened the door, and lay down again.

Now, suddenly, I heard the desperate crying of my little niece, so I tip-toed to my third sister-in-law's door and knocked. I asked why the child was crying so frantically—was she terribly hungry? When my sister-in-law saw me out and about in the middle of the night, she was quite surprised. I told her I had Mother's permission to be out. So she then dared open her door and let me in.

"Let me sleep here tonight," I begged her. "I have just had a bad dream. I am afraid to sleep alone."

"I can't—if Mother finds out, she will scold me into the grave. I just can't stomach it. Let me light the lamp and see you back to your room."

"I am responsible for everything; put your mind at ease."

Ten minutes later Mother came to my sister-in-law's room to look for me. She held up the lantern so it shone on my sleeping face for a long while. At last she said loudly, "Get up. Go back to your room."

"Ma, Sister is asleep. It is all right for her to sleep here just for one night."

Hearing me snoring, my sister-in-law thought I was really asleep.

"All right. But if I don't see her tomorrow morning, I will look to you for her body."

"What a joke—losing a person while we lie on the same bed? What nonsense."

I secretly thanked my sister-in-law. I could not have made my escape without her guarantee.

Now the rain fell heavier and heavier. The entire sky was utterly black.

Lying next to me, she who had suffered such trials and afflictions because of her child had at last fallen fast asleep, like a clay figure.

Then I quietly got up and opened the door that led to the hill path out back. Our black dog barked loudly, and I was afraid that my sister-in-law or Mother would wake up. I felt around for the outhouse and hid in it: the dog then recognized its owner and stopped barking.

Coming out of the toilet, I groped my way along a small path. I decided that this time I would not pass by Lantian. I would invent a path that no one had followed before. But I became fearful when I thought of the coal miners on every hill. It was midnight and pouring down rain. Wouldn't they mistake me for a fearsome ghost and beat me?

Rain ceased for a moment. Suddenly a ray of gray-white light appeared in the sky. Could this be a gift to me from Buddha?

Along my route floated sounds of barking dogs. My heart jumped wildly. I dared not turn my head. I felt the devil's giant hands grabbing at the back of my neck as I hurried along over the steep and rugged hill paths. Mud clotted my shoes, making it difficult to walk. Four times I fell. My whole body was covered with yellow mud, even my eyelids. I no longer cared if people thought I was a ghost and beat me when they saw me in the morning. I ran madly, as if pursued by hordes of enemies, stumbling up the mountains and flying across the flatlands. Then, suddenly, I tumbled down a slope and landed in a small creek. My legs had been torn by countless falls and now my entire body was soaked. Hands and face were stung by thorns, fresh blood dripping. I had become a wild creature, smeared in blood and mud.

Heaven help me! To live or die, to stay or vanish, let it be decided tonight. If I fail to escape this time, let it end here.

I sat on the ground and prayed to the heavens, looking up at the vast black sky. Far away I seemed to see a red light flickering; at first I thought it must be a shooting star. But as I tilted my head toward the coal-black sky, I realized no stars were visible tonight. The strangely flickering red fire floated closer, growing bigger. Perhaps it was a will-o'-the-wisp. When I was little I often saw red lights shining on the mountains at night, and Mother told me that they were ghost fires (they were the same as will-o'-the-wisps). She said that wherever a ghost fire shone, there must soon be a real fire. No mistake, this must be a ghost fire. Otherwise, why was it growing larger?

I was afraid, for surrounding the faraway flame I seemed to see a giant shadow that opened its black arms and rushed toward me—could it be a devil coming to take me back?

Nonsense. The night was rainy, everyone was home sleeping soundly. How could they know I had escaped? Unlikely they'd even dream such a thing. Yet what of this flickering flame, coming closer? I decided I should slip away before it flared on my face . . . to avoid being frightened by a real ghost or being beaten by a human who mistook *me* for one.

So I stood up quickly. But my body trembled uncontrollably. My muddy legs felt as heavy as if they were bound in a massive manacle of chains. So I sat down, closed my eyes. Ah, now I know, it must be the soul of my second brother. He is holding a fiery torch to welcome me, for he cannot bear to part from me. Once he told me that he and I were to each other as a person's body is to his soul: even when the body dies, the soul still lingers. Perhaps he is lonely and miserable living in Hades and has come to fetch me so we can be together. Perhaps he knows my recent sorrow. Oh, Brother—you who loved me the most—have you come to rescue me?

Now I saw two huge and ghostlike shadows standing in the creek torrent, not far from me. The tall one held up a torch and hollered, "Hey, look there, there!"

Blood surged through my body and I started running, but I had not fled fifty steps before a giant hand snatched me.

"Ghost, ghost!" I shrieked, my bones going soft.

"Miss Ming, we are people, not ghosts. Don't be afraid. Come back with us. Your mother is very worried that you must be terrified out here in the dark."

I swore and cursed them for turning themselves into dogs and doing the dirty work of a dictatorial devil.

They paid me no heed and at first they were quite polite. They asked me, in a beseeching tone, to please return with them. But when they saw that I was obstinate, they dragged me away by force.

Not until we neared the family gate did I notice our little black dog running along in front of us. Then I realized that these two men had not been clever enough to find me—it was our little black dog's achievement.

The entire family was waiting in the reception hall, all but the children. The divine lamps had been lit. They looked clear and bright and festive, just as they do during a New Year's celebration.

"Where did you dredge up this ghost? Don't scare everybody. Quickly, throw her out!"

Mother's cruel face was more frightening than the face of the devil himself. My poor sister-in-law. Her eyelids were red and swollen. Stupefied, she trembled as she stared at me. I answered her with a glance of gratitude mixed with sadness and anger. Though again I was being bundled into my prison, I was grateful to her for giving me a chance at escape.

NOW FEWER THAN twenty days remained before the day set for our wedding. Xiao Ming had received a letter of ultimatum that I had sent from Lantian, and he did not dare come back home to be met with my rejection. So the parents in both families were very anxious, especially Mother, who was like an ant on top of a heated pot. During the day she was not comfortable walking or sitting, could not eat, did not even drink her much-beloved wine, and at night she was unable to sleep. When she was not scolding me or cursing me, she was looking for Father to air her grievances, complaining that if he had not sent me to school she would have become a grandmother long ago. She asked why he had let things develop into such an utter mess, with the result that I was *still* not married off. She was most concerned that Xiao Ming might not want me. In that case, she would kill herself.

Everything had been prepared, not only my dowry but also things I would need for daily use, such as food and personal effects and even toilet paper. I had said to Father several times, quite frankly, "Even if you insist on carrying me bodily to the Xiao family, I can promise you there will be only two possible futures for me—suicide or escape. I will never return home. Pa, you had better believe what I say. Don't carry all this stuff over there—it will be a waste to give it away for no purpose."

From hearsay around the house I learned that Father had told Mother exactly what I had said to him. He also told Mother that what I had said, added to the fact that I had already tried to escape twice, led him to believe I really would never allow myself to be united with Xiao Ming.

But Mother insisted on her own view: "Suicide? She deliberately says that to scare you. Escape? After she is married, she will want to guard all her belongings and will hate to leave them. Not to mention that when a woman is in a man's hands, she will become as gentle as a lamb, however strong and ruthless she may be. If Xiao Ming is clever, he will treat her especially well. Mark my words, she will never even think of running away."

Mother was misled by her own cleverness, for she lacked a basic understanding of her own daughter's mind and character. She thought that with plenty of material goods, she could entice me, even change my thinking. So with only ten days left before the wedding, she began sending parts of the dowry ahead to the Xiao family. I secretly sighed for her failed plan. She had taken possessions that she had accumulated by working hard for more than ten years and had unconditionally given them to others to enjoy. What a shame.

I ESCAPED AGAIN—for the third time. But as my sister had predicted, no matter how hard I flew, I could not fly out of Mother's cage.

This time it was not my mother or farmers who dragged me back but my big brother and my brother-in-law. They swaggered along in gentlemen's long gowns and intercepted me at the door of a shop. From my bosom I quickly produced a small knife. Putting the knife to my throat, I said, "If you try dragging me back again, I'll die right now, before your very faces."

My big brother snatched the knife from my hand and put it to his own throat, saying, "If you return home this time and are kept prisoner or ill treated, you can kill me with this knife."

"And kill me too." My brother-in-law grabbed the knife from his hand. "Our two lives must surely be equal to your one."

They spoke very convincingly, but I did not wish to fall into their noose again. I knew what I wanted. I preferred to die on the road to freedom rather than return home.

They saw that reasoning with me was not going to work, that the only way to get me back was to carry me by force. This they did with the help of two strong fellows they had hired earlier for the purpose.

More and more people circled around us to watch the commotion. Soon the road was so jammed with gawping people that even water could not have slipped through. I had put on makeup to disguise myself as a middle-aged farm wife, and the onlookers all laughed out loud at me—all except a few older ladies who saw my worried face and realized I was trying to hold back tears. They cried with me. This did not mean they really understood my pain or sympathized with my predicament, only that they responded emotionally to my hurt expression.

After a two-hour struggle they finally managed to drag me home.

How curious. This time when I returned home my mother spoke not half a sentence. Father only looked at me with a glance that showed his trembling anger. He lowered his head and said nothing. In the reception hall and throughout the house I could hear a murmuring of secret talk, like mice peeling husks. When they all saw me dressed as a farmer's wife, none dared laugh. But Yunbao asked her mother, "Ma, why does Aunt wear such ugly clothes?"

My sister quickly waved her hand. The child did not speak again.

This time I was determined to keep silent no longer. I would argue fiercely with whoever first dared open his or her mouth to scold me. I would sacrifice my life in this last struggle, if necessary. Better to let society curse me as a rebel and as a disobedient daughter than to yield to a feudal code of ethics. My courage was up and I cared not a bit about anything. Quietly, I waited for the bloody tragedy to unfold.

But nothing happened. Everyone remained as quiet as a mute. After I ate a bowl of rice, I lay down to rest.

Now the wedding day was fast approaching and still Xiao Ming had not returned. His reply to his family's numerous telegrams was "Telegram received, return delayed." Or such was the rumor.

The Xiao family had now decided to receive the new bride into their family immediately and to have the wedding ceremony when the groom returned. At first I thought Mother would go along with this, but to my surprise she did not. She feared that I would damage her good name by slipping away as soon as I got to the Xiao place. So she insisted on waiting for Xiao Ming to return before his family could welcome me.

Three days passed and then the matchmaker arrived riding in a sedan chair. "The bridegroom is back, congratulations!" She had come to hurry along the marriage.

Now the entire family was as busy as soldiers fighting on the firing line. Frequently, my sister and sister-in-law sneaked into my room to cry and sigh, their hearts filled with fright and worry that the anticipated tragedy might take place on the night of the wedding, right in the nuptial chamber.

"Oh! If anything tragic occurs, it will be a pity to have lost all your education," sighed my youngest brother's wife. Then my softly sobbing sister began to cry out loud. They did this even though they were sitting right in Mother's room at the time. My sister's tears flowed straight to my heart. They were difficult to bear.

My eldest sister-in-law, my aunt, and my great aunt all came to try to make peace with me. They congratulated me, saying things like "the Buddha will protect you." Sometimes I got very annoyed listening to such stuff, and I angrily shot back, "Let the Buddha protect *you*—I will soon become a Buddha myself!"

Children jumped and laughed in the parlor, which had been decorated with colorful lanterns. Their little mouths were stuffed full of candy sent by the Xiao family, and they were as happy as if it were New Year's Festival.

Now everyone in Xietuoshan was eagerly waiting to watch the amusing tragicomic play that was about to be performed. A most odd creature, a rebellious female, had become their topic of conversation as they drank tea or wine. The entire village was stirred into an uproar by this oddity. They discussed; they criticized; they predicted her fate and her future.

My friend Xiang had been invited to the wedding banquet by my mother. Having seen that my every attempt at escape had failed, Xiang said, "Aunt Ming, you have been suffering for a month. Look at yourself in the mirror. See how skinny you have become. This time I advise you to go to your in-laws and get it over with." She actually voiced these fainthearted sentiments.

Seeing that only the two of us were in the room, I loudly rebuked her: "You have given up the idea of escape? What a coward and weakling you are."

"I don't want to think about struggling. Let the feudal family destroy this life."

"Why are you so weak?"

"A person has limits. I just can't fight anymore."

"All right. Then surrender and submit. Go ahead and follow your parents' orders, go ahead and listen to the matchmaker's instructions. No wonder—you are a devoted believer in ancient tradition."

I spoke in this way just to provoke her. I was quite certain that she would react, at least a little. But I was wrong. She only gave a cold laugh and replied in a tone of ridicule, "You have been struggling a long time, and what do you have to show?"

"Hah! You'll see."

Suddenly, two good friends who had grown up together lost all affection for each other. From then on, each held the other in contempt, each believing the other's ideas and actions to be entirely wrong.

Deep silence gripped us: our eyes stared at the brilliant glare of the fire in the stove.

From the day I escaped and left my native village for the fourth and final time until this very day, I have often missed and pitied Xiang, a mother of three, who was destroyed by ancient tradition.

I HAD BECOME the main character in a puppet show, a curious tragicomic drama. Now the curtain was going up on the final scene.

I actually wanted to play out this performance, not because I had surrendered to feudal society or was moved by curiosity but because I saw how Mother was suffering and I pitied her. I could not bear to see her so heartbroken. I was willing to give her a little temporary comfort. The biggest reason I went through with it, of course, was that I had clearly recognized that what I opposed really was not my mother but a whole feudal way of thinking. I felt that as long as I attained my final goal, I could put up with some short-term sacrifices.

Who would have believed it? I became a bride. Thinking about it now, I feel it was merely amusing and entertaining, not at all the painful and humiliating surrender to feudal society that I once considered it. And what a shame that a photographer could not be found for the occasion. (I must blame my little village for being so isolated.) A picture of me as I rode in the flower sedan chair, sitting all draped in red silk and wearing the phoenix headdress, would have been far more striking than my description.

I wore a pale blue silk top, a red satin skirt (much longer than what students used to wear), and a pair of flower-embroidered red satin shoes. These shoes I would wear only on the day of the wedding, and the next day

I would give them to someone else to use. According to our village tradition, this pair of shoes would prevent all conflicts. And yet many people would *fight* to wear this pair of "lucky shoes." A truly ridiculous contradiction.

I had not cut my hair for half a year, but it still was very short and did not cover my forehead. This disturbed Mother greatly. Xiang's mother was asked to "open my face" and put on my makeup; she used perfumed oil to comb my hair bright and shiny.* Then she began to draw my eyebrows and dab on powder.

"There is no need for makeup, Mrs. Du," I said fervently, impolitely pushing her hand away. "Let me keep my original face."

"It is customary to have this done on the wedding day, no matter who the bride is, but especially when she is such a beautiful bride as you. After I add some rouge you will be like a fairy who has descended to earth—ha!"

I knew quite well she meant to ridicule me, for my skin had been blackened by the sun in my soldiering days, and now my cheeks were covered with dark freckles. She wanted to put powder on me so that I would become a clown on stage. I felt insulted and I firmly refused her good intentions. My clever mother said promptly, "All right, then, let her keep her original face. Natural beauty is more lovable than artificial beauty."

And so the disagreement was resolved peacefully.

I put on the bulky and clumsy phoenix headdress. A large piece of red silk cloth was draped over it so my entire head was covered. When I looked through the silk, everything appeared red. Mrs. Du supported me as if she were leading a blind person. We walked to the reception hall. First I paid my respects to Heaven and Earth and our ancestors. Then I said farewell to my parents and other relatives.

Normally, by the time a bride gets into the sedan chair her eyes are already red from crying, which shows her to be a woman of deep feeling. But I had no desire to cry. I was not in the least sorry to leave my family, steeped as it was in feudal ideas. I simply had no tears to shed. And yet, for no reason at all, the moment I stepped into the sedan chair and heard the

---

*Getting rid of all the hair on the face was called "opening the face."

cries of my sister and sister-in-law, I began to cry passionately. My crying lasted for more than three miles. I did not cry in self-pity. I cried for my mother, who would never see her loving daughter again.

Four men carried the sedan chair. Its four sides were covered by red silk. The door was locked. As we passed through each hamlet or town, people set off firecrackers. The families that did this were allowed to ask that the sedan chair be put down so they could see the new bride. What annoyed me the most were the impolite women who lifted the roof and then reached in with a hand and lifted up my lowered head, all the while making critical comments about the bride. Many times I thought of reaching out and slapping their faces, but I was afraid to disrupt the grand procession. I tolerated it and said, "Please do not touch, just use your eyes to look."

"How rude! The new bride is most foul tempered."

I could not help but laugh to myself when I heard their words.

It was about eleven miles from my home to the Xiao family. We passed through many small towns and over many hills. In our procession were seventy or eighty people. Some carried the sedan chair; some carried dowry trunks. Some were musicians who caused a big commotion by their constant blowing and beating. As I sat in the chair, I lifted up the silk headdress and, using the small mirror that hung at my chest, looked at myself: I saw that I was utterly changed, that I had turned into a clown. I almost laughed out loud. Then I looked at the pair of feet that had worn straw shoes for more than four months and now were wearing flower-embroidered slippers. The sight really did not agree with my eyes. Most depressing of all, this pair of hands and arms that had once held a rifle now wore rings of gold and bracelets of jade, plus various other baubles. How vulgar. Two ancient copper coins hung on the buttons of my jacket. Together they weighed more than a pound. They were most annoying. It was said that these ancient coins were mirrors to shine on the supernatural and that wearing them would drive away all evil. They pulled so heavily on me that I couldn't even lift my head.

Sometimes my mind was quite peaceful as I sat in the sedan chair. The rhythmic and melodic ancient music was very pleasing. Here was an unusual opportunity. I should appreciate the music and think of nothing else. But this mood lasted for only an instant before another thought hit me: why not get hold of a pistol? If I suddenly began firing shots from my sedan chair, I'd scare everyone out of their wits, and they'd be holding their heads and running like rats. And couldn't I calmly escape in that moment of confusion?

Or, better still, I could rush out of the crowd and stand on the table during the worship ceremony, and I would shout curses and let fly some of the grudges that I have been harboring in my chest.

The most worrying danger was the one I might face tonight: if my counterpart was an unreasonable savage, a tragedy might occur.

Yes, I must endure all pain at this moment for the sake of my future. But what will I do if he forces me to consummate the marriage? I absolutely will not stand for it. I will not sacrifice my virginity to a man I don't love. I will put my life at stake and fight. I will not submit.

Perhaps escaping will be more difficult from now on. I must constantly observe my surroundings, every instant, and put my agile mind to good use. If I am determined and courageous, surely I will eventually reach my goal. Never fear or be discouraged, for with your cunning and courage, how can you fail?

I encouraged myself, planning my fourth escape just when everyone thought I had finally surrendered to ancient ways.

The sound of firecrackers became louder as the red sedan chair was carried through the Xiao family's gate. At that moment I could not prevent my heart from jumping wildly, no matter how hard I tried.

A well-dressed woman of forty or so opened the door of the sedan chair and helped me out. Amid the sound of the firecrackers exploding I sat for a while in Huachu's room before going off to worship Heaven and Earth. Huachu was the matchmaker's daughter. She and her mother had gone together to study at the Datong Girls School. I liked her very much. As soon as we saw each other we started to talk, which surprised many onlookers. They said, "Well, the bride was a soldier, of course, so that is why she is different—forthright and not the least shy."

I did not dispute anything anybody said. I did not want to embarrass my father as he escorted me into the reception hall. I was like a wooden puppet, just allowing them to put on the show. I only bowed three times instead of kneeling three and kowtowing nine, but apart from that I performed every number on their program.

"After all, she has gone to school and understands reason," said Xiao

Ming's father, happily boasting to everyone about me. "She is not one who would oppose an ancient wedding ceremony."

Night descended on the bustling scene. The house was crowded with guests who had come to revel and indulge in horseplay. As was the custom, no women participated—though two little girls of five or six were squeezed in amid the men, adding to the commotion. Half this group were relatives; half were Xiao Ming's schoolmates. I handled them quite cleverly by at first letting them indulge in as much horseplay as they cared to and by paying no attention to them. I was like a block of wood, not speaking and not laughing. Then, when they began to speak stupid words that I detest, I put on an iron face and gave them a lecture. In the end they decided there was no fun in all this, and they slipped away before it was midnight.

I deliberately turned the lamp wick very low, until the room was as dark as the inside of a forest. The stove had nearly gone out. I sat by it, quietly thinking of the scene a moment ago when Xiao Ming had tried to slip away and was chased by a group of people. Judging by his forced smile, I understood that he too felt that the situation was uncomfortable and painful.

Like a ghost, he quietly opened the door. My eyes stayed focused on the fire. My head hung so low that it almost touched my knees. With the fire tongs he added some coal to the stove. Then he came and sat by me. "Today you were wronged, but don't be sad. There is nothing a person can do with bull-headed families like ours." His sad voice was trembling. I suddenly felt pity for him.

I answered him as if I were delivering a sermon: "The truth is, society is a large stage and life is a long drama. Everyone is like an actor who must sometimes play in a comedy, other times in a tragedy. And it doesn't matter if the main character thinks the play is worth playing or not. If the actions of a drama can stimulate viewers, the play is brought to the stage and performed."

"So," he said. "Today, did you and I perform in a tragedy or a comedy?"

"From your point of view, naturally, it was a tragedy. But I saw it as comic."

"What do you mean? Are you still thinking about escaping?"

"Pardon me," I said. "Let us just calmly discuss how to end this puppet show."

Ten minutes passed. We were sunk deep in thought. There was not even the sound of a sigh to be heard. At last I, who was the one with a clear head, began to speak about the pain caused by joining spouses who do not love each other.

At first he nodded as if in sympathy with me. But at last he firmly expressed his own view: "You have no love for me. But ever since I was little, I have been in love with you. I cannot leave you. I will continue to love you passionately, no matter how coldly and cruelly you treat me."

"Love cannot be forced, for She is absolutely free," I answered. "No one can force a man and woman together if they do not love each other, and no one can force them apart if they *do* love each other. You love me, that is your choice. I do not love you, that is my choice. I cannot compel you to stop loving me. Similarly, you cannot force me to *begin* loving you. So let us be sensible. Let us plan our future and dissolve the marriage contract. You go marry a wife who is your ideal, who will comfort you forever, who will help you build a family and establish a career. I too will marry my ideal lover and live a sweet and joyous life. In that way we will benefit ourselves and our country. Don't be stubborn in your thinking and make a mistake that will affect both our futures."

We discussed and discussed throughout the night. Still we came to no agreement. Outside our room several village women were eavesdropping, but they could not understand us because we spoke the Changsha dialect.

The second night we again did not sleep. We continued discussing the big question that affected our lives.

His mother began to reprimand him. She called him stupid for wasting these precious moments in conversation: "Since she rode the red sedan chair to my home, she is a Xiao family member as long as she lives, and she will be a Xiao family ghost when she is dead. You are her husband and whatever you say goes. You mean to say that she dares to disobey? Only a dead cat would let a mouse escape from its mouth."

To be honest, Xiao Ming was a kind person, not at all cruel. He did not force me to consummate the marriage. He appreciated my individuality, my ideals, my strong will. He knew that if he were to pressure me, it would only make our problems more serious and more difficult to resolve.

"Are you really so lacking in emotion? Don't we have even the affection of friends? I am not a robber, certainly no wild tiger. I will not harm or eat you. Please believe that I will protect your name and will look after your future. Yet are you still unwilling to give me a little love's comfort? I need a little love, even if you grant it only out of pity. No! I still need it even if your love is false and temporary. Ming, are you really so cruel?" Bright teardrops rolled down from his eyes.

I felt terrible, but his tears could not deflect my iron resolve, even slightly. "Love cannot be given as charity. And surely it cannot be given falsely. I can treat you as my good friend, but I simply cannot give you any love beyond friendship. I cannot give up my beliefs; I cannot become your wife. If you want happiness, then please quickly dissolve the marriage contract and marry another woman."

His tears flew more and more profusely. I handed him a handkerchief, which he returned after he had wiped his eyes.

"It would not have mattered so much if we had dissolved the marriage contract before you had come to my home. But now we have already worshipped the Heaven, the Earth, and our ancestors. Our families are happily celebrating, and your father is still here. It would be difficult for me to face the others if we actually went through with a divorce. And even if I could endure it, my parents would surely not agree to it. Here a good new daughter-in-law runs off as soon as she is welcomed into the family—how could my parents save face? Not to mention that your parents' reputation, and your own reputation, would be greatly damaged. Let us force ourselves to live together until we just can't stand it any longer, and then we will talk about what to do."

When he said this, I felt revulsion for him. This allusion to social standing and social reputation was the last sad gasp of feudal authority. I did not bother to argue with him, for suddenly my mind had turned devious. It is not always good to insist, I thought. It won't hurt to wrangle the final victory by using a little manipulation. So I promised him, quite earnestly, "All right, let's bear it. There must be a way to solve this problem."

Father left to return home on the third day. He knew that we had not slept for two nights and that we had been discussing all night long, but he pretended not to know. Before he left he came to my room and sat for a while. He reminded me repeatedly, "Don't cause any trouble, live peacefully. After the New Year you can go to Datong Girls School to teach." When he finished speaking to me, he said to Xiao Ming, "You know she has a very strong personality—so give in a little."

After seeing Father off, I returned to my room and suddenly began to cry loudly. I was puzzled by this sudden rush of emotions. Perhaps I feared I would never see my father again. I knew he loved me. He was unlike Mother, who was obstinate and unreasonable. The more I thought, the worse I felt. Finally, I fainted from crying.

That night my energy totally collapsed. I opened the green silk bedcover and slept with my clothes on, leaving the pink silk cover for Xiao Ming to use. Like a detective, I waited and watched for his movements. To my surprise, he respected my character and my privacy and went quietly to sleep. I felt grateful to him, but at the same time I thought this was just the way he ought to behave.

Later, I carefully considered the reasons why he treated me so well. I decided it was because he had another purpose in mind. He knew I had struggled for half a year at home and had tried to escape three times. He knew I had already suffered so much provocation that if he did not go along with me, a terrible tragedy would surely ensue.

It was the custom of my native village that the bride and groom return to the home of the bride on the third day after the wedding. This was called "return to the gate." We stayed at my home for two days, and Mother had no suspicion whatever that Xiao Ming and I were husband and wife in name only. After the two days we went back to the Xiao family. Now was the time of the Lunar New Year, and almost every day we had an invitation to go out to eat. Days passed rather painlessly.

Xiao Ming was using the soft tactic in handling me, confident that his temporary sacrifice would lead, eventually, to his possessing me fully. Two telegrams had come from Changsha, urging him to return to work at the public road department, but his mother kept insisting that he stay home. Yet he knew that staying home meant suffering, and he felt he might as well leave now and breathe the air of freedom. He fantasized that someday I would go to him on my own initiative.

On the eve of his departure he said to me, "I absolutely respect your freedom. I, like you, am pressured by family. I had no choice but to come home to act in this play. Now you can do as you wish and, right or wrong, whatever you do, I will love you forever."

I decided to go with him. But his mother refused to let me leave, fearing that I would escape in the middle of the journey. Since my plan was to retreat in order to advance, I obeyed her wish: I would stay and play the part of the virtuous daughter-in-law.

But matters were not so simple as I had imagined. Although Xiao Ming did not violate me, and although he had given me temporary self-governance, he had a larger purpose in view: when he left, his mother was entrusted with the responsibility of watching me, and though that old lady seemed superficially kind, she was, in fact, no less severe than my mother. Claiming she was worried that I might be lonely, she engaged a girl to keep me company while I slept. This girl even followed me into the toilet, which was most annoying. One night I was unable to sleep and tried to open the family gate to watch the moon, but I found that the gate was locked. I then realized that I had been put into a family prison once again. At the time I was not greatly surprised. I felt only pity for these country folks. In their stupidity they did not realize that they could lock up my skeleton but not my soul, that a heart that loves freedom can soar into the sky at any instant.

Both the Xiao family and my family were landowners, and they hired only male laborers, not female servants. Chores such as cooking and laundering were left for the womenfolk. Fortunately, I had been used to working ever since I was small, so I felt no hardship.

I completely changed my lifestyle. I did my utmost to be like the villagers. All day I helped them feed pigs, call chickens, dust tables, sweep floors. I failed only in learning how to start the stove, even though I had been instructed several times. Never did the old lady scold me. Sometimes, when she saw me picking up bowls and chopsticks to wash, she would say, very considerately, "You never did this kind of work when you were in school, so do not fuss too much. You are still a new bride. No one will dare say anything even if you do not do any work."

A short week passed peacefully. I was determined to put up with the temporary inconveniences and to struggle to the end. The matchmaker came to sit with the old lady every day, and one day she deliberately raised her voice as she spoke these flattering words: "I told you before that the bride would be fine once she crossed your gate—and look, who can compare with her in ability to work? Not only is she perfect in both literature and in fighting, she can even handle every household chore. I cannot imagine how many virtues you must have accumulated in your previous life, in order to get such a good daughter-in-law."

"Ha-ha. I should thank you, good Matchmaker, for our fine daughter-in-law. We truly did not think she would be able to take care of a family. *Hah-hah-hah!*" The old lady's mouth was crooked from laughing.

⁂

"OH! IT IS terrible, awful. Robbers! Everybody get out quickly!"

As we were eating breakfast one morning, we heard people's voices suddenly boiling outside and we ran out to look: crowds were hurrying along carrying baggage and bedcovers. Some people were supporting the elderly while also carrying babies on their backs. Some were shouting and some were crying. All were hurrying toward the mountain slopes behind the village. I stuffed my diary into my pocket, locked the gate, and followed the womenfolk to flee the calamity. The old lady and Xiao Ming's sister-in-law had small feet, and it was pathetic to see them taking two steps backward for every step forward. I supported the old lady with my right hand while holding a child with my left. At last we reached the house of a rent farmer, Wang Jiaao, and there we rested. Through the dense bamboo forest we could clearly see thirty or forty robbers moving back and forth through the hamlet.

"Finished, we are finished, your dowry will be gone. Oh! We didn't bring anything with us." The old lady was so anxious that her whole body trembled.

I quickly comforted her: "The common saying goes that as long as you stay in the green mountain, then you have no fear of finding firewood. As long as the people escape, lost possessions don't matter."

She was also worried about her sick husband and about her third daughter-in-law, who was soon to give birth. I wanted to put her mind at ease so I took my chance and, about ten minutes after the robbers had retreated, I went down the mountain to nurse the sick man and to look after the pregnant woman. The old lady thought for sure that I would escape amid the confusion. Instead, I was preparing lunch for them when she returned.

The old lady could not believe her eyes. Excitedly, she said to her husband, "She really is too good. She took care of us when we were fleeing, and even though she herself was hungry she ran to a farmhouse and bought cooked eggs for us to eat. Knowing that I was concerned about you and our third daughter-in-law being left here, she braved danger and ran quietly down the mountain. She really is a heroic and compassionate person."

The old lady was very appreciative. But I felt embarrassed at her praise.

From then on, my good name was established. The entire family, old and young, liked me and trusted me. They no longer feared the unexpected from me. Both the lock on the gate and the servant girl had long since been removed. I knew that my time had come. My travel money was ready, and now I needed only a suitable opportunity to act out my wish.

The opportunity arrived quite suddenly. Just when I was considering how best to escape, someone came and handed me a letter. I opened it and saw it was from Principal Wu of Datong Girls School. He was inviting me to be the supervisor of the sixth grade. I leaped with joy. Then I quickly cooked up some rice and tasty dishes to feed the hired hand who had brought the message. After I had sent him off, I took the appointment letter to ask Xiao Ming's father for advice.

"Just a short while ago," I said, "my father dispatched a man to bring me this letter from Datong Girls School. Principal Wu wants me to be a supervisor there, with an annual salary of two hundred and forty yuan. The school is not far from here, and I could come back often to take care of you two honorable old folks. Every year I will be able to save more than one hundred yuan, which I will use to buy nutritious food for you two. I have come to ask for your advice. I wonder, will you allow me to go?"

After hesitating for about two or three minutes, the old lady wrinkled her brows and asked her husband, "Do you think she should go or not? Our child Xiao Ming should not be against it."

"Why would he be against it? Teaching is a good profession. Besides, it is her old school. And today the close gentleman relative specially dispatched someone to deliver the letter of appointment.* So of course it would not be good to refuse."

I didn't know what to say to thank those two old folks. They were free from all anxiety and so agreed to let me go.

---

*By "close gentleman relative" he meant my father.

On a very bright and clear spring morning (the sun had just exposed half his face above the clouds) I gathered my bags while the children looked at me with lingering eyes. "Aunt, when will you return?"

Naughty Huachu, her hair disheveled, was one of those who came to see me off, and what she said upset me: "Aunt, you won't leave and not return, will you? You must come back."

"Nonsense. Of course I'll be back. I will come back twice every month."

The old lady paid no attention to what was being said, for she was busily cooking eggs and frying beans for me to take along to eat on the road.

"See you again, Ma!" When I jumped on the sedan chair, I used my most intimate voice to call her. I noticed she was wiping her eyes with her sleeve.

Ah, poor old lady, you will never see me again, your daughter-in-law in name only.

I felt a slight sadness at saying farewell, but in less than five minutes I began to smile, for I saw my bright future fast approaching.

I arrived in Datong too early. The school was not open yet. No teachers or students had arrived and no one was around except two school workers.

Oh, this was a chance too good to be true. Did the heavens arrange this especially for me? As I stood in front of the empty building I felt so happy that I could have cried.

I learned from a school worker that the principal would be returning from his village the next day. I thought that if I wanted to leave, I had best go this night. It would be more difficult after he arrived. We were old schoolmates, and he wanted me to be the supervisor of the graduating class. Naturally, he was hoping that if I started teaching, I would at least teach until the end of the semester. But, come to think of it, to desert him even before I started to teach would certainly be ungrateful and unkind—the Xiao family would come and demand to have me, and then what would he do? Then, again, if I waited until he arrived, and then made my escape, he would certainly tell my family or the Xiaos that I had fled, even if he did not send someone after me himself.

Go! I cannot debate any longer!

That evening I hired two strong sedan-chair carriers. Taking advantage of the black night, we followed the small road that wound around Tin Mountain, and made our way toward Changsha.

Early the next morning I got off to walk while the carriers followed me.
I was like a poet, strolling along the embankment of leaning green willows.
Slowly I walked, lightly singing a song without rhyme:

> "Farewell forever, my native village!
> Farewell, oh beautiful place of my birth,
>> With blue-green mountains,
>> And swirling water,
>> With almond and peach trees
>> Sweet as a painting,
>> And willows drooping like silk.
>
> Oh, beautiful village, when I was a child,
> You made me tipsy, drunk with beauty,
>> But now you have buried
>> My love-drunk
>> Youth and left
>> Bright scars
>> Deep, deep in my heart.
>
> Fearsome, fearsome feudal tiger
> Straining to swallow stars so bright—
>> Only struggle
>> Can keep them burning.
>> And so my lovely
>> Native village
>> Farewell forever, farewell."

Parents of Xie Bingying, date and place of photo unknown.

Xie Bingying in Changsha, 1925.

Xie Bingying in Changsha, around
1926, before she became a soldier.

Xie Bingying on field maneuvers while attending
the Central Military and Political School in Wuhan, 1926.

Xie Bingying poses between
two friends in Tokyo, 1931.

Xie Bingying in September 1937, with the flag of the Hunan Women's War Zone Service Corps, location unknown. She formed the corps and led it to the front lines in the war against the Japanese.

Xie Bingying, 1937.

Xie Bingying, 1937.

Xie Bingying at the front line in Luodian, 1937, with Luo Peilan, a member of her corps.

Xie Guoxin, Xie Bingying's youngest brother,
in Guilin's Xi Lin Park in the summer of 1937.

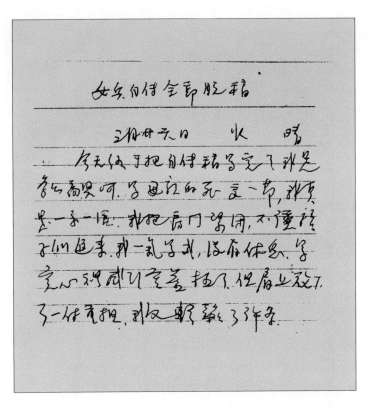

Xie Bingying wrote diaries all her life. Her first book, *War Diary*, published in Shanghai in 1928, consisted of a series of journal entries sent home from the front. This entry, written across the page in the Western style, is from her diary of 1946, when she was in Wuhan:

Woman Soldier's Own Story completed and ready for the printer

March 26   *Sunny Day*

Today I finally finished writing my autobiography. How happy I am. As I wrote the section about Mother, I wept one tear for every word. I tightly closed the door to my room and didn't let children come in, and in one breath I finished it all, not taking any rest. When I was done, I felt quite empty. Yet a heavy load had fallen from my shoulders, and I felt very light and free.

Xie Bingying outside her apartment in San Francisco, 1992.

PART 5 Farewell, Changsha

WHEN I ARRIVED IN CHANGSHA MY FIRST BIG TASK WAS TO WRITE TO Xiao Ming and ask his consent to publish in the newspaper a notice announcing the dissolution of our marriage contract. A week later his reply arrived. He said he was unwilling to comply. So I wrote another long letter. In this one I asked him not only to help make my wish come true but to think of his own future happiness, to consider matters carefully, and not to fall into another disaster. At last he agreed. When the announcement was finally published I became insane with happiness. Immediately, I bought two bottles of wine and hid in my big brother's kitchen and drank until I was dead drunk. I thought about how sad and angry Xiao Ming must be after seeing the newspaper, how he would be tied in knots. Yes, one person's happiness is another's suffering—it is inevitable.

My big brother was displeased with my sudden departure from home, and when he saw the announcement in the newspaper he told me how unhappy he was: "I really do not agree with how you went ahead and made the decision alone and acted on your own in divorcing Xiao Ming. Why didn't you discuss it with me beforehand?"

"Why talk of divorce?" I replied. "I never married him. It is done, Big Brother. Please don't bring it up."

My sister-in-law silenced us temporarily by saying, "Sister has her own ideas. She doesn't need your meddling."

Although I felt much freer while living with my big brother than I had while living at home, I still felt stifled, by both him and his wife. At every meal he felt he had to say a few words to lecture me. And the more his wife flattered me, the more I felt she was actually ridiculing me and sarcastically urging me to get out of her family—fast. This wife was a well-known lady from a town in Xinhua County. My big brother's first two wives had died long ago; this was his third. She was short and fat. She had a prosperous-looking face, soft white skin, and a clever tongue never at a loss for words. In her mouth even harsh and scolding sentences turned into poetic-sounding praise. I often thought she resembled Sister Feng of the *Dream of the Red Chamber,* for she had a sweet mouth and a bitter heart.

Oh! The human sea is boundless . . . where will I find a shore to set my feet?

I was in a daze. I wrote letters to my friends continually, from morning until night. But none of them could suggest a solution to my problem. Oh, for a job—when would I be able to find work that would make me self-sufficient?

IT WAS AS IF the gods were deliberately toying with me, forcing me to taste all of life's bitter flavors. Scarcely had I escaped from a family prison when suddenly I found myself stepping through the gates of a real one.

Xiang was locked in a cage back home and needed some fresh air in her life, so she had asked me to mail her a few books to help her pass the long and painful days. I was just walking to the post office, carrying a sealed package of books for Xiang, when suddenly a young man with a very familiar face appeared before me—"Ming, where are you going?"

"You? When did you get here?"

It was Aisi, a friend who felt quite passionate about me, a comrade from the Wuhan days. We stood and talked at the Eight Corners Pavilion, which at that moment was crowded with people and bicycles. He told me that Molin, another classmate from military school, had come with him to

Changsha and that they were living in the New Peace Inn. He said he'd like me to visit them. So I put the books under my arm and followed him to the inn and up the stairs.

A moment later I seemed to have fallen into a nightmare. Suddenly Molin, Aisi, and I found ourselves locked in iron chains, being escorted to police headquarters through streets packed with noisy onlookers.

Children were singing, "*Ti-ta-ta, Ti-ta-ta, Ti-Ti-Ti*"—kill, kill!

An old lady sighed, "Again they've arrested such a young girl."

"Walk faster, are your legs broken?" A brutish policeman hit me hard in the shoulder with the butt of his gun.

I stopped and cursed him. "Damned idiot! Why hit me for no reason?"

Everyone opened their eyes wide and stared at me.

"What? Are you are afraid of being hit? Tomorrow we'll hit you until your head slams the ground."

I fought down my anger, did not reply. I sped up and kept walking.

We were locked in a jail that had two small cells. Aisi and Molin were put in one cell. I was put in the other, which was stinkier, darker, and smaller by half. The cumbersome iron lock fell into place, *TONG*.

"Hey!" I cried out. "What is this?" My foot had touched something. And now I saw two specks of light.

"A person, like you." A woman got to her feet.

I apologized to her earnestly. "Sorry, but I just came in from the outside. The room is so dark that I could not see clearly. Please forgive me."

"It doesn't matter. I was asleep just now. What are you charged with?"

From her voice I could tell she was not from Changsha. Perhaps from around Liuyang.

"I broke no law. They just arrested me for no reason."

"Where?"

"At an inn. I went there to visit a couple of friends. And just at that moment the police arrived to investigate. They locked us in chains without asking any questions."

"And the two friends?"

"They are locked up across from us."

She looked where my finger was pointing, and saw Molin and Aisi.

Molin whispered in Aisi's ear, but the guard stopped him right away.

"Which one is your husband?" she asked.

It seemed a dumb question. I considered setting her straight. But I remembered the old saying, "Those who suffer the same disease should pity each other." I decided to drop it.

"I'm still unmarried," I said mildly. "Those are my friends."

She looked a little embarrassed.

It was the rainy season, February. The ground was very wet. She and I sat down on thin layers of rotten straw. We had no blankets, nothing to eat. When I sat down I felt countless mosquito-like insects drilling straight into my flesh. I felt so uncomfortable that I had to stand up again.

"The straw is very old and must be full of lice and bedbugs. My whole body is swollen from their bites." She rolled up her sleeves for me to see, but I could not see a thing in the pitch blackness.

"Is there nothing to eat?" I asked, hoping she'd say yes. I was hungry.

"Hah! There isn't even water to drink. Better ask your family to bring some food right away."

"My family doesn't know I'm here."

The guard came over to reprimand me. "No talking allowed."

At ten o'clock that night several police came in holding pistols. The guard unlocked our door. They led me to the judge for questioning. I deliberately walked very fast, scaring them into thinking I was going to escape. They rushed up and pointed their guns at me.

The judge, who appeared to be forty or so, wore a Japanese mustache shaped like a bamboo rain hat. He looked like he might be honest enough, but good sense told me that no honest person would become a judge. He asked my name, my age, my occupation, and my native place. Then, "When did you join the Communist Party? Where is your organization and what are your duties?"

"What? I don't understand you at all—I am a student at the Teacher Training School."

When he heard my reply he grunted slyly, "Huh! If you are not a party member, then why do you have books that show party influence?"

"I bought the books at the bookstore. Do you mean to say that the bookseller is also in the Communist Party?"

"Admit it quickly and we can release you right away. Otherwise, tomorrow you will be shot."

By using this threat he hoped to force me to confess.

"You are holding my life in your palm anyway. So if you want to shoot me, go ahead."

My nonchalant answer brought a violent reaction: "If you did not break the law, do you think we'd dare kill you so recklessly?"

"And I did *not* break the law."

"The evidence is plain, and yet you still deny it. OK, beat her."

A heavy wooden club slammed my leg. I fell to the ground in pain—though not so much pain that I went numb.

"Do you care to confess? If not, we will use the hot pepper water."

I knew that the hot pepper water torture was a terribly cruel punishment. Red pepper powder is dissolved in boiling water and poured into a victim's nostrils, and this makes him bleed from the seven openings of his head. The punishment does not stop until he confesses. Many young people were arrested as political criminals and instantly confessed that they were members of the Communist Party—even though they were not—just to avoid this torture. In this way many lives were pointlessly ruined.

Instantly my brain conjured up terrible images. I felt the world swimming in front of my eyes. I began to feel a chill in my guts.

"Speak quickly. No need to think it over. Do you really want to be punished?"

"Why frighten me like this? Where do you expect me to begin with my confession? I don't know anything."

I don't know what the recorder wrote in his book. The judge said, "Take her back and wait a while, and then we will make her suffer."

I was taken back to the jail. As I passed his cell, Molin quickly put his head close to the iron door and asked, "What did you say?"

I was about to answer, but a gun butt smashed my shoulder. Apparently the guard had been standing right behind me.

My friends were summoned separately before the judge on two occasions. I don't know what they said, but their stories didn't match. The situation was becoming serious. I heard the guard and the night watchman discussing my friends: "The judge said one of them is an important person. He will be shot tomorrow morning."

The woman in my cell was already sleeping soundly. I stood up and put my face next to the iron door and gazed across at my friends, and they sorrowfully returned my gaze. We transmitted everything with our eyes, for our mouths could make no sound. Then I began to notice tears glimmering in Aisi's eyes. I disapproved of this. In the military school we had all shouted the slogan "Revolutionaries do not shed tears, only blood!" So why was he crying about this misfortune?

At my second interrogation I gave the same answers as I had the first time, without a single change. The judge was so angry that his green veins bulged. Yet he did not order me to be beaten, which puzzled me. Instead, he called me into his private office.

No guard was present, just he and I. I knew that now he would try the gentle approach. He figured he could entice me with sweet talk, as if he were coaxing a child. But I answered him stiffly, just as I had on the previous occasion.

"Sit down and we'll talk leisurely. Do you want a smoke?"

"No. Thanks."

"Right now there are many young people with causes. But when they take the wrong path, they sacrifice their lives for nothing. I can see you are very intelligent and no ordinary female. OK—so you were weak-willed, so you mistakenly took the wrong path. But if you will simply repent and reform, you can still have a very promising future. I tell you this for your own good. So, then. Let's have the truth." His eyes flashed frightening light.

Afraid to look at him, I quickly lowered my head and replied in a faint voice, "Judge, I am very sorry. I really am confused. But I have not walked the wrong path, and so I do not need to reform."

"Do you want your head chopped off?" Angrily he threw his cigarette butt onto the ground, hard, and with his large fist he slammed the table. *BONK.*

I was startled. I changed my manner, spoke loudly: "That is not up to me to decide. Because even if you kill me, I still have no confession to make."

I remained obstinate. He saw he was getting nowhere. Finally, he ordered the guard to put a pair of foot irons on me. This gave me a new taste of pain.

Early the next morning my female friend woke up and put her mouth next to my ear and whispered, "How many times were you questioned last night? Are you in danger?"

I told her briefly what had happened. She shook her head and looked at me with worried eyes. She sighed a deep sigh, "I have been locked up for only seven days, and already I have seen five young girls like you come and go. One was only fifteen years old. They came in one day and were dragged out the next. . . . Aye! Will they take you and . . . ?"

I was grateful for her concern. But I didn't know how to answer her.

She went on to tell me, in detail, about her own case, which concerned a fight with her husband. But the punishment would not put her life in danger. "When I get out of here I will bring you some food," she said. "Don't worry. I'll be out tomorrow."

"I'm afraid I may not be around to eat your food," I said. I was just talking.

Yet the thought made her sad and she began to cry. Then I held her hands tightly, putting my head in her lap, and my tears poured down like waterfalls. I treated her like my lover, my dearest friend.

The authorities interrogated us a fourth time, and on this occasion they concluded that we were reactionaries who deserved the most extreme punishment. Apparently they got this idea because we were obstinate in our replies and because they had found suspiciously reactionary letters in Aisi's trunk.

During my interrogation the judge asked me to tell about my family, all the details—and he was stunned when I mentioned my father's name. Apparently this judge had studied for four years at my father's school. This unexpected ray of light saved our lives. The judge allowed me to write a letter, and he promised to send a messenger to carry it to my big brother, who lived outside the north gate. My big brother and his father-in-law, Mr. Long, hurried to the prison to see me. It was after three o'clock that night when they arrived.

Naturally, my big brother stiffened his face and angrily lectured me. But old Mr. Long was kind. He comforted me, saying, "Don't be anxious. We will get you out of here, one way or another."

"Not just me. I have two friends."

Molin and Aisi smiled and nodded.

My big brother remarked sarcastically, "As long as you are here, you might as well relax and enjoy it. A taste of life behind iron bars is not easily obtained."

Aisi and Molin were on their way to see the judge. I spoke a few words to console them: "We now have hope of being rescued." I forced a bitter smile, mostly out of despair.

"Naturally, you have hope, for the judge is your father's former student. But we, we are afraid. . . ." Aisi spoke mournfully, tears filling his eyes.

"Death is death," said Molin, disdaining Aisi's self-pity. "So what does it matter?"

"If I am released, of course you will be too," I said. "If not, I will remain with you, and we will be sacrificed together."

My big brother returned after two hours and told me that I would be released as soon as a trusted guarantor could be found.

"How about the other two?" I asked him anxiously.

"I don't know about them. I don't even know who they are. Naturally, I do not dare speak blindly on their behalf. Anyhow, it is impossible."

He deliberately spoke loudly, as if wishing them to hear.

I said, "No! If they will release only me, then I will sit here to keep my friends company."

"If their lives are—"

"Then, of course, we will die together."

"Why?"

"They were arrested because of my books—it was actually *I* who implicated them. So why should I be released and not them?" I knew my argument was right and fair. And I also knew that, because of me, my big brother could not ignore them. As for the judge, he was my father's student—so of course he could not do anything to me. Fortunately, just at that moment Aisi's friend, Renjun, came to bail those two out of jail.

So on the fourth day the three of us were set free, having been in jail for three full days. Yet when we got out we each ate only one bowl of noodles. The meal cost two yuan and the taste of those cheap noodles was fresh, wonderful, more delicious than sea slugs and sharks' fins. To this very day the taste seems to linger in my mouth.

After leaving jail, I had no more opportunity to see my two friends. Manxia told me that Aisi and Molin had been in great distress when they left Changsha. They feared that I had been driven home by my family. On the evening that Renjun saw them off they had all been quite worried about me.

I was thankful for their friendship.

"EXCELLENT. OPPORTUNITY KNOCKS. Mr. Zhang, the principal of the Fifth Provincial Middle School, wants to find a teacher of Chinese for the affiliated grade school. I've told him about you, and since he was Father's student, he will be very happy to help you. You can pack your bags and go with him to Hengyang tomorrow."*

When my big brother told me this wonderful news, I could scarcely believe it. Could it be true that tomorrow a caged bird would be flying free above the clouds?

This was in the spring of 1928.

My initial plan was that if I did not have a job, I would continue my schooling, though I knew that this dream of continuing my education was only that, a dream, and would never come true. Still, I pursued the dream stubbornly, and even when it was hopeless my fervent mind still pursued it unwaveringly.

But now I needed to live on my own, without relying on family or friends, so I had no choice but to become a teaching drudge and earn my pitiful living by means of the chalk. I had no notion of what was in store for me—that I would no sooner begin living an independent life and earning my living by the sweat of my brow than I would be dealt a serious blow.

From the moment the principal introduced me to the dean of the grade school, I could tell that the dean had a poor impression of me. He could not believe that Principal Zhang would hire such a young female as a teacher. Most of society thought young people were ignorant and only caused trouble, and the dean—quite naturally—was no exception.

I was frightened to think that I had become a teacher. My bedroom was right next to the classroom in which I was to teach a combined class of second-semester sixth-graders and second-semester fifth-graders.

"Heavens! Tomorrow I must become a teacher—what to do?" I stood by the railing, looking at the dusky evening.

That night I did not sleep well. I kept worrying about the next morning. I loved innocent children more than anything, yet suddenly I had forgotten them and thought only of myself, feeling sorry for myself that I was forced to come here to teach instead of being able to continue my studies like so many other people were able to do. I wondered to myself, "What abilities or qualifications do you have to be a teacher of children?"

---

*Hengyang is about one hundred miles south of Changsha.—trans.

I remembered how on the boat from Changsha the principal had told me that I would be a grade supervisor. This meant I must supervise the students at their morning assembly on the field. Also, on days when it was my turn to be in charge I would be unable to leave the office from morning until night. I would need to take names and check the rosters in the morning and evening, inspect the classrooms and the bedrooms, and write daily records of school affairs. If students argued with one another or needed something, they would come to me for decisions and solutions.

I had listened carefully to everything he had said, but now I was thinking that all these matters were much too fussy and that I just could not live this kind of life. Yet how could I escape it?

Morning assembly.

I stood on the exercise field like a wooden puppet. The "at-ease" whistle had been blown, and the children were all tilting their heads and listening to the report by the teacher in charge for the day. Strange, but suddenly their little eyes were staring at me. My face burned like fire. I turned my head to look at the basketball hoop on the east side of the field.

But this is not right, for didn't the principal tell me to supervise the students during the morning assembly?

So I turned my head back . . . and what I saw was even more frightening. More than three hundred pairs of eyes were all fixed on me. I began to tremble from fright, for no reason. I wished I could leave immediately.

Again the whistle blew. The orderly march began and I somewhat recovered my senses. Blindly following the fifth- and sixth-graders, I walked into my classroom.

As I stepped onto the platform I saw three students who were taller than I, and my face again turned red. "Fellow students, I am a big child who has just come out of the Teacher Training School. The truth is, I did not graduate. While I was still one year short of receiving my certificate, I left school to become a soldier. As far as my knowledge and ability are concerned, I really am not worthy to be your teacher. But what I *can* be is your most trusted friend. If there are things you don't know, we can investigate and discuss them together. So I hope you will treat me like a fellow student and not like a teacher."

After I had spoken so modestly, the children all looked at me and smiled. From that moment I became a teacher of children and a slave to the necessity of making a living. Now began my life in a conventional society, and my education as to what life is really all about.

Teaching deprived me of time for reading, but fortunately I received spiritual comfort of a different sort: my children's every move was natural and lovable, and their hearts were wonderfully pure and frank. I had not yet learned how to adapt to my new environment, how to be cunning, negligent, and false when required. I was sincere, loyal, frank with everyone. Aye! This innocent young woman entering society for the first time—how should she know the ways of the world?

In my third month at the school something unfortunate occurred. Not only was I the only female teacher in the entire school but I was very young and I taught the higher grades. And naturally all this made others uneasy, especially the dean of the grade school, Mr. Huang.

Because I kept company with the students all day and because my disposition was like a child's, the students were particularly fond of me, and they respected me, listened to me, and worked extra hard on the subjects I was teaching. They enjoyed talking to me more than to any other teacher. When I told them stories of the Northern Expedition of a year earlier, their eyebrows flew and faces danced.

At that time the young scout troops went to Heng Mountain to give speeches. They told me that Mr. Wang, another grade supervisor, was one of the teachers who took them there. From this I knew that Mr. Wang's thinking must be relatively progressive, that he must know his era and understand the realities of modern China. He had a firm foundation in ancient literature and had read quite a bit of modern literature. Apart from him, there was no one in the school for me to talk to. So I gradually began to have conversations with him, though we had very little time to chat. Every week I was responsible for teaching twenty-eight hours of classes, and on top of this every day I had to correct diaries, look at calligraphy practice sheets, grade notebooks, and correct compositions—all in addition to doing my own reading and preparation for lessons.

Because I was in charge of the children, I was naturally thinking all the time about their welfare. For instance, I felt that the library, the athletic field, and the recreation room should be enlarged and that we should buy more books and athletic equipment for the children. The school library was pitifully stocked with nothing other than a few youth magazines, some books called *Little Friends,* and books about the seven knights and the five virtues. Apart from these there was nothing. On the athletic field were only two broken balls for the children to kick back and forth. The recreation room was even more pathetic. Even the Ping-Pong paddles were bought by the students themselves. On behalf of the students I spoke with Dean Huang about all these needs. Unfortunately, this irritated and angered him and led him to recommend that I "do further study."

Matters turned serious. The principal called me in to talk.

"Dean Huang is somewhat dissatisfied with you—perhaps it is because you are too diligent in carrying out your duties. The truth is, you young people get blamed wherever you go—especially when your heart is straight and your mouth is quick and you are serious about your work." He spoke anxiously, his voice sounding a bit unnatural.

"What? You are not satisfied with me because I take my work too seriously and am too straightforward? Then how should I be?"

The principal's words really confused me. I had been taught to be earnest and responsible in my actions, to work for the good of the people, to sacrifice my own happiness, and, whether dealing with the world or making friends, to be faithful, sincere, and open.

"It is difficult to answer you. But it will be best if you can just get through this semester. Then we will talk again."

"Does he want me to leave?"

"Yes, he has that idea."

"For what reason?"

"He said you and another teacher often speak together openly. He said that in a place like this, where the atmosphere is so intimate and so close, such behavior cannot be tolerated. But more important, I am afraid, it is still a—"

"Still a what?" I interrupted.

"Still a question of his being afraid that you are more capable than he is. You are welcomed by students—"

"Yes," I said angrily. "And now all teachers who are welcomed by students are not good? But that is not a reason at all. As long as the school has male and female students, why can't a female teacher interact with a male teacher? Especially since I have spoken only two or three times with Mr. Wang, about literature."

"Be patient, and for a little while just ignore Mr. Wang—it would be best if you could do this. You can be close to students, but don't acknowledge any male teachers. And we will see what the dean will do to you."

"Ha-ha! Of course this can be done." I laughed loudly.

From the next day on I practiced my "closed-door policy." Not only did I not talk to any male teachers, but I didn't even go into the teachers' lounge. I didn't attend any meetings for teachers or for supervisors, because they were all males. I didn't meet with any man, for fear devils might appear. I didn't talk to any man since this might damage public morals. My sudden change in behavior made all the male teachers curious. I didn't acknowledge them even when they came to my room to borrow books. Gradually, everyone realized why I refused to see visitors. That is when Mr. Wang began to take up arms against injustice, and several other teachers also sympathized with me. But I still said not a word to anyone. I only clenched my teeth, taught my classes, and corrected my papers.

One night the dean came into my room. I thought of ordering this visitor to leave, but he had already sat down on the bench.

I deliberately piled false smiles on my face as I spoke. "Mr. Huang, what is the purpose of your honorable visit?"

"Nothing. Let us talk freely."

"Sorry, I do not receive male guests."

"Ha! Then, I will leave."

He could only open his mouth and laugh—only heaven knew how I felt at that moment—and he said, "Your knowledge is lofty and deep, your teaching methods are excellent, the students are receiving great benefits. But you are making too big a personal sacrifice."

I knew the intent of his words the moment he opened his mouth. But I pretended that I was an idiot and did not understand him at all.

"Sacrifice? Why would you say such a thing? I have already received great satisfaction from the job—and even if I had not, I should do it as my duty, to serve my country."

"Well said, well said. A smart and able talent like you is just right for pursuing education. You surely have a future of boundless opportunity."

He was making detours with his words, but instantly I intercepted him and told him, "Yes. At first, I was going to continue my studies, but Principal Zhang insisted on hiring me to come and teach at your honorable school. And because he is a friend of my father's, I could not refuse. I could only accede to his request. But I will be gone as soon as summer recess begins. Thank you for your concern."

My words tasted slightly sour and slippery, but after I had spoken them my heart felt much lighter.

After he left I went to the principal and talked for a long time. The truth was that Dean Huang had a relative waiting to solve the problem of the rice bowl, and that is why he wanted me to leave quickly. Anyway, I could not tolerate it there any longer. I did not want to wrangle with a person who would wrest a rice bowl away by force and who was a dishonest schemer. I actually sympathized with his relative, who no doubt was worse off than I was. So I made up my mind to leave. I left the school just ten days before the students in my class were to graduate, and I left in secret. But strangely, all the students learned of my leaving, and they formed a line and came down to the riverbank to wish me farewell. Many of them were crying.

"We will meet later. I beg you to work hard." My eyes were red, I could not speak anymore. I looked at them earnestly, then got onto the boat.

I left Hengyang in such a hurry that I was still owed a month's salary, and I had brought with me only a twenty-yuan banknote.

When the boat began to move, I could not hold back my tears. The children were standing there as if in a trance. Some used their sleeves to wipe their eyes. Some waved to me. Lovable little angels, when will we meet again?

I NOW SEE that under the ancient authority of Chinese society a woman—especially a single young woman—cannot stand on her own two feet. Yet I will not give in. I must be prepared to endure even more hardship, suffer more attacks. For I cannot escape reality and live as a hermit. Most of all, I cannot let myself be discouraged or surrender to the past.

Go, then, for the earth is vast. Must not the future await me somewhere, if only I can stand hardship? Go, and let no one trace my footsteps. I wish to quietly begin a life of lonely drifting. I am like falling leaves of autumn: my resting place is where the wind will blow me.

Yet what about Aizhen? Hasn't she been writing every day to ask me to save her? I should pity her and help her, so I will write a letter inviting her to go to Shanghai with me. And Aisi's good friend, Renjun, who sympathizes with me—I should tell him which boat I am taking so I can give him a final farewell. I am definitely leaving Changsha. I have no idea when I will return to my native village. Perhaps never.

I will not tell my big brother, for he has inherited all the feudal thinking of the past, and I'd be flinging myself into the net if I went to see him. I have lived the life of a prisoner, but I will endure it no longer. I will not agree to escort my own life back to the grave from which it escaped but a moment ago. Other than Renjun and Aizhen, I will let no one know, not even Shurong or Shanshan. Yet how about Manli? Poor child. How sad she will be when she hears I have left.

Twilight fell. Renjun, Aizhen, and I boarded the boat.

Aizhen acted exactly like an escaped prisoner, for she feared that her family would pursue her. Renjun knew we were feeling anxious, so he kept up a steady stream of amusing stories to help us forget our predicament.

"Quiet—listen—is it the inspector?" I heard sounds of quarreling outside. I pasted my wide eyes to the slits of the cabin to look out. Aizhen quickly jumped down from the upper bunk and crowded next to me to sneak a glance.

Renjun was a little nervous, frowning. "Don't be afraid, let's discuss—"

After all, he was an experienced person, a man who knew the ways of the world and could be perfectly calm even while realizing that probably there would be trouble if the inspector came.

"Discuss what?" Aizhen softly interrupted.

"How to handle the inspector." He lit a cigarette.

We sat down and began to talk. His voice was so faint and feeble that I had to listen closely to hear what he was saying. Within a short ten minutes we were ready for the inspector.

Then, for no reason, I suddenly remembered what had happened here four months ago, and this frightened me: Renjun and Aizhen could be implicated because of me. I mulled it over in my mind for a long while. Then I said firmly, while clenching my teeth, "Mr. Renjun, you had better leave soon. And Aizhen, do not go with me. Because if anything happens when the inspector comes, well, I'm afraid . . . it is just not worth it."

Aizhen began to cry. "You don't want me with you? Then I'll jump into the Xiang River and drown myself. Sister, you are cruel. I told you long ago that only death lies before me unless you help. Can you be so cold that you would watch my family destroy me? Sister, I will follow you wherever the road leads—if to life, that's good, and if to death, then so be it." Aizhen's tears splashed my heart. I felt so sad that I could not speak. I wondered what to do.

Renjun said to Aizhen, in a threatening tone, "Don't cry. If the waiter hears, he'll come knocking at our door."

I felt I ought to offer more explanation so I said to her, "Of course, it was just because I wanted to save you that I got in touch with you and asked you to escape with me. Look—except for you and Renjun, no one knows where I am. Sure, part of my plan is to find myself a future in Shanghai, yet it is for your sake that I am leaving here in such a hurry. But now I am overwhelmed by a thousand depressing thoughts. If something unexpected happens to me, what would happen to you? Let's say we *do* get out of here safely. It is still possible that your family's search for you will lead them to this boat. Then I would certainly be branded as a criminal who has abducted you, and Renjun would be suspected as an accomplice. If that happens, what a mess! Or let's pretend that all I've mentioned is really no problem—even then, if my brother somehow hears news of my departure, and if he rushes to the boat to drag me home, wouldn't it still result in a terrible situation?"

Aizhen was sobbing and even Renjun was beginning to feel bad. But fortunately he pretended to be calm. Like an older brother comforting his sisters, he said, "Don't think such complicated thoughts. Be calm. Actually, it cannot be as serious as you think. Perhaps tonight will pass peacefully, as it has up until now. When the boat whistle blows tomorrow morning, you will be sailing away to freedom and leaving behind this sea of sorrow."

BANG! BANG! BANG! Sudden frantic knocking exploded at our door.

"Who is it?" I said, using my Changsha accent.

We three looked at one another, our faces white.

"Inspection," said the voice outside.

The door opened and in walked two military policemen with rifles and bayonets strapped to their backs, plus an officer and ten or more soldiers and sailors. Suddenly our cabin, which could barely accommodate two beds, was so crowded that water could not leak through it. Passengers were pressing close to the door to watch the commotion.

Renjun moved toward the door, but he was stopped by a policeman with a pockmarked face. "Do not move—are you thinking of escaping?"

"Why would I want to escape?"

"Why are you moving?"

"What business is it of yours if I move?" Renjun was so angry that he appeared to be on the verge of punching the man, but luckily the military officer tactfully stepped between them and reprimanded the policeman, saying, "Why all this uproar? Conduct your inspection in a proper manner."

After our luggage, bedrolls, and little handbaskets had been thoroughly searched, a tall military policeman (a fellow who was more genial than the man with the pockmarked face) asked me, "What is your name and where are you from?"

"My name is Xue Yingzhi."

"And she?"

"She's my younger sister."

"Younger sister?" He looked at Aizhen closely, from head to toe, as though he didn't believe me. "Why is she taller than you?"

"There are many sons taller than their fathers in this world."

My answer made the people outside laugh.

"If you are sisters, why do you not resemble each other in the least?" This officer was deliberately making it difficult for me.

"There is a common saying, 'Ten sons have ten faces.' People are not made from a mold. Naturally, each person has his own face."

"How flippant! Dare you be so bold!" The pockmarked face pushed angrily forward. Renjun saw that things were not going well. He quickly touched my hand, hinting that I should beware. Immediately my face became very accommodating.

"What is their relationship with you?" asked the tall one, turning to question Renjun.

"These are my cousins from Hankou. They live on Jishengsan Road. They came here to visit my mother for two weeks, and I am seeing them off." Though Renjun was full of resentment, he had no choice but to endure their insults. There was no reason whatever for them to ask about his relationship to us in such a leering tone—suggesting that Renjun was somehow disreputable.

"Where do you work?"

"At the Bureau of Salt Affairs." Renjun showed them his badge as he spoke. The pockmarked face walked over and glanced at the badge, then screwed up his lips and walked off in silence. The rest followed. The officer was the last one out. As he left, he made this disgusting remark: "When you are in the cabin with these two *young cousins*, you should not close the door—understand?" He then he eyed Aizhen with a leering glance.

I almost started cursing. Renjun's face was red with anger, but he dared not react. He could only hold his breath and swallow his voice.

"We have passed the first barrier," said Aizhen, behaving exactly like a child. She even jumped up with joy.

Renjun quickly waved his hand. "Quietly, quietly—they have not left yet."

I smiled. "We have peacefully passed a barrier more dangerous than the one at a ghost's door."

But Aizhen's face fell. "Two more remain."

"The one I face is unimportant," I said in an almost deliberately needling tone, "but you can count on having left the tiger's mouth only when the boat departs."

This made her angry. "I am not afraid either. Just like you said, at worst we would die—but what is so frightening about that?"

I asked Renjun to leave: "Mr. Renjun, thank you. It is almost ten o'clock, the curfew hour. Please go home to rest."

But he seemed uneasy about our spending the night on the boat. "I'll sit a while longer. I am afraid someone may come to cause trouble." He looked out the round window. Then he glanced at us.

"Never mind. The curfew is on, so our families will not be able to come after us. You had best go now." I begged him to leave. I could find no other way to express my gratitude for all he had done.

The big hand on the clock now showed three minutes to ten. Renjun was forced to say farewell. As he stepped out the door, he turned to us and said, "I wish you peace and comfort the entire journey. Send me a letter right away when you reach Hankou."

DEEP AND STARLESS NIGHT. Already midnight. The curfew was on, the shore dead silent. Not half a sound. Not a single vendor of water dumplings or wantons or fried sweet balls to be seen. The city of Changsha lay covered in blackness: electric lights appeared like stars, creating a tint of twilight. It was summertime, and yet the lovely nightscape was the cold color of autumn. Sailors and passengers on the *Dongtingwan* had all fallen into dreams. Only Aizhen and I, in cabin 13, were still awake.

Somewhere outside on the steerage deck an old lady coughed, a child cried.

The heat of the day had completely retreated; night wind blew cool from the river, and little waves hit the prow of the boat, *tung-tung-tung*. I turned over and, stretching my neck, looked up at Aizhen in the upper berth. "Zhen, are you awake again? You'd best sleep a little."

"I . . . I . . . I can't sleep. I am afraid my family will come after me."

"What? Crying again? I told you, crying is useless. Why bother being frightened, now that you have decided to escape? Could it be that you miss your family?"

"Not at all, no. I am just afraid they will come after me and take me back. If they do, they will force me to get married. Then I am finished."

"Why worry so much? Surely, they must think you have gone to your aunt's. That is why they have not been looking for you. They would have been here long ago if they had thought you were on this boat. Why would they wait till now?"

"Maybe they think I took the train. I left home this afternoon at around three o'clock. So my family must have taken the night express and rushed to Hankou to catch me."

"If that is the case, it will be dangerous when we land at the harbor."

The two of us were like a lonely vessel moving over boundless seas in the black of night on a perilous voyage, passing wave to wave, unable to see a lighthouse or to distinguish east from west, south from north.

Aizhen had just passed sixteen. Ever since she was a baby she had been cared for and spoiled by her grandmother. At thirteen she was sent to Hengcui Girls School to study. Being a very smart girl, she learned to paint with watercolor in the first year, and in the second year she switched to studying Chinese painting. She received very good marks and every teacher praised her talent. Amid the love and admiration of her schoolmates, Aizhen lived the happy life of an angel, unaware that life has worries and pains. Seen from her eyes, the entire world was a brilliant spring day, a beautiful painting, and everyone in it was a happy god or goddess of spring.

She sang the praises of life and beauty and felt that beauty and love were life's most necessary ingredients. Without love she almost could not survive. Lacking beauty (she thought) was to be a skeleton without a soul. She said love and beauty were the sustainers of her life. Then, in the year she reached her fifteenth birthday, her school hired an art teacher who was about twenty-two years old. This new teacher was the very model of a modern man, with a strong body, a suave manner, and an uncommon talent for art. His temper was as sweet as that of an ancient unmarried girl, yet his spirit was as brave as that of a warrior.

The already-mature Aizhen fell in love with him the moment he arrived. But he was a young man with a goal; he taught at her school for only half a year before going off to study in Shanghai. Aizhen fell ill from unrequited love, and her weak heart began to taste the flavor of pain. She cursed life and said that to be human meant trouble and distress. She said that happiness and fortune were all words to fool people and that to be human is to suffer. From the day the man she loved left, she thought only of destroying herself.

Here was news to catch people's eyes: a fifteen-year-old girl has thrown herself into the river.

Aizhen was gasping for her last breath when a fisherman rescued her. The fisherman took her to the police station and then escorted her home. Her father knew the reason for her suicide attempt, but no one else in her family understood what had caused her to want to die.

"Do not ask her why she wanted to jump into the river," her father advised his wife and his mother. "Let her recover first." He could not mention the pain in his heart. He was a well-known educator who had founded a middle school and a grade school, and now his daughter had created a sensation of the sort that society likes to use as a topic for conversation and as a subject for criticism. It shamed him to the point that he could not show his face anywhere. He decided that during this winter he would marry Aizhen to Xu Xuanzong, a man to whom she had been matched thirteen years earlier.

Xu Xuanzong was a playboy. His father was a well-known gentleman from Xinhua County. He had both money and power. Mention his name, and people knew him. Xuanzong, having been born and raised in that kind of family, naturally spread gold around as if it were soil. He was short and he had coarse yellow skin, and he had a temper as fierce as a tiger's. He understood nothing at all other than eating, drinking, whoring, and gambling. Clearly, he had no qualifications to take Aizhen as his wife—she who sang the praises of beauty and love.

Her spirits gradually recovered after her heartbreaking experience. Contrary to everyone's expectation, she changed her view of life. She now pursued life wholeheartedly and despised herself for having been so weak as to do something stupid that would shame her forever.

Aizhen's family had originally planned to solve the whole affair in the summer of the following year, but now they wanted to move the wedding date ahead. That was why Aizhen was so anxious to leave Changsha. I thought of how her parents would hate me to the bones for having helped her escape. But I could not watch someone sink in a sea of despair and refuse to hold out a helping hand.

"Oh, Ma! I don't want to go back, I would rather die. . . . I'm afraid, afraid to return. . . ."

I was awakened by Aizhen's talking and crying in her sleep. Quickly I got up and held her nose to wake her up.

She sat up suddenly and, wiping tears with one hand, trembled with fear and pointed at the window. "Look out the window—is my mother here? Sister, I'm afraid."

"No, there is nothing. Everyone is asleep. Don't make noise and wake them. Lie down and be quiet."

Despite what I said, I too was frightened. I looked out the window and thought I saw a dark shadow walking on the bridge. A sudden breeze blew into the room; I shivered.

Maybe my brother is here, or perhaps her family?

I hid this terrible suspicion, gave not even the slightest hint of it in my expression.

Softly, I opened the door to go out. But then, fearing Aizhen would notice (for she had just lain down), I drew back and walked toward her, to listen. Already she had fallen asleep again. In the corners of her eyes and on her cheeks were traces of tears. Her pale white face was like a corpse's, very scary.

The night was still. Only the sounds of waves, of rushing wind, of snoring passengers on the deck.

In the western sky a cold bright half moon lingered. A few scattered stars flickered faintly, like glowworms. Gradually, earth sank into utter stillness, into profound, mysterious, frightening dark. Wind rushed in waves over my frail body. If not for the railing, I might have been blown into the river.

The inky shadow I had seen through the window now seemed to be hiding at the prow of the ship. I imagined it might be a devil come to seize me. Suddenly, a voice startled me—"Hey, what are you doing standing here?"

A huge shadow stood before me.

I stared wide-eyed . . . and recognized the fat cashier who had sold us the boat tickets. "The room is too hot. I came out to get some breeze." I forced a smile.

"The wind is quite strong—your sister did not come out?"

"A child does not mind heat. She is sleeping."

I got worried when this fat cashier asked about my sister, thinking he might have some ulterior motive. So I quickly returned to the cabin, closed the door, and lay down on the bed.

Bang, bang, BANG! BANG! BANG!—urgent knocking at the door.

Aizhen cried out loudly, "Ma, I'm afraid!"

The knocking became more urgent.

"Who is it?" I asked, as casually as I could.

"I am looking for someone named Wang," said the voice outside.

"No, there is no one here named Wang."

"Please open the door and let me take a look."

"What is there to see? I told you there is nobody here named Wang."

"Open the door and we will talk."

I thought it must be Aizhen's family pretending to be looking for a Wang. But having gone this far, there was no point being afraid. Aizhen was holding me back with all her strength, but I ignored her and opened the door.

Instantly, a red beam darted in as two men in long gowns shined a flashlight on my face. Smiling, they immediately said, "Sorry we disturbed you."

"It doesn't matter."

The two men went to knock on the door of cabin 23.

Aizhen spoke breathlessly. "Sister, touch me and you will find my entire body covered with sweat, yet my head is ice cold. I even stopped breathing just now. I thought they were coming for me."

I smiled bitterly and said, "It is as if we are scared by the sound of the wind and the cry of the cranes, and terrified that every tree and tuft of grass might be a soldier in ambush. We fear whatever moves. I hope the boat gets under way quickly, for we cannot stand this much longer."

Soon afterward I heard the *chang-chang-chang* sound of iron chains, and I knew the anchor was coming up. Through our small window darted a ray of light the color of a fish's stomach. I stood and looked out. A throng of people were busily working—it was time for departure.

"We are free." I held Aizhen's head and kissed it madly, and she was so happy that she was crying.

"Sister, it is our world."

The giant engine wheel began to turn, the whistle shrieked to the sky, the river water roared as if stirred by a thousand soldiers and horses. Gradually the boat turned east, slowly at first, then faster, and an instant later it drove into the center of the Xiang River.

Farewell, Changsha!

I stood on deck holding hands with Aizhen as the wheel of red sun rose out of the eastern water. Smiling, we welcomed the new morning, new sun, new life.

THE *DONGTINGWAN* STEAMED for a day and an evening before reaching Hankou, and there we stayed the night with Mutang, who, like me, had been a female soldier. The following evening Aizhen and I boarded the steamboat *Ruihe* and paid for a hanging bed on the steerage deck, intending to share it. This was the first time I had ever been on a large steamboat. Passengers crammed the corridors and filled the decks and were almost piled on top of one another in some places. With a huge effort we pushed through mountains and seas of people, and at last we found our space. The sweaty odor of third-class passengers was more suffocating than ammonia.

A smiling fat waiter came over to solicit business. "How can two people sleep in one bed? Why don't you buy a cabin?"

Perhaps he thought we should not be in the middle of all this filth when he saw that we wore neat student uniforms and had friends to see us off. He had no idea that all we possessed was seven yuan.

We were in the largest steerage cabin, which had more than three hundred bed spaces. Our row was by the riverbank, next to a line of small round windows. Each row had upper, middle, and lower bunks. Unfortunately, we were on the lower level, where light was frightfully dim. Across from us our neighbor was arranging a plate to smoke his opium; suddenly, a strange and foul odor pierced my nostrils and almost made me throw up.

The departure gong sounded. I took my pillow and blanket out of my basket and put them on the bed plank. Aizhen asked, "How can two people sleep on this small platform?"

"Try it first. If it doesn't work, we will take turns sleeping. We will each sleep half a night and sit half a night, and the problem is solved."

"Where will we sit?"

"On the plank."

"How can we sit in such a low spot?" Aizhen complained. "Look, won't my back break from bending?"

I quickly comforted her. "Never mind. The nights will be very hot and we will most likely not sleep. Besides, the moonlit nights are beautiful, especially on the misty and boundless Yangzi River. We will walk on deck to watch the moon."

And we did just what I said. When night fell we didn't sleep, just stood by the railing and watched the moon and the stars. The moon was glistening white, the scenes on both shores as clear as if seen on a sunny day. High mountains, farm dikes, villages, forests—all were perfectly sharp in the moonlight. The river's waves were golden, as if they had been splashed from the sky. The sound of the engine was urgent. The foamy waves pushed up by the prow of the boat were lovely, powerful. The crowd lying along the sides of the ship was mostly refugees, clothes torn to threads, boys completely naked, girls wearing only torn trousers. Most of them sat with lowered heads, snoring. Moonlight shone on their pale and skinny faces. One glance told me that they were people who had suffered a lot to eke out a living.

Aizhen had not slept the previous two nights, so tonight she went to bed first. Mesmerized, I watched the moon and the white clouds racing each other, and the falling stars secretly crossing the river.

Aizhen had no sooner lain down than she fell dead asleep. She could not be awakened. I didn't want to make her suffer; I preferred to suffer myself.

So I curled up to sleep behind her back, with my two feet dangling just off the floor. In less than ten minutes my entire body was numb.

Strange. Even on this sort of bed I entered dreamland.

I was making coarse yarn in a very large Japanese cotton mill, and just as I was turning the machine with all my strength, a strand suddenly broke and the machine stopped. I tried to connect the broken yarn, but all at once an iron stick fell on my back. Uh-oh. The foreman had come. I thought I had better hurry and repair the yarn and begin working, but I was so nervous and fearful of the foreman that my fingers got caught up in the machine, and an instant later fresh blood dyed the white cotton red, and three of my fingers were gone.

"*Ahhhh!*" I cried out loudly, waking suddenly from my dream.

An old man in the upper bed had carelessly dropped his rice bowl on my head, and fresh blood now was dripping fast, dyeing my clothes red.

I could not help but holler, and this startled many people awake, including Aizhen. Now the old man quickly used his face towel to wipe the blood off me. A young person, who looked like a student, spoke to him angrily for being so careless. The waiters all came to comfort me and offer apologies. I couldn't lift my head because it hurt so much, and I couldn't hear clearly what they were saying. But I was alarmed when a round-faced, big-eyed waiter came to scrutinize me like a detective—his two eyes probed my whole body. At last he chewed out the old man in the upper berth and ordered him to move out immediately so I could sleep in his space.

"Sorry, please forgive me," the old man begged in a trembling voice. "I was careless. I did not hit her on purpose."

Actually, how could he be blamed? If my head had not been sticking out I would not have been hit. It was I who did not have the money to buy a second bed.

"You broke someone's head—it is not a trivial matter."

The waiter was again talking about fairness, like some sort of knight-errant.

Aizhen said softly next to my ear, "This waiter is very strange. Why is he helping you like this?"

I gave her a quick wink and she dared not make another sound.

"No problem," I said. "It is not painful now. Thank you all."

Actually, my wound felt as if someone were pounding on it with a hammer.

"I will go to the cashier and get some cuttlefish bone powder for you to put on your head," said the waiter. "Then you will feel better immediately." And he left.

I was suddenly frightened.

Why is he so courteous to me?

Aizhen again fell asleep. I sat until dawn with my eyes wide open, holding my head with both hands.

Breakfast time. The passengers in the third-class cabin usually ate only two meals of coarse rice each day, with no accompanying dishes. At every meal a waiter brought in a barrel of tea that looked like dirty water, and the passengers drank it as if it were soup. I bought two pieces of dried bean curd but Aizhen thought this was not enough. She asked why I had not bought salted eggs and fried Guilin fish. I told her that all we had was three yuan, and we had yet to tip the waiter.

When suppertime came that same round-faced, wide-eyed waiter suddenly showed up with two bowls of snowy white rice. He also gave us salted fish and pickled turnip roots wrapped in paper.

"We don't need these side dishes—please take them back." I didn't dare accept his favor. After all, I still didn't understand why he was giving us special treatment.

"It doesn't matter, I won't charge you." He hurried upstairs. We then realized that he was taking care of the first-class cabins.

"He wouldn't have put poison in the food he brought us, would he?" Aizhen had taken a mouthful and she spat it out immediately.

"You are a fool. Why would he want to poison us? We're not rich."

A very good meal, indeed. We continued eating until there was not a single grain of rice left in our large bowls.

Dismal night again descended. But even before the sky had completely darkened, Aizhen was sleeping soundly, like a bug. I felt terribly tired, but I didn't have the heart to awaken her and make her take her turn standing guard. I had slept the first half hour because of my headache, while she had stood outside—and I don't know what time it was that she came in and fell asleep with her two feet pressing on my chest like rocks. This had awakened me and I found my body wet from sweat. Across from me the smoking devil had begun his work again; the odor was so unbearably foul that I immediately went outside to take in the breeze.

Strange, a long bamboo chair had been placed in the empty corridor. I saw no one around, so I sat down. But then I saw the round-faced waiter walking toward me, and in embarrassment I jumped up and apologized. "Sorry, sorry!" I felt an inexplicable terror.

"I knew you were dead tired last night, so I put out this bamboo chair for you to sleep on tonight. A while ago I went to look in on you and saw you were sleeping soundly, so I didn't dare to awaken you. Now you can sleep here."

His manner made me even more suspicious of him—and yet, after observing him closely for a while, I felt as if I had seen him somewhere before.

Don't guess blindly . . . of course I haven't seen him before, for this is the first time I have been on this boat.

I gave him a stern look. "Thank you for your help, but I don't feel like sleeping—you can remove it."

He smiled. "Perhaps you don't dare to sleep. Then sit for a while."

I actually sat down.

He began by addressing me as Comrade Xie and he said he had seen me at the Xianning Chamber of Commerce. He asked if I recognized him.

"No, I have not been to Xianning and I have not seen you before. You must have made a mistake. My name is not Xie."

"Don't stand on ceremony. Yesterday as you came aboard the boat you made an impression on me, though I caught but a glimpse of you. Then, when your head was injured, I paid close attention to your voice and your manner. That was when I decided for sure it must be you. Not until this afternoon was I bold enough to bring you a little rice and food to eat. You don't have to be afraid here. No one knows."

"But I don't know what you are talking about—I really am not the person you imagine."

I was afraid that he was a spy and was testing me with these words. Several times I sternly denied my name. He had no recourse but to take a step further, explaining, "You must still remember Mr. Qian Yuanjie, from the Xianning District?"

When I heard the words *Qian Yuanjie*, I thought the waiter must be a good man. Gradually, my suspicions faded.

He earnestly continued his story—"Originally I was the executive director of the Sailors' Union. Later our group delegated me to be responsible for organizing a labor union, so I asked for a month's leave from work. Didn't you represent the political ministry, and didn't you give a report at the big meeting for women representatives—the meeting sponsored by the chamber of commerce for workers, farmers, merchants, and students? The chairman was the secretary of the labor union, Comrade Liu. I was in charge of organizing that event."

By now I believed he was speaking the truth, yet I was still a little suspicious. Why was he able to work here safely as a waiter?

He smiled at me. "Now, can we talk—without you suspecting me to be a bad guy?"

"Why are you here?"

"My movements in Xianning are known by very few people. When I took leave to go there I used the false excuse that my mother had died. Now that I have returned and everyone sees that I do only the work of a waiter all day long, of course no one suspects anything—but never tell a third person what I have just told you."

I suddenly felt almost as if I had met a relative from my native village— I anxiously wished to know what had happened to those brave and honest farmers, those lively and progressive youths, those still-unliberated women during the year after I left Xianning. "Can you tell me what happened to the people around Fengkou and Xianning, what they went through in the disasters after we left?"

"Oh, it was tragic." He sighed a long, cold sigh. "When you came to Xianning the repressed people all thought that the saving stars had arrived. They had been under the iron hooves of local gang members, corrupt officials, landowners, and warlords—and now suddenly they thought they would be liberated, forever freed from pain. Who could guess that before a month was up they would return again to their life in hell—actually, even worse than before. The warlords returned on the second day after you left. They did not stop to inquire. They shot women who had cut their hair short, shot young people. On the day they entered the city they sprayed machine-gun fire into a crowd of more than a thousand farmers and young people and women. A number of extremists were among the crowd, no doubt. But two-thirds were innocent young people and village women. And those others who had escaped the revolutionary army—the local gang members, the corrupt officials, the landlords—they also returned as soon as they heard that the revolutionary army had left, and immediately they began slaughtering people. Now they have all the power in our district. Almost all the strong young men have been knifed and turned into ghosts. The farms grew more deserted day by day. The fields filled up with stinking corpses. The odor of blood could be smelled from several miles away. Yes, the homeland, the whole pitiful place, has become a site of slaughter."

I listened quietly. My heart felt infinite sorrow. This result had been foreseen by everyone. But we did not think it would be as terrible as what he had described. I asked about the chairwoman of the Women's Association at Fengkou, and he replied, "She has long since become a martyr."

"Our hope has vanished as quickly as a canna flower. Oh, I never imagined that the situation would change so quickly. . . do not be disheartened. The new society is fermenting under this repression. The great period will soon arrive."

I comforted him with these words, at the same time comforting myself.

When we saw that someone had come outside to cool off, we stopped talking right away.

Later I gently pushed Aizhen to waken her and tell her the happy news. "Zhen, that round-faced waiter is someone I knew on the military march in Fengkou—no wonder he is so concerned about us. We need not be afraid now. He said he will take us to Mr. Sun Fuyuan."

"That's great," she cried joyfully. "Wonderful."

I felt like a desert traveler who is suddenly handed a glass of dew and who will drink it even if it might prove poisonous: I quickly grasped the unexpected comfort of having met someone I knew.

The summer weather changed rapidly, difficult to predict. On this evening all those people who previously had slept bare-chested under moonlight were crowded into steerage. Children began to wail. Outside, a thunderstorm was pouring down tubs of rain. All this immediately made you think of those rich people in the officers' berth or in the big dining room—were they drunk in their dreams? Or were they appreciating the smoky and misty landscape of rain, perhaps gazing through their binoculars while listening to sounds of nature's music, *shhhi-li shhhi-li shhhi-li*?

From the start the steerage deck had been so crowded that even water might scarcely have moved amid the throng. Now, with this large group of newcomers, the cabin was more crowded still; scarcely room for a needle. Waiters had difficulty walking, were constantly complaining—

"Move it! A good dog does not block the way!" A waiter (he held a pot of boiling water) hollered angrily at a young man curled up in a passageway.

"You are the dog! A waiter so bloated with his own glorious power must have been raised by a bitch."

When I heard this last sentence I knew the young man was from Changsha.

The waiter suddenly put down his kettle of boiling water, but too roughly—the boiling water spilled onto the foot of a child who was drinking his milk. The child cried loudly, *WHAA-WHAA,* and now the waiter and the young man were brawling. A complete mess. The passengers all stood in a battle line and tried to help the young man who had been insulted and the child who had suffered for no reason. The waiters teamed up and shouted insults as if they were about to attack the passengers.

"These brutish waiters bully only the passengers in steerage," cried a rough and violent villager. "As soon as they see rich people in the restaurant, or in the officers' quarters, they don't dare so much as fart."

Instantly the crowd broke into fervent applause.

"Right! Right! These waiters are only flunkies, servants of the rich."

"Think about it. Whoever our parents may be, we are all humans. So why should we suffer the insults of others?" A middle-aged woman (who had not spoken a single word for two days) spat this out, angry at the unfairness of it all—she surprised me.

Our three days and nights aboard the steamboat were drawing swiftly to a close. I felt bewildered as we sailed into Wusong Harbor. I floated, lonely as a vessel that has lost its anchor, over a vast and violent sea of waves and billows. I flew like a lone goose who has left its flock and is sadly crying across the sky, over the Pacific, over the Himalayas, to all corners of the watery, airy world. But heavens, where is my resting place?

Waves of coldness washed upon me.

And when I arrive in Shanghai, what will I do?

As I stared at the vast white waves of the rushing Yangzi River, suddenly I beheld a new vision: flow, only flow like water, and you will find your future. Even if what lies ahead are dangerous sandbanks and shoals, still flow swiftly forward like water, and you will surge upon a new life anytime you wish, and realize your dreams.

The shrieking steam whistle woke me up like a bugle call to arms. The boat was nearing the Yihe wharf. Trams, buses, horse carts, motorbikes . . . tall smokestacks, neat rows of foreign buildings—before my eyes appeared the vast civilization of a city.

"We have arrived, I will take you ashore," said the round-faced waiter, full of smiles. He came over to help us carry our luggage.

We left behind the reeking smoke and sweat of the third-class cabin and stepped out onto Bund of Huangpu, full of new hope.

Volume Two

PART 6 Shanghai Days

THE WAITER LED US INTO A VERY POSH ROOM ON THE THIRD FLOOR of the Peace Hotel. He vanished even before our luggage appeared, closing the door behind him.

New doubts. "So why did he bring us here, not straight to see Mr. Sun?" I glanced at Aizhen.

She ran to the door and tried to open it. "It is locked from the outside. He must be a white slave trader."

Or a government agent, I thought. I looked out the window: the drop to earth was more than fifty feet; a jump would flatten us. Best to wait and see what game our waiter was playing. I knocked on the wall several times, and was answered by silence.

"Waiter!"

More silence.

Aizhen clutched me. "What if he is a bad person? I'm scared."

"Of what?" I said, trying to comfort her. I assured her I would soon concoct a plan or two for handling our devious waiter. "There are two of us—we could bite him to death, if nothing else."

Bold talk, yet I was trembling.

An hour passed. Still no sign of the waiter. I was now certain we had entered the tiger's mouth, and I was becoming nearly desperate enough to try a window leap—but just then we heard murmurs in the hallway, and someone (it sounded like the waiter) called, "Hey, Miss Xie! Open up, please!"

"We can't—it's locked from the outside."

"No, there's no lock out here. Turn the round thing to the right—it's a spring lock."

So I turned the knurl and the door opened.

"Sorry to keep you waiting so long. I've found out there is a bus that goes to Hatong Road, but not directly to Mr. Sun's place. So I have called a ricksha."

Only then did our fears begin to fade. Evidently we had caused this whole farce simply because we were too ignorant to open a door. We laughed at ourselves.

The waiter stared at us, dumbfounded.

Yet even after I was seated in the ricksha I kept turning around to look at Aizhen, wondering if we might be split up and dragged into an empty alley. Until I had actually laid my eyes on Mr. Sun, I just could not calm myself. I was wrong to keep suspecting an honest man who was helping us, but in this sordid society that engulfs us, how can a sensible young woman not be skeptical?

"At last, you have escaped—ha!" cried Mr. Sun Fuyuan, standing up exuberantly under a bright electric light. "Bingying, we celebrate you!" He held his glass high to salute me. "From this day you are free and can begin your new life."

Boldly I drank a full glass of Shaoxing wine, in a single gulp.

"Good for you," said he, "and have another glass. You have suffered enough this past year. You deserve a bit of consolation."

Mr. Sun's sympathy touched a deep well of sadness within me. I drank two full bottles of wine that night. By the time the ricksha carried us off toward the apartment Aisi had rented for us, I was perfectly drunk and oblivious to all human affairs.

ON THE TENTH MORNING after our arrival in Shanghai I got out of bed, put on my clothes, didn't even wash my face. I opened my manuscript to start writing where I had left off the night before. Suddenly came a violent knocking. I opened the door. In rushed a bunch of policemen, all pointing their guns at me and madly shouting, "Put up your hands!"

I raised my arms like a zombie. I followed them downstairs, as if in a nightmare. Luckily, Aizhen was gone; she had left for her friend's home the day before. She would have been petrified.

Several gendarmes hurried to the front of the building and arrested Aisi before he was even awake. They shackled our wrists, shoved us into a large truck waiting in the alley, drove us to a police station in the French Concession, and took us into the interrogation room.* The moment that I noticed that our guard had let his attention stray, I whispered to Aisi, "What could this be about?"

"Who knows?" he replied, his face ghastly white. He seemed even more nervous than I.

"Mr. Hua!" I shouted, suddenly spotting someone else I knew. "You're here too!" He wore an ancient long gown, his hair disheveled.

"Rotten luck!" said Mr. Hua angrily. "I had just arrived at your place to see you, and they arrested me for nothing whatever."

The gendarme slashed at us with his leather whip, whipping each of us twice.

And now suddenly Meng Chao, a poet, stumbled into the cell with us, and when he saw me he groaned, "Are you a ghost? I was looking for you at your apartment, to deliver your royalties, and suddenly . . . this!"

The gendarme whipped him.

At that point we decided to talk as loudly as we pleased. This so enraged the jailer that he put us into separate cells.

They locked us in the damp and dark for two days and two nights without food. I felt as if I had fallen into five miles of fog. Why was I a prisoner

---

*Foreigners controlled areas called "settlements" and "concessions" in many parts of China. Settlements were thought of as Chinese soil governed by foreigners. Concessions were leased land and were viewed as foreign soil where the leaseholder could deny entry, residence, and the right to own property to nationals of China or other countries. Shanghai contained a French concession and an international settlement. In the late 1920s the number of foreigners in those two enclaves exceeded 60,000; the number of Chinese, more than 300,000. The population of the metropolitan area was more than three million.—trans.

when I had committed no crime? During those two terrible days nobody so much as mentioned interrogating me. Nobody brought food or even so much as a drop of water to drink.

In my cell were four other women. One was a murderer; two were robbers. The fourth had a husband who had not paid a gambling debt. This last woman looked to be about thirty-five, and she had her child with her.

"Do the police intend to starve us?" I asked. "How do they expect us to go for two days without food?"

"You are still dreaming about eating?" the middle-aged woman said. "You are damned lucky they don't kill you. This is where they dump the most violent criminals. What are you in for, murder? Kidnapping?"

When I heard those words my whole body began to tremble, and I sternly replied, "Neither. I am neither a murderer nor a kidnapper."

"No? So why did they arrest you? What a joke."

"It is a joke, yes. I don't know why they arrested me."

The oldest thief laughed in disdain and said, "It is all right, we are not the judge. You can tell us."

"I am telling you, I did nothing."

The jailer walked toward us and we all shut up.

By the third day I could no longer stand the hunger and thirst, so when the jailer began washing the hall with a rubber hose, I said, "Hey, just one mouthful of water, OK? Have a little pity!"

"Then open your mouth, you stupid pig!"

Suspecting nothing, I opened it. He shot a cascade of water into my face so hard that I couldn't even open my eyes, but the water dripping from my hair satisfied my thirst a little.

Three of the women had been starved until their eyes bulged. They were as thin as jackals. They lay curled up in a corner, moaning. The two-year-old child cried day and night. Urine and shit were scattered all over the floor, and the place stunk so foully that I felt I couldn't survive much longer. Bands of flies made our cell their playground and at twilight the mosquitoes, huge as horseflies, came swarming out in gangs to attack us. Their bites kept me from closing my eyes all night long.

Let it end, bury me here!

In the silence of the lonely dark, pitying myself, I cried until daybreak.

The next thing that occurred was unbelievable, unforgettable—I actually ate shit. Here's how it happened.

The middle-aged woman's husband had at last gone to trial and was to be released the following day, along with his family. Meanwhile, he asked the jailer to toss a glutinous rice ball through the iron window of his wife's jail cell, and this the jailer did. Unfortunately, the rice ball fell into some of the little child's shit. But the woman swiftly snatched it up and offered me a third of it. My subconscious mind kept crying, "Disgusting, disgusting," yet a hungry hand was already reaching out of my throat to grab that rice ball. Instinctively, I popped it straight into my mouth—all the while trying to pretend I had not seen what I actually had seen a moment before.

Ha-ha! How beautifully fresh and sweet that rice tasted. Never in all the banquets I'd ever attended had I tasted anything so wonderful. Even to this day the flavor of that moment lingers in my mouth, and I feel deep gratitude toward that woman.

They interrogated us once but did not tell us what we were charged with, only warned us that the charge was so serious that in a few days we might be put before a firing squad. Then, by a stroke of luck, Meng Chao was suddenly released. He went straight to Mr. Sun to tell him of our predicament. Mr. Sun came to the jail with quantities of bread and fruit, knowing that Aisi and I would be starved. But the miserable jailer refused to let him see us and demanded a bribe of thirty yuan just to let him send in the food. Mr. Sun angrily hauled all the food back home with him and made a plan to get us out on bail. On the fifth day we suddenly were set free. We left that foreign prison and went to Mr. Sun's house, and there we whooped it up and drank exuberantly.

Mr. Sun kept shaking and shaking his head as he said, "You were in serious danger—foolish bugs. Did you know you were living in the house of robbers? You nearly lost your lives for nothing."

"So *that's* why they locked me up with a murderer and robbers. If you had been two days slower in coming to help, I might not have gotten out at all."

"*Might* not?" he cried. "If it were a political dispute, it would not have been this serious, but robbery is punishable by death."

Springing us had not been easy. He'd had to plead in French with the judge for two long afternoons, and finally he was forced to use his own life as a guarantee in order to get us released. Eventually those friends who had landed in jail—landed there simply because they knew me—were released. My main regret after I got out was that I had lost my little bit of luggage.

Mostly it was books and manuscripts. They vanished and were never returned.

⚘

MR. SUN FUYUAN and Mr. Lin Yutang were the only people in Shanghai who both sympathized with me and could give me any help, but Mr. Lin was in Beijing at the time so I could discuss my future only with Mr. Sun. He urged me to pursue a college education. He said he would negotiate on my behalf for a tuition waiver and would pay for my book and board expenses himself.

Though I had long dreamed of continuing my studies, I felt uneasy. I had always believed that one ought to live by one's own effort, not depend on family or friends. I preferred to get a temporary job as a laborer, save up some money, and then continue my studies. So I repeatedly asked Mr. Sun if he could give me a recommendation for factory work, but he always insisted, "I have no connections in factories—so what can I do, young lady?"

"Then I'll find someplace to work as a maid," I said. "I'm quite good at emptying chamber pots, mopping floors, and doing chores of that sort."

"Well, then, you may as well be a maid right here—and in the evening you can write essays for *Contemporary* magazine. Ha-ha! This fine female soldier has turned herself into a servant."

He thought I was just being playful. After he'd had a big laugh he went off to edit his manuscripts, for at that time he was editor-in-chief for the *Contemporary* monthly.

Unable to find work, I again sank into depression. But luckily Yanghua came to me one day and suggested I take the entrance test for the Shanghai Academy of Arts, saying, "The academic dean, several professors, and also the dean of students at that school are quite famous in the cultural world. The tuition will be waived if you are accepted, and you can pay for books and board and other miscellaneous expenses with money you earn from your writing."

Without more thought I boldly took the test and passed. I entered as a second-year student in the Chinese literature department at the Shanghai Academy of Arts, and I moved into a room in a dormitory in the 1014th alley of Xiafei Road. The room accommodated eight or so, but school had not opened. So I was there alone, enjoying the pure bliss of solitude in a clean bright place filled each day with sweet warm sunlight. I felt almost completely content. Sometimes, when I thought back to my life in the family prison, it seemed as if all that had taken place in another world altogether—and then sometimes I would think that I was only in a dream and that before long I would be caught by my mother and forced to return home.

Poverty now made life a struggle. In two days I had eaten only four small pancakes as a substitute for three normal meals. Still, I was able to read books that I liked, day and night, and I really could not have been any happier.

On the evening of the third day, as I was lying on my bed reading a book, the principal's wife brought in a young lady all dressed in black, her face sadly white beneath the bright electric light. She looked exactly like a wax figure, her face beautiful, her body gracefully shaped. She would have been a true classic beauty if only she had not worn thick, black-rimmed glasses to correct her nearsightedness, and if her lips had been thinner.

The young woman broke the silence, smiling as she asked, "Have you lived here long?"

"I moved in only the day before yesterday. Are you from Shanghai?"

"No, Hangzhou. And you?"

"Hunan."

She unpacked as I continued reading my book. She seemed to be a modern well-to-do girl, judging by her clothes. I would never have guessed that she, like me, was a runaway.

From the start we were good friends, and later close ones. We had been together for only a day when, to my surprise, she freely confided in me all the details of her fight with her family:

"My father and brother are officials in Hangzhou. My family is quite wealthy. Ever since I was a child I have lived the life of a spoiled princess—and yet my views are modern. When I entered middle school I began to participate in various political activities. I was general secretary of the Hangzhou Women's Association. Later I quietly left home because the political situation had changed and the government ordered my arrest. From the time I was very young until that moment when I left home, my fate had been determined by the orders of my parents and the words of the matchmaker. My fiancé was the oldest son of an official, but his only talent was for wandering around all day; he did not work at a proper job. So I decided to dissolve my marriage contract with him. Now that I've left, I'll never consider returning to Hangzhou—so long as this whole marriage problem does not catch up to me."

Her words sounded exactly like my own when I had left home. I was so happy that I hugged her: "Manman, how can your sadness be so like mine?"

United in sorrow, we became intimate friends.

For a whole week I lived happily, until suddenly three married women moved into our rooms. They spoke with Sichuan accents and wore strange-looking clothes that made everyone shake their heads as soon as they spotted them. Their long, tight-fitting Chinese gowns, bright red with pale green trim, were ugly and utterly vulgar, and their shoes had heels at least three inches high. On their faces they smeared thick layers of rouge. As soon as they arrived they announced that they wanted Manman and me to move out of the big room and into the back room. We, however, would not agree to this unreasonable request; we had moved in first, and we felt we had the right to live where we were. But soon the principal's wife began to argue on their behalf. I finally decided that if we stayed in the same room with these three we would surely never live another happy day, so Manman and I gave in and moved to the low, narrow, and very dark apartment in back. When classes started, all five of us had board contracts with the school kitchen. Forced to sit at the same table, we often quarreled. Those three didn't attend classes regularly, only made a showing—and sometimes they did not even do that, sometimes merely putting on their flowery, colorful, and captivating clothes and going out to see movies and eat Western meals. On rainy days they would play records and practice the fox-trot in their room. At mealtime they never waited for us to return from class but instead quickly polished off all the accompanying dishes—so when we came to eat we found nothing left but a little soup and cold rice. This so outraged Manman that she called them outright thieves.

One day, as I stood on our sun deck looking around, I heard the voice of that tall fox fairy say, "Why bother entering the university if you cannot afford to have clothes made? You would be better off as a good-looking beggar. See how dirty her whole body is? Let's never let her eat with us."

This made me tremble with anger. Clearly, she was speaking of me. I felt like pounding her. But Manman told me to ignore her and treat her as an uneducated bitch. From then on we ate separately from those three. The little back-room apartment became also our dining room.

MANMAN TOLD ME that tomorrow another student was arriving to live in our apartment, a girl called Zhenzhen, who was both her good friend and her enemy—her enemy in love.

Manman gave a bitter laugh. "Cui wants her to live with me so that it will be more convenient for him to come and visit both of his lovers." Cui was the male lead in this drama. Also Manman's executioner.

"Can you stand it?"

"I love Cui, so what can I do? It will hurt, but . . ."

"And the future?"

"Somebody wins, somebody loses."

The next day the new girl moved in, a tall and very strong girl whose skin was dark like an athlete's. She spoke the Hangzhou dialect, just as Manman did. Though her eyes were not large, they were very lively. She walked and spoke faster than Manman, seemed quite talented and capable, and was altogether lively and lovable even though she lacked Manman's innocent beauty. She enrolled in the music department and every morning was off to practice the piano. Manman told me the girl did not like reading literature or taking any part in cultural activities, holding the view that the ideal of womanhood was to be a virtuous wife and loving mother.

"So what is Cui's philosophy? What does he believe in?"

"Universal love."

"But, surely, loving two people at the same time and place is impossible."

Manman smiled bitterly, and said sadly, "No doubt a tragedy is in the making."

She was right. It happened before the month was up.

I remember clearly how cold it was that winter evening. I had just come in from outside, and as I entered the door I saw all three of them in a pile, embracing, their faces depressed and sorrowful. I quickly retreated to the sun deck to avoid them. I wondered whether to stand there and take in the breeze or to find a friend to chat with. Suddenly I heard a violent noise on the stairs and Zhenzhen came flying toward me. She grabbed me and kept crying, "Bing, Bing!"

I held her as tightly as a lover and said softly, "Don't be sad, Zhenzhen— what were you arguing about?"

"I want him to leave me, to love Manman—but he won't. It is all too . . ."

I didn't know what to say. The truth is that Cui was selfish. I thought of telling him so. Yet I also felt that love is a private matter—so why should I elicit everyone's contempt by butting in?

More noise on the stairs. Manman appeared on the sun deck and told Zhenzhen to go downstairs—but at that moment Cui also appeared, and he tried to tug them both back downstairs. But Manman clutched me, would not let go, her eyes bright with liquid pearls, her head pressed on my left shoulder. I could hear her rapid heartbeats.

"Don't torture yourself," I said. "Look, there are many things more important to do in life than to be in love."

Manman replied, trembling, "I want to be released. If this continues, I will kill myself."

"No love is worth suicide," I said. "Suicide is for fools."

Cui came up again and dragged her downstairs. I stood on the sun deck looking at the night scene and wondering how it all might end. After four or five minutes the three of them hurried downstairs to stroll in the streets. As they left, Cui apologized to me, "Sorry that tonight we made you suffer out in the cold."

I answered him indifferently. "No matter. Good luck." Then I went back into the room to sleep.

The women did not return until after twelve o'clock. Neither of them spoke. They just got undressed and went to sleep. The next day Zhenzhen rose early as usual and went to practice the piano. Manman and I chatted at home.

"Did you settle things last night?"

"No. But I have at last made up my mind not to act any longer in this endless tragedy."

"Good idea."

Her eyes fell on the self-tutoring Japanese language book. I tried to persuade her to focus her affections on learning and on her future career. She was a very intelligent woman and had actually been making progress until now, step by step. But the whole affair concluded unhappily. Manman could not escape the web of her affections. She was betrayed by Cui's lies, and in the end she gave up her youth and her future for nothing at all.

SOON ANOTHER SHORT TRAGEDY played out in that same apartment.

Aisi, Molin, and Qi had been my schoolmates at military school. We had all been in love with literature and soon we became good friends. Aisi studied children's literature and liked socializing. Qi, a poet, was silent and deep and often melancholy. Molin, an essayist, excelled at dealing with people and was chairman of every meeting. All three liked me very much and I treated them as my own brothers. Aisi was the oldest, Qi the youngest of the men. We four made big plans for our future:

"It will be best if none of us ever gets married. Like brothers and sister, we will organize a large family and live happily together. Each of us will have a job—early to work and late to return. On Sundays we will all go out together and see a movie or ramble in the wilderness."

Such was the foolish hope we had, an impossible ideal.

We left school and were separated. Qi often wrote to me but I never imagined he could ever love me as fervently as Aisi did—Aisi who, during that year that my mother had kept me locked up, brought a girlfriend all the way from Jiangxi to Xinhua to see me.

Not long after Manman's problems ended in disaster, Qi took leave from the army and came to visit me in Shanghai. Aisi had been coming around to see me every couple of days. I knew the day would soon come when I must cut him off and hurt him. He was too impassioned, too in love with love, as if he could not survive without it, while I was much more absorbed with learning and studying. After watching Manman's recent disaster, I was on guard not to be sucked into the whirlpool of sentiment. I intended to avoid the shocks she had suffered.

And so? I fell in love with Qi. Intellect is intellect; sentiment, sentiment.

While on the march, Qi wrote beautiful poems and mailed them to me, and always he would pick a leaf or a flower—wherever he was—and send it in his letter. He wrote his letters in very small characters—almost like sesame seeds—and never scribbled. He filled my ears with his passionate love yet never asked, "Do you love me?" He knew how to suffer, for his family had been terribly poor. His father had died early, which meant that the four mouths in Qi's family relied on him to survive. My reasons for loving him? Simple. I hoped I would someday have the power to help him. And I was intoxicated by his lovely poetry.

When Aisi found out that I was in love with Qi, he was miserable to the point of madness. The two of them lived together and one morning I went to see Qi. Aisi would not say a word. He only sat there like an idiot, watching us talk. I knew that the whole situation was wrong. We spoke briefly and then I left to return to school, but Aisi chased after me and grabbed me. "If you discard me, I will kill you," he said.

I had no intention of listening to what else he had to say. Surely love cannot be seized by plunder and pillage, or forced by sheer power and pressure. One loves whom she wants, and no one else has the right to interfere. He had pounced on me like a crazy person because he was suffering, yet I could not forgive him.

An empty ricksha passed by and I jumped into it and asked the driver to pull quickly—but Aisi stopped the vehicle with his arm and screamed, "I won't let you go! I'll be damned if I'll let you leave before you have answered me!"

"Answer you what?"

"Swear that you love only me."

"I don't love anyone but myself."

I kept repeating these words. Which made him feel utterly hopeless. He had no way to control me. He could only watch the ricksha fly away with me.

In my classes on that day I heard not a word that was said. Manman noticed that I was upset and she comforted me. I felt that if Aisi realized that I truly loved Qi, he would do something terrible. Murder or suicide. I decided that it was better that I should suffer the pain of giving up Qi by asking him to leave Shanghai immediately. Then I could concentrate my energy on learning and on keeping Aisi happy by staying friends with him—while not allowing him to talk about love.

A short and small shadow silently rushed into my room at twilight, almost as if Qi and I had arranged this meeting. I told him all that had happened on the street that morning, how Aisi had stopped the ricksha. Qi thought quietly and finally he said in a determined voice, "Then I will take tonight's express train to Nanjing and change for Hankou. I certainly will not stay here and make it difficult for you."

I could not answer him. My heart hurt as though pierced by needles.

"Let me love you forever in my heart," he said, holding back tears. "Don't be sad that I must leave so suddenly."

We heard a sound on the steps. Qi thought it was Aisi, so he quickly ran downstairs. I stood on the terrace and watched his far-off shadow disappear among the electricity poles.

That night Qi stayed in his room and tossed back four or five bottles of wine and got stinking drunk. Our friend Lin Xi told me that Qi did this because he was disappointed when I did not come to see him.

One often tends to sympathize with those who are unfortunate, and after Qi had left Shanghai not a moment passed that I did not think of him. In his letters from Nanjing, Jiujiang, and Wuhu, I learned about his hard life on the ship, and I felt very sorry for him. When I thought of his uncertain future, I felt even worse. He was like a younger brother to me. I remembered how we used to sing "Flowers of Tangdi." I had always compared myself to Nieying and Qi to Niezheng, and I knew I must love him with all my love and use all my power to help him. Though we were far apart, day by day our souls grew closer.

My feelings for Aisi gradually cooled, naturally. He felt terrifically sad and often he asked Manman about my state of mind. She would reply, "Lately, she is very focused. As if afraid of love, she works hard at her research and studies. You should hide your feelings and not always be bothering her and making her uncomfortable."

I never imagined that a person like Aisi, so steeped in passion, could also prove to have good sense, but one day he came to me and said, "I think we are both too young and, really, I should not spend every day intoxicated in fantasies of love. Your spirit of study has impressed me. I have decided to go to school. Tomorrow I leave for Beijing by way of Tianjin. I came just to say farewell. Goodbye, then. We will meet again."

Instantly I began to feel lonely. I had not imagined he could be so strong and to the point. That night I saw him to the boat and we talked all night. He still was dreaming about winning my love in the future. He did not realize that, as far as I was concerned, there was only friendship left between us.

❧

HOW WELL I remember that quilted cotton jacket, so full of meaning.

Keqin and I had become such good friends while she was a nurse at Xiangya Hospital in Changsha that people laughed at us, calling us lesbians. Afterward, whenever she wrote to me she enclosed beautiful picture cards or pretty and delicate paper dolls that she had cut out of foreign magazines and newspapers. She was an unaffected, beautiful, and loving young woman, and we formed a deep friendship. Yet after we both arrived in Shanghai our attraction to each other was not as strong as it once had been, for no longer were our ideals and interests the same: she liked to dance and she quickly became popular in the social scene, while I was just beginning to live a bohemian's life of poverty. Still, old friends stayed as old friends, and we were always concerned about each other's lives.

One morning, as the north wind was blowing and making us shiver, Keqin tugged at my jacket and asked me, very concerned, "It is winter, yet you still wear this single-layered jacket—how can you make it through the day?"

"I don't have money to have a quilted jacket made. So I will just have to put up with the cold."

"Here, if you don't mind old clothing, you can wear this thin quilted jacket."

I took from her hand—without hesitation—a soft and light jacket, pale yellow with bands of flowers. Perhaps she had worn it for a long time, and worn no coat over it, for it looked rather dirty. The inside was torn in several places but the outside was still intact. As soon as I held the jacket in my hand I felt my body temperature rise. Quickening my footsteps, I hurried back to the dormitory, and as soon as I entered the door I smilingly told Manman, "I have a quilted jacket. Look what a pretty color it is."

Manman answered indifferently, "Too bad it is used."

I knew that she was thinking about another problem.

From that moment on I never felt cold, even when snowflakes tossed about on the ground and the entire city of Shanghai became a silver-white world. While others wore fox-skin coats and felt the chill, I wore only this thin jacket, running to and fro through the streets, and really did not feel the least bit chilly. Sometimes I even found that the jacket was too warm when I walked a lot, and at those times I preferred to take it off and put on my single-layered jacket instead.

But my feet suffered miserably in those days, for I had only a pair of cloth shoes that I had already worn through rain and sun and snow, and by now those shoes had no heels at all and had holes in the toes: snowflakes often would sneak in the front and crowd right out the back. I had two pairs of socks but they were torn to shreds and had mends on top of mends. Whenever it rained or snowed I would come back with a pair of wet feet and go out the next day with the same wet feet, for I did not have a stove to dry the socks, so I thought I might as well wear the wet socks to bed. As a result, a stinky coverlet and stinky feet were inevitable. I had to listen to the insults of those three women from Sichuan, but fortunately Manman and Zhenzhen never objected to my dirtiness.

Earlier I'd also had a short overcoat that a big passionate fellow named Ruihua had given me when he left the country. The outside of the overcoat was black and the inside was made of lamb's wool, and it was very light and warm. As he had put it on me he had said, "I hope you will dress up like a boy, so I am giving you this coat. When I return, in three or five years, you can become my friend if you have kept it."

I wore his short overcoat for more than two weeks, and I did not care if others jeered. Later, a poverty-stricken friend asked me for it so he could support himself by selling it to a pawn shop. He also pawned the gold ring my fiancé (in-name-only) had given me.

In the end the torn quilted jacket was my only possession. I used it as a coat during the day and as a coverlet at night. I will never forget Keqin or those hard days when I suffered from hunger and cold.

INCREDIBLE. I HAD NOT HAD a meal in four days. I had started out eating four baked cakes a day or two little hard rolls. Then I had cut my ration to two baked cakes. Then to one. In the end I could not even pay for boiling water: I had not a single copper coin. When thirsty I could only open my mouth, stand under the faucet, give a twist, and let the water pour into my mouth until my stomach ballooned with coolness and pain. The experience was unspeakable.

Finally I became so hungry that I just could not stand it any longer, so I decided to go to the Spring Tide Publisher's Bookstore to borrow money. I knew that Director Xia or Director Fang would lend me three or five yuan—but I also knew that they were seldom in the shop and that the clerks would not dare to act on their behalf. So chances were nine out of ten that I would come away with nothing.

Even so, this day was the happiest of my life—it was the day my *War Diary* was published. On the large door of Spring Tide Publisher's Bookstore was posted a very fresh and titillating multicolored advertisement for my book. With a curious heart I walked in, pretending to be a customer. From the bookshelf I picked up a copy with a bright red cover. On the front of it was a picture of a little soldier riding a buffalo, drawn by Mr. Feng Zikai's daughter.* I wanted only to look at it. I had no need to buy it, for I knew I would receive at least ten complimentary copies.

I shyly said to the cashier, speaking very softly when no other customers were in the shop, "I'm afraid I have no money—could you please pay me a few yuan of my royalty?"

"I cannot. Royalties are paid only twice a year, and now is not the time."

"But I need an advance right now—I can't wait. Really, I would not be here to borrow money unless I was desperate. Don't you believe me? I don't even have enough money to ride the trolley home—I came here on foot."

Hunger burning in my stomach had made me suddenly forget all shame. I boldly told him of my misfortune.

The cashier gave a cold, unsympathetic laugh.

But the junior clerk was different. "You wait awhile," he said. "Definitely more than a few people will buy your book, and you can take all the money we receive."

At this the cashier gave the junior clerk a sidelong glance with an angry eye, but since I was there, he dared say nothing; he just pounded harder on his abacus.

---

*Feng Zikai (1898–1975) was well known as a painter, an author, and an educator.—trans.

I became a temporary store clerk. When customers came in to buy my *War Diary* I wanted to personally hand them the book. They did not know that I was the author, of course, and several customers were angry at the way I wrapped the book. But when the junior clerk was about to tell them who I was, I quickly stopped him with my eyes—which always caused the customers to gaze at me for a long time, in confusion, before at last leaving the store somewhat discontented.

By twilight I had received five yuan. On my way home I didn't take the third-class trolley car. Instead, with toes high and spirits dancing, I flew up into the first-class car. The ticket seller hastily directed me to the car up ahead. "Go to third class," he said—perhaps believing that since my clothes were very old and torn I must be a poor egg who could not afford to ride first class. Quickly I grabbed my five bills and waved them in his face. "Hey! Give me my change."

He lowered his head and said not a word.

On the trolley I happened to sit next to a young man who was reading my *War Diary*. He tried to persuade me to buy the book, but I deliberately provoked him by saying, "No, I don't agree that women should become soldiers, so I don't want to read that book."

He was most unhappy to hear me say this. He went so far as to scold me for my stubborn opinion. "A twentieth-century female should not be driving in reverse," he said angrily.

When the car reached Carter Road I got off and, with fluttering heart, ran to find Guangguang. She and Yuanzhen were so poor that they had no way to get through the day. When they saw that I was very happy they guessed that I must have gotten some money. Immediately they asked me for a share, and I gave them two yuan. Then I took the rest—more than two yuan—and treated them to a meal at a small restaurant. When I returned home I had only a few coins left, but I was not worried. Having eaten a full meal, I could stand hunger for at least three more days.

It was during this period that I learned how to drink. When a person descends to such poverty, she looks at gold as if it were feces. I often wondered at those money slaves who worship gold as if it were life. Why do they make themselves suffer by refusing to spend even half a coin? I care only for spiritual delight. Material suffering, however bitter, cannot bend my thinking or my willpower even slightly. When I have money I divide it among poor friends, or I go to restaurants to indulge in food and drink, or I buy lots of my favorite dried shrimps, dried beef, duck gizzards, duck liver, and candy. When poor, I go alone into the streets to drink the northwest breeze, or I hide in my room to drink tap water, or I stay completely covered in the nest of a comforter and sleep for two days. Or I read interesting novels to pass the long and frightful hours.

If someone asks, "How does hunger taste?" then I quickly answer: "Friend, please eat nothing for four days, and you will have tasted hunger."

I believe hunger that is even more bitter than death or the most terrible suffering. Sometimes you hear your ravenous intestine crying *goo-goo*. Sometimes you feel a giant snake inside you trying to bite through your stomach and emerge through your torn flesh. Sometimes you are so hungry that your head spins, your eyes see stars. When you try to sit upright you only fall over. You try to walk but your legs are so sore and limp that you can't move them, even by dragging. Sometimes sour water from your stomach surges up into your mouth and makes you want to vomit, but you can't. Other times hunger is so unbearable that you want to bite flesh from your own elbow and swallow it raw. At such moments I finally come to believe that ancient saying: You can never eat your own child, but you might eat someone else's in exchange for yours. At this very moment there are places where such tragedies are happening, hungry people taking the flesh of a dead person to boil it for a meal.

Even at this miserable stage of poverty I must say that I—this hard set of bones—still did not buckle, did not bow to the rich. Above all, I still opposed the traditional female path of seeking a rich husband. Hunger only deepened my knowledge of the present society, only strengthened my will to live.

It taught me a precious lesson.

I COULD NOT have been unluckier. Two years earlier I had been attending the Central Military School when it was closed by the authorities, and now the same thing was happening at the art school. The authorities seemed to think that all of us young men and women students would turn into outlaws if they did not shut us down. The truth is, nobody had committed any crime and we should not have had to suffer this crazy retaliation.

The incident began this way.

First, workers on the electric trolleys in the French Concession went on strike, and some people claimed that students at our Academy of Arts had encouraged them. In addition, students from the academy ran a night school attended by a large number of common people, and the authorities did not like this. Finally, the Literature and Art Research Society, which had been established at the academy, stirred up the students' enthusiasm for publishing newspapers and posting them everywhere on walls. These various activities made the gendarmes at the foreign police station furious. They looked upon all students at the Academy of Arts as reactionaries, and they were frantic to concoct an excuse to come and search us—partly to look important and live up to their supposedly awesome reputation, partly to gain merit with their superiors so they could get themselves promoted.

I was just stepping out of the dormitory on my way to school when a fellow student said, very agitated, "Don't go. The school is surrounded by police, and they have already arrested enough professors and students to fill two large trucks. They have confiscated the sign for the night school, the printing machine, and the textbooks. Is this maddening, or what?"

"You mean the French Concession gendarmes are making arrests again?"

"Yes. Luckily Torn Trousers escaped again this time—because if they had laid hands on him, he would not have gotten out alive."

Everyone at the academy knew Torn Trousers. He was actually the principal of the common people's night school. His real name was Li Te. He was a quiet guy who always acted very responsibly and conscientiously. The first time our school was searched he was in a meeting, and though all the others were arrested, he flew out the window with the nimbleness of an expert thief—but as he did so a policeman tore a large hunk of material off his trousers, whereupon all the gendarmes cried out, "That torn trousers is escaping—grab him, don't let him get away."

After that, Torn Trousers became notorious.

"The foreign police are coming to search our dorm—let's hurry up and hide the books," cried Manman, panting for breath as she hurried toward me.

We returned to our dorm on the double, wondering what to do about the novels and the books on literature and art, for it would be a pity to have to burn them. The police would surely search under the bed, so how could we hide them? Then I thought of a way: we tied the books with rope, dropped them out the window, then threw two pieces of clothing over them to cover them up. We hoped the police, seeing the clothes, would merely think that some laundry had been blown off by the wind. And the trick worked. When the police came around to inspect, they only glanced at the clothing on the ground and took no more notice.

A horrible situation. Our schoolmates were imprisoned, cold, hungry, suffering the insults and cruelty of the jailers. The jailers were spraying our women with a water hose, and Keqin was crying and screaming because of the frigid water. Their lives were in danger if we did not think of a way to get them out.

That same evening Torn Trousers, Liu, and others held a meeting in our apartment to discuss ways to rescue them. We decided that the first step was to send food and clothing. The next was to learn whether those who had been captured had friends or parents in Shanghai, people we could enlist in the rescue effort. We also decided to begin soliciting donations to hire defense lawyers.

Matters soon turned more serious: the school gate was closed, cordoned off by police, and marked with crisscross strips of paper. Now the gendarmes worked frantically, searching like hungry hounds for whoever opposed them. For some reason the school would take no initiative whatever while all this was going on. We asked the principal to help with the rescue, telling him that not only students but several teachers had been arrested, yet he only wrinkled his brow and looked very unhappy. "This is already the third time they have searched us," he said. "We are living in imperialist times. We live on their leased land, and yet we oppose them— so naturally they hate us. What can I do? If they do not allow us to operate the school, we can only close the door."

To hear this was devastating, like hearing thunder in a clear sky. We were Chinese, living on our country's own soil. Didn't we even have the freedom to keep our own school open?

Manman and I went back to our cold empty room and sat quietly, facing each other. The ticking of her watch broke the frightening silence.

Manman smiled. "You were lucky," she said. "If you had left for school a little earlier, you would now be suffering the cold water torture."

"I ought to thank my youngest brother for that. If he hadn't sent me money, I would not have been writing him a letter of thanks. But Manman, now what do we do?"

"What *can* we do? The school is closed."

It is amazing how quickly fate can arrange calamities. I had figured I would have at least two years of peaceful study after entering the Academy of Arts. I never imagined that within six months I would again be forced to roll up my bedding and hit the road.

"So what will you do, Bing?"

"Work as a laborer—that is my only choice."

"But you would never stand it—you'd best dream up some way to continue your studies."

Our two hearts were tangled like hemp and we had no notion what would be best to do. The Academy of Arts and its more than three hundred passionate young people—so lively, so brave, so full of life—filled us with wonderful memories. Also, Manman and I felt deep affection for each other: I could not do without her, nor she without me. Yet she, unfortunately, had Cui. Those two souls were entangled and not to be parted. Otherwise, she and I might have stayed together and been quite happy.

"Friendship between women will not last long, because they all will marry." I did not remember who had said it, but I was again struck by this melancholy truth.

The school was closed and I, like a dog whose owner had died, walked irresolutely through the streets all day long. Slowly, our schoolmates were released from prison. About half returned to their homes. Manman went to Cui's arms. As for me, in the freezing depth of night I faced a five-filament electric bulb and kept company with the shadow on the wall. I felt very lonely.

I buried my head in books to seek comfort.

PART 7 Beijing

JUST AS I WAS FRETTING ABOUT WHAT TO DO NEXT, I RECEIVED A registered letter from my youngest brother, mailed from Beijing and forwarded to me by Mr. Sun. My brother had enclosed a money order for thirty yuan. He wrote that he hoped that I would go immediately to Beijing and take some supplementary courses of study so I would be ready to take the entrance exam for the Women's Normal University the following summer. In his letter he also enclosed an introduction to a Mr. Tong, who soon would be going to Beijing and would be able to look after me on the journey.

I ought to have been happy for another chance to study, yet I vacillated. At the moment nothing fascinated me more than the prospect of living the bohemian life in my apartment in Shanghai, a town where everything was lively and progressive. Stay away from Fourth Avenue for a few days, for example, and by the time you went there again the bookstores already would have put up more newly published books and magazines. Everyone was terribly interested in reading and writing. Shanghai was a gathering place for the literati.

Yet I am grateful to my third brother for offering to pay my tuition and for rescuing me from utter destitution. When at first I hesitated to accept the offer, Mr. Sun said, "How very strange you are. Here is your opportunity to study—would you throw it away? Not to mention that your third brother loves you and is concerned about you."

He convinced me. In the end I boarded the ship for Tianjin—I remember very clearly it was May First, Labor Day, and only one close friend came to see me off.

When I first arrived in Beijing I lived at the Hebei Women's Association.* After a week I moved to the *Republic Daily News* office, where Xiaolu and I took turns acting as chief editor for the newspaper's supplement. But within two months the newspaper stopped publishing, and I was forced to go back to living at the Women's Association. Day in and day out I read only books concerning literature and art. I never studied at all for the university entrance exam.

Most of all I loved buying books at the Culture Bookstore, which was managed by the Yang brothers. They specialized in books on modern literature and art. One brother was the man who had encountered me on the trolley in Shanghai and had tried to persuade me to buy my own *War Diary*, while I had pretended to disapprove of the book. Later we became friends. Aisi was studying at the Normal University. Eventually he became deranged (so I heard) and began desperately chasing after a Miss Zhou. He broke a window in her house and not long afterward he was sent to a mental institution—another victim of love.

When Big Sister Tie moved to Beijing we stayed together for a while in a small house, washing our own clothes and doing our own cooking. Eventually she moved to Tianjin, and afterward I passed the entrance exam for the Women's Normal University.

Qi was now working for the Merchants Steamship Company in Tianjin, and our affection for each other was growing day by day like spring grass and trees. Yet it was to be but a brief dream, a canna flower that blossoms for only an instant and then wilts.

I lived for six peaceful months at the university. My third brother paid for my tuition, books, food, and miscellaneous expenses. He even had a long coat made for me. It didn't keep out the freezing cold but it was quite warm compared with the torn thin cotton jacket I had worn on snowy days in Shanghai.

---

*She arrived in 1929.—trans.

But as bitter luck would have it, my third brother suddenly returned to Changsha to teach, and, since he earned less money there than in Beijing, he stopped supplying money for my schooling. This was a shock. It would be a shame to lose my chance to study, yet if I stayed in school and depended on selling my writing in order to eat, I could not see how I would earn enough to buy clothes, books, and all the rest. Luckily, two friends saw how poor I was, felt pity for me, and let me teach their classes for them. I recall that I was paid one yuan per hour at the Anhui Middle School and a mere seventy-five cents per hour at Dazhong Middle School.* Every week I taught twelve hours of Chinese literature and corrected ninety-five books of compositions. Some people assured me that it was beneficial to teach and study at the same time, but I considered this only empty talk. In fact, it was very painful to do both. I sacrificed a great deal when I had to miss my own classes in order to teach classes. Correcting papers was most troublesome. Frequently I worked past midnight before I went to bed. Strangely, at that time my body was almost as strong as if it were built of iron. I did not feel tired even when I had not slept well for several nights in a row. My routine was this: I corrected papers until midnight and then, when the entire dorm was quiet, I began to write. My writing career was pitiful. Because I liked to voice my discontent, several large newspaper supplements did not dare publish my work. A friend who was an editor for the *Huabei Daily News* had said to me several times, "Can't you write essays that are a little less controversial?"

"No, I can't," I replied. "I can't survive as a writer if I abandon truth."

Only one small paper welcomed my writings at that time. I received a pitiful fifty cents for every thousand words, but the payments were never late and I got paid every month. I used many pen names—Ziying, Village Matron, Yingzi, Gelei, Linnuo, and so on. Sometimes, when I wrote a lot, I earned more than ten yuan per month. This, together with my teaching salary, gave me a monthly income of more than forty yuan. At a quick glance it would seem that I should have been able to scrape by. Yet the cost of transportation alone was seven or eight yuan a month, and I had to help Big Sister Tie. How comfortably could I live under those conditions?

---

*One hundred Chinese cents equaled one yuan.—trans.

I shared a single room with women named Chaoren and Yunxian, and we ate together in the food hall. At that period of my life I had a huge appetite. At every meal I ate three large bowls of rice and two steamed buns. Because our appetites were big, we did not have enough money to pay for all our food, so we had no choice but to be corrupt and take advantage of the kitchen. It was customary for us to ask for the bill after we had finished eating our meal (this was a snack bar and people either settled the bill after each meal or charged it in the ledger).

"How many bowls of rice did you eat?"

"Five bowls of steamed rice and two bowls of rice gruel."

"Ho! Three people ate so little?"

The short cook's tone was always suspicious and sarcastic.

"What do you mean? Do you think we are telling you less than we actually ate?"

In the end our imposing manner made him swallow his grievances. He lowered his head and walked away. No doubt others took advantage of the kitchen like we did, for suddenly one day we noticed a guard standing next to each rice barrel. At first we did not understand why, but we were enlightened when I carried my empty bowl to the rice barrel and the guard quickly took the bowl from my hand and, very respectfully, filled it with rice.

"They are serious. Tomorrow we had better go and buy bigger bowls," said Chaoren, and we laughed until the rice sprayed out of our mouths.

On one occasion I owed the cook more than seven yuan, and he followed me around every day, demanding that I pay the debt. This made me so afraid of him that I did not dare go near the food hall, and for four days straight I ate only sweet potatoes and toasted pancakes.

At the time of the Lunar New Year in 1930 I sneaked away to Jingfen's to hide from my creditor. When I returned, Yunxian told me that the cook had already come to look for me at least ten times and had even asked our old woman servant, Chenma, to give him my trunk as collateral. Later, because Chenma guaranteed that I would pay when I returned, he stopped making trouble. How could he have known that inside my trunk were only a few torn garments and some manuscripts, letters, and books?

❀

WINTER. SNOWFLAKES TOSSED about the earth.

The visitors' lounge at the Women's Normal University was crowded with young men dressed in Western attire and holding ice skates in their hands. They were politely waiting for their young ladies to join them to go skating in North Sea Park. As for me? I pulled in my neck, carried the lecture notes under my arm, and waited on the icy street for the electric trolley. The snow was falling heavily and my entire body turned white. My nose drips quickly became two small icicles whenever I did not wipe them off immediately. Some days even the electric trolley could not operate because of winter weather, and then I tramped step by step through the snow. I remember that one snowy morning I walked from Shifuma Street to Beixin Bridge, where the Dazhong Middle School was. I heard not a sound as I entered the gate, so I knew classes had already begun. I did not want to waste time, so instead of stopping to rest and to warm my hands by the stove in the lounge, as I normally would have done, I ran straight to the classroom. As a result, on this day my fingers were as stiff as a dead man's. I could not hold the chalk. I dropped it. I held my fingers close to my mouth and blew on them, and then picked up the chalk again—and dropped it again. The students, seeing how cold and pitiful I was, all cried out, "Teacher, go and warm your hands and then come back to teach us."

I walked toward the stove and pressed my two hands tightly to the hot iron, feeling no pain, until the skin on my fingers was scorched yellow.

That evening the dormitory was even more bustling than usual. Young ladies sat next to the warm air duct knitting sweaters for their boyfriends. Some played records. Some were singing "Dream Lover." They laughed together, ate chocolates, swapped love stories. They seemed as happy as angels in heaven. As for me, I chewed a few broad beans, drank a glass of boiled water, and felt infinite pleasure.

Night deepened. Now the young women were all in sweet dreamland . . . now only the *sa-sa* sound of my pen touching paper.

Write—write for your life.

I struggled forward into the dunes, like a camel under a heavy load.

HONG HAS BEEN DEAD for fourteen years, and I scarcely dare to imagine the tragic scene of his death. I fainted when I saw his picture and read of his death in the *Shanghai News*. Now willows may sway and sigh in wind over his grave, but I don't know where he is buried, nor when I will ever be able to grieve there for his lone soul.

Hong was my second brother's best friend, and he was my revolutionary comrade when I was in the military. He was in love with me before I met Qi. He was strong and handsome, had a talent for public speaking, and was a fine athlete. Although he studied education at the university, his specialty was politics. At one time I loved him very much. He was an intelligent, able, and passionate man. But we broke up because his family situation was very complicated. Also, his character was not like mine, and he did not like it that I was studying literature.

Since we had parted in Hankou we had not seen each other and had never written. In the winter of 1930 he heard that I was in Beijing and decided to travel from Guangzhou to see me.* When Hong passed through Hong Kong, a good friend of ours told him that I was living with Qi and would soon be giving birth to a child. He advised Hong not to disturb my peace of mind by visiting me. But Hong did not listen to the advice and came anyway.

What a coincidence. Both Hong and Qi rode the same express train from Tianjin to Beijing, and they arrived to see me within a few minutes of each other.

When a messenger handed me a visitor's slip with Hong's name on it, I was startled and hardly knew what to do. But he had come all the way from Guangzhou and I felt that if I could not love him, I should at least treat him as a very good friend. Weixu said the same thing: "You are old friends, why not see him?" So I decided to go to the university visitors' lounge.

We had just sat down and been together for only a few minutes when suddenly Qi appeared. I was startled again, but I quickly calmed down and introduced them to each other. Actually, they had met before, in Hankou. But now they pretended not to recognize each other. I invited them both to go out to eat.

"I'll treat you two," Qi said quickly. The smile on his face seemed forced.

---

*Guangzhou is about fourteen hundred miles south of Beijing.—trans.

"No, no, I'll treat you two," said Hong, a bit ruffled yet more natural than Qi. "Beijing is my second native city."

When we went out the gate I led them to Qieyi Restaurant in the Rongxian Alley, a Sichuan restaurant where the dishes were pure and agreeable to the mouth and where my friends and I often went.

The three of us talked casually as we ate our meal, without the least unease. But later, as we strolled in the Central Park, the moods of both men changed. Qi fell silent, as if deep in thought, and walked with slow steps, and Hong for a while kept looking from me to Qi as if he were envious. Then Hong finally lowered his head, like Qi, and walked in silence. I could not stir up any conversation. The other men and women we passed in the park were mostly in pairs or alone; very few were like us, a group made up of two lovers and a friend strolling together. When I suggested that they might be tired from their trips, and perhaps should get to bed early, the tension eased a bit.

"The day after tomorrow is the thirtieth on the lunar calendar," Hong said, just as he was about to leave us. "I would like to invite you to celebrate the new year with me."

"Oh, no need for that," I said quickly—I saw Qi's eyes gazing elsewhere, so I knew he must be unhappy. "We will come to see you another day."

"It is rare that the three of us can get together," Hong insisted, "so why don't we celebrate this new year together?"

I refused again and, holding Qi's hand, returned with him to his brother's place east of the city.

Fearing that Qi might suspect that I still loved Hong, I skipped my classes at the Women's Normal University and stayed in his little room and kept him company day and night until the day before the Lunar New Year. On that day I needed to participate in an evening literary discussion and attend a banquet with my schoolmates. I told Qi that I had to go to the west side of the city, adding that I would stop by to see Hong if there was time. He agreed. But he said that he hoped I would return home before nine o'clock since his younger brother would be coming to celebrate the new year with us—and his brother had even bought chicken and wine for the occasion.

The evening turned out to be a very busy one. By the time the literary discussion was over, it was already seven o'clock. When I walked into the Women's Normal University, the concierge handed me several visitors' slips, so I realized that Hong had come to look for me several times. As I had Qi's consent to do so, I went to see Hong. Then I returned to the banquet. I figured that it would take only ten minutes to get back home and that I'd certainly be there before nine. How could I have known that, due to the heavy snow and the lack of passengers on New Year's Eve, the electric trolleys had already stopped running? I called for a ricksha but the driver was a cripple. He limped, and by the time he had dragged me to my destination, it was much later than the time Qi and I had agreed upon.

The foul odor of alcohol pierced my nose as soon as I walked through the door into the pitch-black room. Qi was already snoring. With great difficulty I felt around for the matchbox to light the lamp. I saw the floor piled full of broken wine bottles and smashed bowls and dishes. I regretted having gone to see Hong, regretted that I had not walked back—which would have been much faster than riding in the cripple's ricksha. I regretted even more that I had not dragged Qi with me to go see Hong. What could I say? The big mistake had already been made. I could only beg Qi for forgiveness.

"You, woman, you are not a good sort. I understand everything. Obviously, you love Hong and still deceive me. Hong is more handsome than I, more capable, has more money, has better position—go, love him."

How could these words come out of Qi's mouth? At first I thought it was just the sleepy talk of drunkenness, so I did not reproach him. Instead, I begged his forgiveness. But as his senses became clearer, his language became harsher. I had no other way of showing my feelings, so I grabbed a knife to cut my throat—but Qi snatched it away. No matter how I tried to explain the reasons for my late return, Qi would not believe me.

"I don't even understand my*self*," he said angrily. "So how can I believe in or understand someone else?"

So it was his misunderstanding that caused our anguish and breakup, and then all that was left was regret.

"You have abused my love," I said in a moment of pain. "You don't understand my character or believe anything I say, so I will let you keep your misunderstandings forever. I will not live with you."

My spirit was shocked; my thoughts had turned to ash. I had little interest in living.

❧

I WATCHED MY STOMACH getting bigger every day and I knew that the child would soon be born. I worried a lot that I would not have enough money to support my baby, so I asked Yunzhang, who was the principal of Daming Girls Teacher Training School, to find me a position teaching Chinese literature, but my doctor was very much against my going to Daming. He pointed out that I would be giving birth in two or three months and that the jolting road would be hard on the unborn child and could cause a miscarriage. So I wrote to Qi in Tianjin, asking him to send some money as a responsible father should, so that I could use it to care for our child. When he returned to Beijing for the summer recess, however, he had only thirty yuan to give to me, which was not much. On the day after his return our child was born, a beautiful girl with big bright eyes and a little mouth. When she cried, her voice was splendidly clear.

At first Qi was very happy. Every day he would come to see me at the hospital and would hand me a pink envelope containing a poem or a love letter. One day Mrs. Zhang, the woman in the next bed, said enviously, "Such a young student—I thought he was your younger brother. Who would have thought he is the child's father?"

I smiled, feeling fortunate and proud. The child's cries erased our past misunderstandings. I prayed that from then on we would be happy together.

But my life suddenly took a turn for the worse when I returned home, for by then the thirty yuan had been spent and I could not afford to buy chicken and eggs, which I needed. I had no money to hire a maid so I had to launder my own clothes and the baby's diapers, and I had to do all the cooking and sweeping. I was poorly nourished so my milk was getting thinner by the day. The child cried night and day because she did not have enough to drink. I finally resorted to buying milk powder to feed her.

Then I fell ill. On the second night of my illness I asked Qi to fix some milk for the baby to drink at eleven o'clock, a task he quickly forgot because he was playing his beloved game, mahjong. Our neighbors, Shikai and Yangma, heard the child crying, and I asked them to fetch Qi—but twice he simply ignored them.

After all, a woman's heart is soft; finally Shikai came over to fix the milk. But either she mixed it too thin or the child was purposely being naughty, for the child refused to drink even one mouthful. She cried nonstop for more than two hours and then went to sleep, exhausted. That night I wrote Qi a very long letter in which I implored him to pity the child and to temporarily give up playing mahjong. I expected him to apologize. He only wrote on the back of my letter, "From now on I will not play mahjong."

I could not understand why, but Qi's attitude toward me was becoming more indifferent and more cold, and he was becoming more and more unhappy. I dared not look at his iron face. When he spoke with others his face was full of smiles, but as soon as he faced me it was as if I were his enemy. No matter what we talked about, he would wrinkle his brow and become deliberately distant and perfunctory in his reply. I thought it strange that he would sit in a daze until twelve or one o'clock each night and not go to bed. Sometimes I could hear the tip of his pen touching the paper, making *sa-sa* sounds, but before he had written for even ten minutes I would hear the sound of paper being torn to pieces. Several times I was tempted to pick up the pieces to see if he had been writing a letter to me, perhaps asking me to break off our relationship. But I was afraid to upset him.

To be honest, I loved him even though he treated me so coldly and indifferently. Perhaps, I thought, his heart has changed in these few days because he is worried about how we are going to live and how his mother, brother, and sister are going to survive. Yes, this must be the reason. Love cannot be eaten as food; we are not idealists. I should forgive his indifference toward me, and we must love each other even more in these distressing circumstances.

But Qi still suspected my loyalty to him, and we finally parted.

⁂

"IN PRISON, COME help quickly."

At twilight on a very hot summer day, the postman handed me a postcard on which those simple words were written. I would have suspected that someone was playing a joke on me if it were not for Qi's handwriting and the stamped seal of a prison. But what was this about? He had just arrived back in Tianjin four days before, and now this?

That evening a friend came from Tianjin and told me how Qi had been arrested.

"It was bad luck. As soon as Qi arrived in Tianjin he went to the Northern Bookstore. It so happened that the military police were making an inspection there. The manager was arrested, and Qi was implicated and clapped into prison with him."

Our baby had been born a mere twenty days earlier, and now this unlucky incident. I was anxious and distressed. I had implored Qi to stay home a while longer to help me take care of our child, but he had insisted on going to Tianjin to find work. Who would have thought that he would be falsely arrested and sent to prison even before he could find a job?

I walked toward that tall forbidding-looking prison, and my heart jumped wildly. I did not need to look at him. I could imagine how terribly worried and perplexed he must be, how awful he must feel. I visited him three times, and each time we had very little to talk about.

"Can you hire a lawyer to help release me on bail?"

"Where would I get three hundred yuan?"

This was our conversation. I knew he would feel desperate when he heard my reply, but I could not lie to him. I spent a lot of time and energy looking for a lawyer, but with no result.

Nobody could imagine my despair as I visited my lover for whom I felt no love. If this had happened six months earlier, before we had separated, I would have been more concerned about his situation in prison, and surely I would have visited him every day. But as it was, it cost more than three yuan just to buy the train ticket from Beijing to Tianjin, and after I arrived in Tianjin I had to take the trolley, then eat my meal, and then buy pickled vegetables, salted eggs, bread, and roasted meat to bring to him. So each time I visited him I had to be prepared to spend ten to fifteen yuan, quite a large amount at that time. I would begin to save the money a week before my visit by not eating rice and instead buying only two fried pancakes or sweet potatoes each day. Sometimes, after I arrived in Tianjin, I would carry the things I'd bought for him and walk to the prison instead of taking the trolley.

"What is he to you?" a curious guard once asked me. "Why must you cry every time you see him?"

"He is my older brother. I am upset because he is locked up even though he committed no crime."

I was so pathetic that even the guard was moved. Whenever he was on duty he let us talk longer than was allowed, not hurrying us even when visiting time was up.

Qi sent me two postcards each month. He wrote that prison food was terrible and that he hoped I would bring more food when I came to see him. He also hoped that I would bring books about literature and art. Sometimes he missed our child and asked me to take good care of her, yet my feeling for him was now more pity than love. I sympathized with his misfortune and I felt the unfairness, indignity, and injustice of what had befallen him. But I really had no power to help him. I would never have gone to see him in prison if I had been a woman without feeling, for even in prison he did not apologize for the way he had treated me. He had a friend who was editor of a newspaper in Hankou, and he sent this friend a long satirical poem describing me as a female who desired glory and wealth, a cruel woman who had broken up with him so that I could marry a person with money and position. His editor friend knew these mean-spirited lines were written when Qi's nerves were shot, so he did not publish the poem and instead reprimanded Qi for having written it. I was not at all angry when I heard about this. I understood that Qi was in a depressed mood. When a passionate, lively, and innocent young man is one day suddenly imprisoned, naturally he will experience a change of mood and attitude—particularly if he has also recently suffered a blow to his love life. I felt it was unnecessary for me to explain myself or advance arguments about how I felt. I knew the day would come when facts would prove what kind of woman I was.

I dared not think about our future. There was much he did not understand about me. And he did not believe in me. I made up my mind to break with him for good. He was narrow-minded, melancholic, wavering, indecisive, opportunistic—completely incompatible with my character, which was straightforward, frank, outspoken, determined, decisive. I preferred to face the pain and end our relationship forever, but how could I hand him such a blow while he was suffering in jail? I just couldn't.

I remember the last time that I visited the prison. It was just before I left Beijing. As if I had had a premonition, I made a point of bringing him more food than usual on that day. I had the feeling that I would never see him again. Before I even opened my mouth to speak, tears started rolling down.

"Why are you so sad—are you leaving Beijing?"

"No. I am thinking of bringing our child to live near the prison because it is too costly for me to travel back and forth like this. Anyway, I should bring the baby for you to see. She is truly adorable."

Qi bowed his head and made no sound. I could not tell if he was reminiscing about the days when we were first in love or thinking about the child's future.

He said in a gentle voice, "Don't think about the past; take good care of the child."

Suddenly, for an instant, my love for him was restored. I wanted to hold him and kiss him deeply and say to him, "Qi, let us love each other."

But we were separated by the iron window and could not even touch each other's fingers. Then a guard at the inner door made us stop talking and pushed me in disgust and said, "Why are you still standing here? Get out! Go quickly."

I remained standing at the same spot, dazed. I wanted to watch poor Qi carry the food inside. When I saw his shadow disappear at the corner, my heart suddenly jumped wildly.

Oh no! When will I ever see him again?

I felt faint. A multitude of sparks leaped in front of my eyes and I felt my head splitting as if it were pressed by a heavy rock while both my legs twitched as if I were having spasms.

I walked out the gate. But then I ran back toward the visitors' lounge like a crazy person.

"Haven't you seen him already?" asked the guard, whose face was even more cruel than before.

"I forgot to say something. Please, let me see him."

"Absolutely not." He pushed me out. "Come next week."

I endured his insults and swallowed my tears as I walked out the gate. I turned my head to look back—it was as if Qi had run after me. I imagined him staring vacantly at my shadow, sighing.

I MOVED TO Shoushuihe to be close to the Women's Normal University. I really could not care for the child because I had to attend classes and also teach, so I decided to hire Liuma. Nutrigent, a powdered milk substitute, cost only a yuan a pound at the time, but I still did not have the means to buy it. Sometimes friends gave me one or two pounds and I would then instruct Liuma not to mix it for the child until she was crying very loudly from hunger. Liuma saw through my poverty and was unhappy about having to work in my home. I had thought that utmost sincerity would move even heaven—wouldn't my sad misfortune catch a woman's sympathy? I thought I would treat her as affectionately as if she were my own mother. I hoped she would take care of my child as if it were her own. The result? My tactic failed totally. Like most servants, she looked out for herself and would rather work like a horse or a buffalo for a powerful, wealthy family than to work for an average person who respected her and treated her as an equal.

One day, as the summer recess was quickly approaching, I had to attend a staff meeting at Dazhong Middle School. I returned home an hour later than usual. Liuma had finished eating. I asked her to heat up the cold leftover rice and accompanying dishes. She answered me in an unhappy tone, "When it got so late and you did not come back, I thought someone had invited you to eat out, so I went ahead and ate."

"It doesn't matter. You got hungry while waiting for me, so naturally you can eat first. But why don't you want to heat up the leftovers for me?"

"It is not because I don't want to. I am trying to save you a little firewood. It is OK to eat cold food when the weather is hot. Do you know that the landlord came again today to ask for money? He said you already owe him three months' rent. At three yuan a month, three times three equals nine. If you don't pay in the next two or three days, he will be asking you to move, without ceremony."

Her manner was as hateful as that of the landlord. I was furious at this point. I could not imagine Liuma would bully me like this. I looked at the child's face. It was streaked with tear stains. Her pants were wet through; Liuma had not changed them. The dirty diapers from morning were still piled in the corner of the room and had not been washed. I really could not tolerate it any longer, and I scolded her angrily.

"This is how I am." She started to pack her clothes as she talked. "You go and find someone better than me, because I am not working here any longer—I'm leaving immediately."

I thought, what a mess. If she leaves, how will I take care of the child? I can't carry my child while I listen to lectures. What's more, I can't possibly hold her while I teach my classes. Even if I find another servant, I might end up with someone just like Liuma. Over and over again I thought about it and finally I decided to humble myself for the sake of my child. I carried my grievances in my chest and, holding my child in my arms, I went to ask for her forgiveness.

"Liuma, you should think about me. You have a kind heart. When you see that I am tired and haven't eaten all day, you should pity me for my hardship. Even if you don't like to heat up the food, you should at least bring me the cold rice. Also, it is your responsibility to take care of the child. Why don't you change the diaper when it is wet—and why haven't you washed her dirty clothes from last night? I have no way to keep you if you must go. I do ask you to please stick it out for a couple more days. You can go when I have found another person."

Seeing how politely I spoke to her, and that I did not scold her again, she momentarily gave up the idea of leaving.

I handed her the child and, without eating anything, ran quickly back to school where I lay on the bed, covered my face with the coverlet, and had a satisfying cry. My eyes looked terrible when I got up. The dormitory counselor asked me what the matter was. I told her that I didn't feel well because of a cold.

How could I endure this kind of life? Even Liuma sneered at my poverty. No wonder the landlord came to press the debt day and night. My nature is such that I hardly borrow anything from my friends. I would rather die of hunger than tell others about my sufferings. But what would I do with the child? Because of her I had to support a home and a servant. If I listened to my friends and put her in an orphanage, I would never get her back and it would be the most regretful event of my life. And if I gave her to a farm wife to raise in a village, my mind still would not be at rest.

I stirred these thoughts around and around in my head and still came up with no suitable solution. So I wiped dry my tears. I returned to Shoushuihe, not hungry at all, and I lit the coal-oil lamp and started to write essays that would earn fifty cents per thousand words.

"Miss, when is mister coming back?" Liuma suddenly asked this one evening.

"He will definitely come back this winter, and then we will have money," I lied.

"Why doesn't he send you money now?" she asked, as if she did not believe what I had said.

"He is at a place where no drafts can be sent," I answered indifferently.

❧

YICAI KNEW THAT I was having a very difficult time caring for the child. He and his wife, Xiaoyan, made a special trip from Tianjin to visit me and suggest how I might solve the problem: "Let us take her to Tianjin and we will hire a wet nurse to live in our home. You can work here with a peaceful mind. You can come visit her every month or every two weeks—whenever you miss her."

This was truly the best solution at the moment. Yicai even promised that he would pay the wet nurse's wages and buy the child's shoes and hats and all her clothes. This way I could save some money and send it to Qi's mother. But in my heart I really did not want my baby to leave. She touched my spirits with her every laugh and every cry. There were many times that I thought of committing suicide but was saved by her smiles.

Yet after thinking it over for a day and a night, I accepted their offer without reservation. I decided that early the next morning I would let them take my child to Tianjin.

"We have already hired the wet nurse. She hasn't come to our home yet because we were afraid you would not want to give the child to us. We will ask her to come tomorrow. I have already prepared the milk powder, bottles, and nipples that we will need on the trip." Xiaoyan was afraid that I still did not feel comfortable, so she carefully explained all this.

"Of course, I'm not worried, but the thing is, the child is quite naughty and often cries loudly for an hour or two in the middle of the night—and, I am thinking, won't that interfere with your sleep?"

"A small problem, that. The important thing is for you to put sentimentality aside, not to miss her too much," Yicai said.

I knew he was right: I should fully accept their kind offer, for it is true that I act too much according to emotion. With just a bit more reliance on good sense and reason, I would be able to look more indifferently on family and children. Then perhaps I would actually be able to make a few small accomplishments in my literary career. As it is, I have been unlucky half my life and I have managed to do nothing whatever but suffer.

That evening I started to pack up my child's clothes. Normally, after she had been fed she would sleep for two or three hours straight, but tonight she did not want to sleep, which seemed strange. After she had finished sucking my breasts, she only wanted to lie in my arms, and soon afterward she fell asleep. She cried loudly as soon as I put her on the bed, so I again picked her up and held her in my arms.

I repeated this process ten or more times and the result was always the

same. At last I reached my limit. I angrily hardened my heart and slapped
her several times on her small behind. I thought that if I gave her a warning, she would sleep a short while, and in ten minutes I'd have tidied up
everything. To my surprise, the more I slapped her, the more she cried, and
the more she cried, the more I could not put her down. As soon as she lay
against my body she fell into a deep slumber. Did she have a premonition?
Did she know I was going to send her away?

"What, is the child awake already?" asked Yicai when he arrived, just at
dawn. "Have you packed all her clothes?"

"No. I had to hold her all night. She would not go to sleep unless she was
lying in my arms, but as soon as I put her on the bed she began to scream.
So I had no way to pack her clothes."

"The child senses what is happening. She must not want to leave you,"
said Xiaoyan, crying with me, "and I see you don't want her to leave, and
that is why your eyes are swollen from crying. We will wait till next time to
take her with us."

But Yicai insisted on taking the baby away on this day. "There is a common saying, 'Long-term pain is not like short-term pain.' Why don't you
just take a deep breath and give her to us? Your child is our child—you can
put your mind at ease about everything. There will be a wet nurse to care
for her. She will be much more comfortable than if she stayed here."

Again I made up my mind and gave the child to Xiaoyan so that I could
pack her clothes. It was really strange. The baby began crying brokenheart-
edly as soon as she was in Xiaoyan's arms.

"That's it, this child will definitely be a strange creature when she grows
up. She understands even when she is only a half-year old. I don't dare take
her away. Let her stay with you and suffer," said Yicai, almost angrily.

Xiaoyan stood expressionless, feeling bad. She didn't say a word. I felt
awful. I didn't know what was best to do. If I insisted on giving the child to
them, I would be afraid she would cry day and night, causing problems. If
I did not give her to them, our life together would become much harder.
How would I keep her alive? My milk was decreasing day by day, while her
appetite was increasing. Soon winter would be here, and I would need
more money to have warm clothes made for her. More miseries.

"Since the child is so peculiar that she can't leave you for even an instant,
she must have had a premonition. Then we had better leave. We'll wait

until she can be apart from you, and then you can send her to us. We sympathize with you and we will help you. We are your friends from beginning to end. You don't need to stand on ceremony. Just write and tell us whenever you need help."

Only with my tears could I thank Yicai for his parting words. I carried the child and saw them to the door. They left without my offering them even a glass of water to drink. Liuma was still not awake. I cried until finally I awakened the child with the dripping of my tears. Her eyes opened, looked at me once . . . and then closed again. At this point I deliberately tossed her onto the bed, yet she didn't make a single sound. I thought of running after Yicai and Xiaoyan and asking them to take her away. But my legs went weak and my heart went sour as I walked near the door. I didn't have the courage.

I DESPISED MYSELF for being unable to live without love. Solving the problem of Qi had not been easy, and I had solved it only by using the I-don't-give-a-damn-about-anything method. Now the problem of the child lay before me.

Society was certainly too cruel, blocking young, pure, and promising people from developing their abilities. Everywhere brilliant youths were met with heavy blows that ended only when they could no longer survive. I was one of this group of young people. I was viewed as a criminal simply because I had edited a women's monthly, performed publicly in plays, and joined a literary group. A niece of a friend quietly told me what people were saying. She thought I should leave Beijing immediately. I just couldn't believe it. The whole thing seemed unbelievable, like a dream—that fate should afflict me with all these problems.

I had no time to hesitate or ponder. That same day I decided to take the night train and return to the South. My friends, who were all very loving and protective and concerned about me, spent lots of energy raising money for my travel. They reminded me again and again to take care of my health, not to despair, and to continue to struggle for the bright future ahead.

I realized that my diploma—once so nearly in my hands—was now out of reach. Actually, I was not too disappointed. What I felt bad about was leaving Beijing. The town had made a deep impression on me, and leaving it was like leaving a lover. Before coming to Beijing, I had been used to a wandering life. I could rest anywhere, could endure any pain. But Beijing had made me linger. I can scarcely describe the sorrowful scene when I held the child and climbed onto the train to leave the city. The baby was crying in desperation because she was parting from her wet nurse, so Mr. and Mrs. Xizhen hurriedly boarded the train and held the child while I mixed some powdered milk with boiled water. But the baby would not open her mouth to swallow it. To bring the wet nurse with us was absolutely impossible, and I didn't have even one drop of my own milk with which to trick the baby. After three days and four nights of crying, the child was actually gasping for breath. Luckily, when we arrived at Wuchang I met a woman who could give her some milk to drink. Her little life thus escaped its first brush with death.

In Wuchang we took up lodging in a very low and dark loft. I depended on my writing to survive. Qi's mother treated me very well. She was not aware that Qi and I had separated and would never love each other again. She was anxious about her son, who was in prison, but my child and I comforted her all day long and helped ease her many worries.

The news about why I escaped from Beijing had quickly reached Wuchang. My friends advised me to go to the countryside to stay for a short while in order to avoid other troubles. Feeling injured and full of resentment, I left Wuchang.

❀

I ARRIVED IN Changsha like an escaped criminal and dared not look up any of my friends. I went alone to Kuntao Pavilion on Yuelu Hill, on the west side of the Xiang River, to live in quiet isolation.

Mr. and Mrs. Zhu were still the caretakers of Kuntao Hut. They greeted me with smiles, but my tears poured down as I remembered when I had accompanied my second brother here four years earlier so that he could convalesce from his tuberculosis. I had spent a drunken springtime of fragrant flowers and prattling birds, watching the sun rise over the Xiang River and watching it set beyond our hilltop.

I had no wish to see this little building again. It had broken my heart. But

I had no other place to go. I lived in the same small room where I had lived before, painful as it was. I didn't even have the courage to walk through the door into the large room next to mine where my brother had lived.

I was already miserable when I arrived, and seeing this old place made me even more miserable. I imagined being buried in the green maple gorge where blood-red maple leaves would cover me and the gurgling little creek would play a sweet dirge. But then I thought of my child, and I again abandoned all thoughts of death.

I returned to my little room and continued to write.

After I had been at Yuelu Hill for more than ten days, my youngest brother urged me to go back home to see Mother. To be honest, I missed her very much. But she still wanted the last word in our dispute, and she had not asked me to come home—and I would never surrender to my family. Luckily, an excellent excuse arose: Father's seventieth birthday was approaching. He wrote and asked me to return home, so I took the boat to Xinhua.

Mother was a woman who loved to win. When she thought of me she often cried, yet she pretended not to care about me, pretended to dislike me, even refused to admit that I was her daughter. At Father's birthday dinner party she would not acknowledge me even after I had called her Mama several times. After dinner when I poured tea for her she nearly smashed the cup. After listening to her waves of angry scolding, I lay down on the bed and closed my eyes, pretending to be very tired and sound asleep.

At about ten o'clock she quietly got up from the bed opposite me and, without throwing on any clothes, used a match to light a very small coal-oil lamp. She lightly walked over to my bed and picked up the fallen blanket from the floor and covered me with it. She touched my right hand and said to herself, "Her hand is icy cold, the cover must have fallen long ago."

I wanted so much to open my eyes and see her expression but could not. I had to keep pretending, to learn what else she would do. And, yes, I witnessed a most wonderful scene.

The light of the lamp came closer and closer, flared on my face: a blast of intolerable heat hit me. Several times I thought of covering my eyes with my hand. Mother shone the lamplight on me and looked at me vacantly. After two or three minutes she sighed heavily and said, "Ah! She is thin. She is much thinner than when she left home."

With her soft hand she lightly caressed my face, my temples, my hair strewn on the pillow. Suddenly an icy-cold tear dropped onto the corner of my mouth. I moved my head slightly, to show that I had been startled awake. I wanted to open my eyes and hold her face in my hands and call her "dear Mama!" But an unknown power prevented me from doing so. I heard the sound of Mother blowing her nose. Then, moving with slow steps, she returned to her bed. With my tongue I licked Mother's tear. The taste was not as salty as usual. At first it had a bitter taste; afterward, a strange sweetness. I was overwhelmed, wanted to arise and kneel in front of Mother's bed and beg for her forgiveness. I had given her much pain during these four years. Just because I wished to be free and happy, I had made her lose sleep, and because she had not heard a word from me, she had prayed to the gods and inquired by divination what had become of me. To what end? Having struggled these many years, what had I gained? I had broken free of the ancient marriage system but had fallen into a bitter sea of romance. I thought of telling her how during these past four years I had swallowed the world's bitterness and borne the afflictions of fate—been in prisons, experienced starvation, given birth to a child, and now was still living a wandering life, my future uncertain. Mother! When will I truly gain freedom and happiness?

Naturally, I could not tell her all this. It would have broken her heart. I snored softly and continued to pretend I was sleeping. An hour later she was still crying because of me. Oh! The loving heart of a mother.

In Xietuoshan I had two different kinds of feelings whenever I met an old acquaintance. On the one hand, I felt great pride as I showed the person that I was successful in every aspect of my life. On the other hand, I felt tremendous anger and shame as I recalled how I had sat in the sedan chair as a bride after failing several times to escape.

When my old friend Xiang came to see me, her face looked haggard and her eyes dull. I could see the pain in her heart. We only chitchatted, for many people were around. Afterward she quietly told me that Xiao Ming, my ex-husband, had married a village girl and that they had a child. I silently wished him happiness, feeling quite pleased.

"Aunt Ming, you have won and I have become a miserable sacrifice to feudal society. I'm sorry I didn't follow you."

"Xiang, don't be. Life is not so simple. I still have not found real freedom, and even now I must struggle continually in a very depressing and uncertain situation. Be patient. Surely the day will come—if you don't lose heart—when you will be able to hold your head high."

I comforted her, and both of us sighed softly at the same time.

My great aunt said to Mother, loudly, "After all, she is your daughter, and even if you slap and scold her, she can't leave her own family."

"I just didn't think she would ever return home," said Mother. "I am astonished she actually came back. Her disposition seems much better. Maybe she won't make me angry anymore."

I stayed home for only one short week, but during that time my mother's deep love—that most high and natural love of a mother for her child—moved me to tears. From now on if I did not work at being a good person instead of wasting my days being depressed, I would not be able to face my own conscience. I would, most important, not be able to face my mother. I made up my mind to give my child to Qi's mother. I would torture myself about her no longer. I would go to Shanghai to find my own path.

When it came time for me to leave, Mother did not try to stop me. Just as when I had left home for Changsha to go to middle school, she prepared cured meat, dried fish, and salted eggs for me to eat on the road. With a heart full of fresh hope, I happily left my native village.

PART 8 Japanese Attack

MY CHILD HAD JUST TURNED ONE YEAR OLD. ON A PITCH BLACK NIGHT, my eyes full of tears, I kissed her farewell. Then, carrying two old and torn suitcases, I stepped onto the *Ruihe* steamship, bound for Shanghai.

In Shanghai it took me less than three weeks to finish writing two books, *Young Wang Guocai* and *Letters to Youth*—more than 140,000 words. Day and night I wrote continally in a never-to-be-forgotten room in a place we called the Black Palace. I forgot to sleep, forgot to eat. Sometimes, when my stomach groaned, I went to the co-op at Fudan University to buy small steamed buns. I ate with one hand and wrote with the other. Sometimes my hand would still be holding the bun while I dozed, and my head dropped onto the desk; a mouse would come and snatch away my bun, upsetting the ink bottle. I was not the least aware that my manuscript had been stained. During those days I didn't even talk to my friends when they came to see me. Eventually they got used to my strange habits and never disturbed me unless I first said hello to them or went to their rooms to chat.

Quite unexpectedly I received 650 yuan for my two manuscripts. How happy I was! This was the first time in my life that I had been paid such a huge sum. I went almost crazy with joy, could not even sleep. I wrapped the money in several sheets of paper and hid it under my pillow at night, for fear it would be stolen. Within a few days I had decided I would use it to go abroad and study in Tokyo.

Since childhood I had loved the joys of travel, the sights and sounds and smells of mountains and seas. When the *Empress* carried me from Huang-pu harbor into the East China Sea, I felt as full of joy as a little bird that has escaped from its cage. I watched huge waves of a boundless jade-green sea under snowy-white clouds. My heart felt like a seagull, one moment soaring, the next plunging—for though I felt sad at leaving my country and dear friends, when I thought of the bright future ahead I temporarily set aside my worries and felt infinite joy.

On the ship the only person I knew was Mr. Qin from Guangdong Province. He was studying literature at Waseda University in Tokyo, and he enthusiastically told me all about Japan's most famous scenic spots, its most delicious foods, its delightful little netsuke carvings. He described the character of the Japanese people and suggested that I be quite careful in selecting friends among them.

I was often deep in conversation with Mr. Qin, which made the Japanese sit up and take notice. And when he actually served me rice at supper, all the Japanese women opened their eyes wide and stared in surprise, and then lowered their heads and whispered to one another in small, secretive voices. This was truly a strange sight to them, for in Japan it was always women who served men. On our ship I had my first authentic Japanese meal, but I did not like it much.

At last, the ship arrived at Nagasaki, and he and I went gaily ashore to enjoy ourselves—but we didn't enjoy ourselves for long. What was this? What were these shocking words that danced before our disbelieving eyes, shaking us to the core? Could we be seeing right?

IMPERIAL JAPANESE ARMY OCCUPIES SHENYANG!
ARMY OF CHINA DEFEATED!
ZHANG XUELIANG ESCAPES!*

"Mr. Qin, what is this about?" My voice trembled. "Are we dreaming?"
A Japanese newspaper "extra" with many passages circled in red was posted next to the three-page *Rising Sun News.* Mr. Qin read them closely.

---

*In September 1931 Japanese forces attacked and captured the walled city of Mukden in northeastern China. Chiang Kai-shek ordered General Zhang Xueliang to avoid risking his troops in battles with the Japanese and to withdraw south of the Great Wall, which he did. By the end of the year Japan occupied all of Manchuria, China's northeasternmost province.—trans.

"What a disaster! What a debacle! I can't believe all this could have happened in the two days since we left Shanghai. Why didn't our army resist? Can it be true that we have lost our northeastern provinces?" He finished reading the headlines, shaking his head incessantly. "I just don't believe it," he groaned. "It must be rubbish, pure rubbish."

I felt terrible, about to cry. I too doubted that all this could be true. I knew that the Japanese had a habit of manufacturing propaganda.

Suddenly we were not much in the mood for a stroll. Every high-stepping Japanese on the street became even more proud after spotting us two Chinese. We lowered our heads and, hiding our anger and shame, returned to our ship.

In an empty cabin we sat discussing whether we should go on to Tokyo as planned or immediately change ship and return to Shanghai. I thought we should go back but Mr. Qin disagreed, arguing that after coming this far we should stay, since even if we returned instantly to Shanghai, we could not go immediately to join in battle to recapture the Northeast. No doubt in Tokyo we would suffer provocations, but we would find many overseas Chinese students there, and, when it became necessary to do so, the entire student body would return to our country. In short, he thought we need not be hasty. He analyzed all the pros and cons of the situation in detail and concluded that since this was my first trip to Japan I should travel here for at least three months, so I would not have made the journey in vain. I followed his advice, because he was older, wiser, and more experienced than I.

Dawn. We arrived in Tokyo. Suddenly I felt sad and alone as I watched piles of luggage being pushed along the train platform. Crowds of unfamiliar faces. Waves of wooden-shoe sounds and staccato Japanese voices. A small motor car took me and my luggage to Higashi Nabano Women's Dormitory.

The first Chinese friends I made were Miss Guo Jianer and Miss Liang Zuosi, both from Guangdong. Guo was studying at the Japanese Women's University; Liang, at the higher division of the Teacher Training School for Japanese Women. Both were fluent in Japanese and liked to wear Western clothes. I also made friends with Miss Wang Wentian, who was from the Northeast. She had been in Tokyo for only a little more than a month. When she heard the news that the Northeast had fallen, she lay in bed crying all day and her eyes swelled up like apricots. Her friends went to comfort her in groups of threes and fives, and the first time I entered her bedroom and saw her tear-blurred eyes, I too wept.

"Miss Wang, crying is pointless," I said. "We must seek revenge. The Northeast is lost only temporarily. The day will come when we will take it back."

Such talk was of little help to her, but what else could I say?

The funniest thing that happened in Tokyo was when, on the very first evening, Guo took me to the dormitory bath hall. I was completely startled when I saw everyone standing around nude. I quickly retreated, thinking that I must have entered the wrong room. Guo said, "No mistake, no mistake—this is the public bath—go on in." She then explained, "This is not like our country—here we all bathe together. Don't be shy. Take off your clothes in this room first and then go into the public bath through that door."

Hearing this, I became even more embarrassed. I picked up my clothes and turned away. "I will wait until others have finished, and then bathe."

"No, no—I am afraid that if you wait until all the others are done, it will be after eleven o'clock, and by then the water will be dirty. Come! What is there to be afraid of? You were a soldier."

She laughed at my timidity and I laughed at her amusing words—for did she really mean to say that soldiers have no shame?

I asked her to please leave, but she said, "I also want to bathe. Since I came to Tokyo it has become my habit to bathe every night. If I don't, I can't sleep."

This made it even more difficult for me. It wouldn't have mattered if she were a total stranger, but to bathe with someone I had just met was awkward. I had never had this experience in my life, and I could not escape my feudal notions on the subject. At last I bathed in my underclothes, which made everyone in the bath hall laugh out loud. But bathing with clothes on was really too inconvenient, so on the next occasion I waited until the others had finished before I went in. Unexpectedly, as soon as I was immersed in the pool the door opened and a smiling young woman with her hair in a bun bowed to me and said, "Good evening." It turned out this was Yoneko Yamabe, the twenty-year-old maid from our dormitory. She not only waited on the dorm supervisor but had to sweep all the rooms and corridors of the dormitory. Every day she was busy until late at night and had not a moment's rest. She endured all this toil and I never saw her idle or looking unhappy. Her disposition was most gentle and affectionate.

"Miss Xie, I already knew you before you arrived. I heard you are a woman writer in your honorable country." She combined Japanese with Chinese in her first attempt to speak to me.

I smiled and answered her, "No, no."

"I enjoy reading novels more than anything, and I want to make friends with the Chinese. I would like to go to China someday. Miss Xie, are you willing to teach me to read Chinese?"

"Yes, very much so. But first you must teach me to speak Japanese."

From then on we became good friends. Whenever I returned from classes and was sitting alone in my room, she would ask outside the door, "May I come in?" And when we saw each other her first words always were, "Don't you feel lonely?" But whenever I invited her to sit down, she would only stand. Sometimes she looked at my photo albums, other times asked me about words. When she saw pictures of me in my military uniform, she was surprised and said, "You looked entirely like a man. You were truly very brave. Miss Xie, do you know how much I like you?"

As she spoke, her eyes quietly sent the message of love, and she gave me a captivating smile. My heart had a floating sensation as if I were a young man who had discovered for the first time that he was passionately loved by a young lady.

AT SEVEN O'CLOCK each morning we finished eating breakfast and then, carrying our book bags, we walked to Higashi Nabano station to catch the trolley. The trolley stop was about three hundred yards from the dorm and on the way we passed through a scenic village. As we walked by its bamboo fences we could not help but admire the evergreen trees and the flowers and the small houses amid flowery gardens. One morning, about a month after I had arrived in Tokyo, Wang and I were passing along one of these quiet lanes, with bamboo fences on either side, when we saw three seven- or eight-year-old children up ahead, playing with marbles. When they saw us coming, one little boy called from afar, "Chinese, slaves of a dead nation!"

We both cursed at the same time, saying, "Bastards!"

They threw small stones at us. We threw several back. But we kept walking because we were afraid that their families might come running out. We made two turns in the lane, and as we were nearing the trolley stop we could still hear the three little bastards calling in their high-pitched voices, "Chinese, slaves of a dead nation!"

Being constantly provoked and insulted made living there more and more difficult. All the Chinese students felt the pressure. Our hot blood was bubbling and boiling constantly, our avenging hearts forever jumping—which shows why it is often said that greater force brings greater resistance.

Who would have thought that we would be able to convene an assembly of more than a thousand people—the entire Chinese student body in Tokyo—while we were living in such a repressive environment? At the Youth Association we held a large memorial service for our dead compatriots in the northeastern provinces. The gathering was convened by the Overseas Chinese Students Association for Resistance Against Japan, which had held four secret meetings in preparation for this assembly. We had decided that the meeting time would be very early, six in the morning, to avoid problems with the police. Those committee members who were responsible for decorating did not sleep all night. They hung scrolls, pasted slogans, decorated the chairman's platform with garlands of flowers—they were busy until the sky was light. To our surprise, more than one hundred government detectives and police officers swaggered into the Youth Association meeting hall at five o'clock, looking as fierce as if they imagined they were confronting their biggest enemies. They stood in rows of four, guarding the main entrance. About that time our fellow students began arriving, and as they entered, one after another, each person was thoroughly searched by the detectives. Every fountain pen, even, was confiscated and examined over and over again before it was returned. Soon the meeting participants were pouring in like the tide, and the detectives could not continue their scrupulous inspections. Our fellow students saw what was happening and crowded into the hall. Then those bastardly guards became even more savage and boorish. They strode right into the meeting hall and tore down the portrait of our country's founding father. They tore down the words "Avenge the insult, wipe out the disgrace" that were hanging on the chairman's platform. They tore down all our scrolls and slogans. Our faces burned in anger. All of us were rubbing our fists and palms, preparing to confront them.

We could no longer wait for six o'clock, so the chairman immediately declared the meeting open. A most somber and moving occasion it was. Everyone felt more sorrowful than if his or her own parents had died. All of us stood without a sound, silently mourning our Northeastern compatriots who had died for our country.

The chairman announced the reason for the meeting—but he was dragged down by a government detective as soon as he said "Japanese imperialists." Then a second person ran up to the platform. His speech was even more fervent and stimulating, but he too was dragged away by a detective—and was slapped twice hard on the face. Immediately a third and fourth speaker got onto the platform, but they were violently dragged down. By now the meeting hall was in turmoil, all of us shouting simultaneously, "Down with Japanese imperialism! Revenge for our Northeastern compatriots! Long live the Republic of China!" When we began batting their heads with benches, they pulled out their handguns and fired a few rounds, thinking they could suppress us—*pa-pa-pa-pa*. But this only stirred our hatred. Our cries became more violent. We took turns punching them in the chest—and we felt very good doing it. Unfortunately, the sound of gunfire became intense, and then they began arresting the people who were speaking on the platform and the people who were throwing punches. At last they forced us to disperse and warned us that all who had come to the meeting would be given three days to leave Tokyo.

Government detectives guarded our dormitory all day. A new atmosphere enshrouded us, a desire to return home. Whenever we met, our first words were, "When are you leaving? Have you packed your bags?"

Mr. Qin was among those arrested. He and other students in prison were questioned three or four times a day and were repeatedly threatened with, "If you don't repent and admit your mistakes, we will have to shoot you."

"It is not wrong to love our country. If your Japanese law lists patriotism as a crime, then shoot us."

Such replies confused the militarists. Later, unable to bring the affair to a satisfying conclusion, they asked Qin to represent all who had been arrested and to write these words on a sheet of paper: "I will never oppose the Grand Japanese Empire." He did so and thus the lives of more than ten prisoners were saved. What a ridiculous gesture of deception and self-deception.

From then on, our hatred for these Japanese militarists was even more deeply rooted in our hearts.

LEAVING TOKYO IN the fall of 1931 was like leaving hell: we were freed, reborn. When we saw that two out of three passengers on our ship were schoolmates, we went almost mad with joy.

With wounded hearts we returned to the land of our ancestors. As the steamship neared Huishan Harbor, we all stood by the railing, madly waving our handkerchieves, raising arms in the air, not caring that no one came to meet us. We treated everyone as if they were our own friends and relatives, so long as they were Chinese. We even smiled and waved at the longshoremen, a group we normally considered obnoxious.

I returned to Shanghai and went to the Black Palace to see my old friends, but everything had changed. The bustling Black Palace of the past was now just empty rooms, cold and lonely. Perhaps this was because it was winter. All the people I visited kept their doors tightly shut. All had very painful memories of their lives after September Eighteenth, though none of them had—like some of us—been physically attacked.* They expressed themselves in mild terms, saying, "We should quickly think of a way to recapture the Northeast, for the longer we wait, the more powerful the enemy will become."

No kidding. Who was not aware that we must act quickly to recapture the Northeast? But we were all bare-handed scholars, powerless. Those fist-rubbing, palm-wiping good men in Tokyo had no sooner returned to Shanghai than they had sunk out of sight. We had no contact with one another, no future plans. I could only pass the placid days in my apartment. Yet how mysterious. Why had all the students who had studied abroad sunk so suddenly out of sight? This question was soon to be answered. Perhaps on the night before the storm the air must always be stifling and still.

---

*On September 18, 1931, the Japanese began an attack that led to the fall of the walled city of Mukden in the Northeast.—trans.

I REMEMBER SO clearly the night before the famous January Twenty-eighth. At a little after three in the morning I finished writing a novel of more than 200,000 words—*Abandoned*. Though weary, I did not feel like sleeping, and since the main character in the novel was sleeping in the next room, I dragged her out of bed to read through the manuscript with me (little caring whether she was sound asleep). She rubbed her eyes and asked me in a melancholy tone, "Have you used me as the subject for your writing? I am afraid that reading it will depress me. I don't feel like it." She shook her head slightly and was about to lie down again.

I held her up. "But it is just because you are my theme that I must ask you to read it for me and tell me honestly if you see anything in it that is not right. I will certainly follow your suggestions to make corrections."

She actually sat up and read it all in a single breath. Eyes filled with tears, she said, "My actual experiences didn't seem to be so hard to bear, but after reading your story I feel totally heartbroken."

I raised my head and looked toward the window, for I sensed a ray of dawn spying on us. I turned off the electric light. Sure enough, day was just breaking. Who could have imagined that on such a still and tranquil morning a war would erupt, startling sky and earth?

Now thin and scattered sounds of gunfire could be heard; slowly, they thickened in the morning air.*

That evening I was still sitting in front of my desk, concentrating all my mental energy on correcting *Abandoned*, when suddenly I was startled by sounds of several cannon shots, followed by a confusion of voices in the alley. People were running, some shouting in fear and surprise, some discussing in loud voices. Lisao came rushing down from the roof into my room, crying out in her Hunan accent, reproaching me: "Miss, it's not

---

*Japanese marines landed at Shanghai on January 28, 1932, and exchanged rifle fire with the Goumindang Nineteenth Army in a Chinese residential district of the city. This was the sound of gunfire Xie Bingying heard that morning as she was finishing her novel. Soon the Japanese began bombing the city, and then launched a full-scale attack. In the fighting that followed, thousands of Chinese civilians died or disappeared. Hundreds of thousands lost their homes. Many Chinese crowded into the International Settlement and the French Concession, trying to escape the fighting. Japan threw three divisions at the city before the Nineteenth Army, which resisted fiercely, was forced to give up.—trans.

good! You can see the Japanese setting fires. The houses around Tiantong Buddhist Convent and North Sichuan Road must be all burned down. Half the sky is red. Come quickly and see for yourself. Shanghai will soon be gone, and you are still writing."

Quickly, Shanshan and I ran up to the roof, and we saw that Lisao was right. Half the horizon was ablaze, red flames and yellow-black smoke were shooting straight up to the top of the sky. The *pee-pee pa-pa* sounds of explosives, guns, and cannon wove a tragic and moving war symphony. Now the vendors selling extra editions of newspapers were shouting in husky voices as they ran from streets to alleys. Everyone's surprised heart was cloaked in suspicion and fright. People now, having read the extras, knew that the inevitable disaster of war had finally arrived, but who would have thought that our cultural essence, the Commercial Press Publishers and the Eastern Library Publishers, would both be swallowed by the blood-red flames?

Shanghai was sucked into the whirlpool of war. Large groups of students joined the Nineteenth Army to fight, and all the students who had returned from Tokyo became active, joining an army unit or performing various sorts of cultural work in barracks, each carrying a gun or holding a pen to fight the enemy.

In these exciting days I felt as if all the insults I had suffered in Tokyo would at last be avenged. All day I worked in the ambulance corps of Baolong Hospital, nursing wounded soldiers at the front line. All night I edited and wrote for a weekly magazine called *Women's Light*. I was so busy that I didn't have time to sleep, and yet I felt not the least tired.

Shanghai was roaring angrily. Workers, merchants, students, office clerks, and teachers—all were anxious to join the fight and resist to the end, sacrificing everything. Each day material gifts for our soldiers were transported to the front line by countless trucks and small cars. The fighting record of the bold Nineteenth Army was published daily under big headlines, along with reports from newspapers around the world that praised the Nineteenth Army as troops of iron and steel that made the enemy's guts go cold. With blood and flesh our soldiers faced the enemy airplanes and cannon: one lieutenant had his stomach shot away and his intestines were spilling out, yet he held on to his rifle and still rushed toward the front, and even when he stopped breathing he still held his rifle tightly.

Like dragonflies, the enemy's airplanes spread over the entire sky. But the brave Nineteenth Army, undaunted, often shot them down with rifles.

LITERARY CIRCLES IN SHANGHAI joined forces and organized the Shanghai Patriotic Writers Association for Resisting the Japanese. We did propaganda work and often, in order to collect material for our writing, we rode to the front lines in vehicles that carried the delegations of consolation. During these exciting days I got to know Bai Wei, a woman writer from the time of the May Fourth movement. Strong willed and sharp thinking, she had made strenuous efforts to break away from her feudal family and fight the feudal society. Everyone knew her poetry and novels but none knew of her poverty-stricken life. She was ill, she said, for 300 out of every 365 days, and she often just lay in bed in an upstairs room. She had a few friends who visited her. She did not have a servant. She had to wash clothes, cook meals, and mop floors even when she was ill. Sometimes, when she felt a little better, she would go into the city to shop, riding in a pushcart because this was cheaper than a ricksha.

"The cannon fire of January twenty-eighth has cured my illness. I want to go to the front line with you," said Bai Wei, very excited. But when we saw her skinny and sickly body, we all agreed that she should not go. She came to all our meetings, which stirred and cheered her spirits, though still she lacked energy and looked very feeble when she walked.

At this time the head of the women's corps, Miss Zhong, happened to be in Shanghai, and she very enthusiastically accompanied us to the front. I remember that on one occasion she and I and a number of writers got into a large truck loaded with gifts for the troops and went to Tiantong Buddhist Convent, which was on the third line of defense. Electric fences and sandbags were everywhere, the situation very tense. We first carried the bundles of gifts into a captain's office, but he was talking with someone on the phone and was too busy to even take time to say thanks. A soldier said, "We don't need gift packages, only manpower."

These words exhilarated us. Not wanting to disturb their concentration, we hurriedly returned to where the truck had been parked, carrying with us that soldier's admonition. Suddenly, a fusillade of bullets sang through the air past our heads—we instantly dropped to our knees and crawled. But we couldn't find the truck. It was gone. All those who had come with us had fled. So we had to walk all the way back.

When we returned to the foreign concession, Miss Zhong said, "So, after all, it is true that those who have not been to the front line are cowards. They fled for no reason."

In the days that followed we were embarrassed to read in the *Literary News* successive war essays by these so-called famous writers who had fled from the front but who truly felt no fear of being ashamed. From this I learned that a writer need not go the front line in order to write very moving essays.

Amid the beacon fires I got to know many sorts of writers. Some truly loved their country, made no noise, buried their heads, and worked hard. Some wrote proclamations and slogans all day and acted as chairmen in meetings. And yet there was another sort, those who were afraid of being called cowards and who would talk, every time they opened their mouths, about going to the front line, and who would write, whenever their mouths were shut, about joining the troops—yet who, as soon as the cannon sounded, would hold their heads and flee like rats, their butts burning and piss flying.

The blaze of war became more fierce. But just when everyone was ecstatic and excited about sacrificing all for the final victory, we received the order to stop fighting. The heroic battle was finally ended at the end of March by orders from above.

ALTHOUGH THE RESISTANCE FIGHTING near Shanghai had stopped, every citizen's heart was still aflame with hatred for the Japanese militarists and alight with adoration for the officers and soldiers of the Nineteenth Army. Everyone constantly recalled heroic tales of the fight and wished that soon the beacon fire of war would reignite and signal us to destroy the enemy.

Those of us engaged in cultural work were likewise angry and unsatisfied. We longed for freedom, longed to recapture the Northeast. The January Twenty-eighth war of resistance ignited the fire of hope, hope that war would lead to victory, a hope that soon the Northeast would be recaptured. But reality turned out to be not so simple. The government had made comprehensive war plans and now gave the order to stop fighting. Some officers and soldiers wept so bitterly at this that they lost their voices, not happy that their fresh blood should have flowed in vain, preferring to fight to the finish, to the last soldier and the last gun. But army commands are as immovable as mountains, and obedience is a soldier's sacred duty. They had no choice but to stop fighting.

Depressing times, yet we stayed active. Shanshan, Bingxian, Zhiying, and I had done women's work since January 28. During the fighting we did ambulance work at the front lines while managing *Women's Light* weekly. We never accepted grants from organizations or individuals; each of us had pulled money from our own pockets. Now the women's movement was at high tide, surging forward, just as it had been during the days of the Northern Expedition. Many uneducated women worked under our leadership. They were less complicated than the educated sorts. Straightforward and passionate, they carried out their duties without backstabbing or gossip. They were of one heart, willing to sacrifice everything in the fight for women's emancipation.

Though superficially free, Shanghai was actually in chains. China had been put into the inferior position of a colony, and every imperialist nation now turned its thoughts to how to repress us. Some Chinese imagined that they would enjoy more freedoms by living in the foreign concessions than by living on their own soil. They were mistaken. Consider what happened as we prepared for the March Eighth Woman's Day celebration.

On the afternoon of March 7, we were holding the last planning meeting for March Eighth. We had mapped out the parade route for the following day and had prepared all our flags and slogans. In addition to publishing essays related to March Eighth in a supplement to *Women's Light*, we printed two small booklets that we set in the new no. 5 type. These two pamphlets we had edited with great vitality, and their content was quite substantial. We were convinced that they would be a fine gift for March Eighth. To our surprise, they later became the evidence for a crime.

Like a pack of wolves, gendarmes charged into the office of the Women's Association and, asking no questions, indiscriminately arrested whomever they saw. They caught everyone at the meeting in a single net. I did not attend because I was sick, so I did not learn the terrible news until the morning of the eighth. I jumped up out of my bed when Zhiying rushed over to tell me what had happened.

"Then today's commemoration and parade are not going to be held?"

"How can we hold them? Everyone is locked up in the foreign police station."

"What if we convened another group of people?"

She replied, after some thought, "Maybe it is possible. But we must all face the fact that we will be arrested and taken to the foreign police station."

So at last we decided to suppress our incendiary anger. We discussed methods to rescue those who had been arrested. Meanwhile, we sent them items for their daily use and tried to boost their morale. Contrary to everyone's expectation, poor Shanshan, Bingxian, and the others languished in prison for more than three months before they were released.

PART 9   A Traveling Life

I AGAIN BEGAN MY WANDERING LIFE.

Little Hang and Hong had written to ask me to visit them in the isolated village of Longyan. This village was located in western Fukien Province, which is where the Nineteenth Army had retreated and built a new society. (Earlier, the Communist Fourth Army had originated in this same place and had forcibly occupied the area for four full years.)

Longyan was strategically located, difficult to reach, and set amid beautiful landscape. In April I traveled there, and as I walked from Longxi to Longyan my heart was filled with happiness. I was so overwhelmed by the beautiful scenery that I felt I wanted to travel the world forever, never stopping. A steep and lofty mountain lay between Heqi and Shizhong, and between these towns the Nineteenth Army had built a road that spiraled round the mountain. To the right of the road plunged a bottomless abyss. Alongside the road were lush green trees and fragrant wildflowers, so that as you walked along you felt no weariness at all—you felt as if you were strolling in a park where your feet did not want to stop, where you were ever drawn on and on by the feeling that still more splendid scenery must lie ahead. It took me just two days to reach my destination.

When I first arrived at Longyan, I was treated by Hong and Little Hang as their distinguished guest, but because we were old friends they felt free to play a trick on me.

On the third day after I arrived an orderly came to me and said, "Reporting to Madam. Has Section Chief Xie arrived yet? Please ask him to attend the meeting."

"There is no Section Chief Xie here," I answered. "You must have made a mistake."

He left, looking disappointed.

Soon afterward another person came looking for Section Chief Xie, and I now began to wonder what was going on. Finally I caught up with Little Hang and he admitted that a committee had already issued a statement announcing that I was to be a section chief. They had not told me this right away, figuring I needed a few days to rest after I arrived in Longyan. Also, they feared I might not accept the position. The orderlies, of course, had assumed that the new section chief must be a man, and that is why they called me "madam," thinking I was the new section chief's wife. I had to laugh, though I was angry.

At that time the person in charge of Longyan was General Cai Tingkai, and Hong was the chairman of the committee for reconstruction of western Fukien Province. He had married a nurse from Guangdong Province and they had a baby boy. I was very happy for him and I visited his home frequently. We chatted about our life in the Northern Expedition and about the unfortunate episode in Beijing. Those long-ago days seemed like a dream to both of us.

Then, one day, something happened that surprised me.

Hong took from his shirt pocket a package wrapped in plastic, and he smilingly asked me, "Guess what's in here?"

"I cannot guess," I said.

Hong's wife, Yuqing, said, "I know. It's a love letter from his lover."

"Really?" I said, thinking Hong must have a lover. I watched him, smiling in much the same way Yuqing was smiling.

"I will let you see it, but only for a glance," he said, and he very carefully opened the plastic wrap. It was a short letter that I had written to him during the Northern Expedition. Just when I reached to grab it, he quickly put it back into his pocket.

I felt very bad, realizing that Hong had not forgotten his feelings for me and was not entirely loyal to his wife. I knew I would be heartbroken if I were in Yuqing's place, and immediately I felt like leaving Longyan to avoid causing any problems between them. Fortunately, my wish soon came true and I drifted alone to Xiamen.*

WHEN I FIRST ARRIVED in Longyan my friends had arranged a feast to welcome me, and there I met a crippled principal. This principal was very short, perhaps barely more than four feet tall. Both of his feet were lame and he labored when he walked—he looked just like a duck, swaying left to right. His face was very thin and his four limbs were as dry as sticks. Only his two bright eyes infused him with vitality. His clothes were made of coarse blue cloth, and anyone meeting him on the street would certainly mistake him for a beggar. Few would imagine that he was actually an educator who promoted women's rights.

We indulged for a while in idle chitchat, and then I asked him how he had come to establish his school. He blinked and, speaking in a humble voice, answered me in detail:

"To begin at the beginning, it was forty years ago that I started my school. I was only twenty then and had not read much. Yet my ideas were very modern and I opposed society's repression of women. I felt that males and females were equally humans, and I did not understand why males enjoyed privileges while females were repressed. I wanted to respect the female sex, to elevate female rights. I was determined to establish a school for girls that would give women in poor villages and isolated rural areas the opportunity to study, so that after they graduated they could work in society just as men do and not be humiliated by men. I began by respecting my wife. In the third year of our marriage she still had not given birth and someone suggested that I marry a concubine, but I utterly rejected this idea. My wife has kept me company from that moment to this day, and during these forty years we two—this old pair—have depended on each other and struggled together for the sake of the school."

All this he spoke with exuberance and in one breath, leaving no room for

---

*Xiamen is a coastal city, about sixty miles from Longyan.—trans.

anyone to interrupt. He swallowed a mouthful of tea, then continued to speak:

"My family was very poor, so where could I get the money to establish a school? Luckily, I had learned skills in physiognomy, palm reading, and fortune-telling, so I went alone to many large ports, first Xiamen, then Shanghai and Nanjing, then Hankou. I earned money every day, and I saved all I earned except what I spent each day on two simple meals. Because guest houses cost money, I sometimes slept under the eaves of people's houses. After living like that for five years, I had saved more than three thousand yuan. I then returned to establish the Equal Rights Girls School. This building was already standing. I was the principal and my wife was the school's labor force. Besides sweeping the classrooms and the courtyard and the corridors, my wife cooked meals and washed and sewed and mended clothes for the students. She was also responsible for duties such as enrolling new students and ringing the school bell. The school was founded in 1904, so this year will be its thirtieth anniversary. But it was a feudal period in those days. People in Longyan thought I was a madman because I did not take my hard-earned money and use it to buy property but instead wanted to establish a school. They were certain I suffered from a mental disorder. Many old educators actually opposed me openly, saying that I was untrustworthy and that I had established my school merely as a ploy to seduce virtuous young women from good families. That kind of talk made me tremble in anger."

At this juncture he became very excited. He opened his eyes wide and curled his lips in indignation—and in so doing he splashed two drops of spit onto my face. I could not very easily use a handkerchief to wipe it off, could only let it dry by itself. Taking advantage of a moment when he was not looking, I moved my body slightly to the left. "We owe you a great deal for your struggle with the forces of feudalism, but what happened next?" I was eager to know how his work had progressed.

"Eventually my school was established. In the beginning only four students came to register, and I accepted them. Each day they attended four classes plus two sessions on sewing. I taught the classes; my wife, the sewing lessons. Those four students could be called the pioneers of women's emancipation in Longyan. Caring nothing for family pressure and opposition, they came promptly to school every day. Unfortunately, two of them were persecuted by their families until finally they got married, so they were unable to exert any influence on the society. The other two had very good marks, and when they graduated, they became my teaching assistants. They never married. They made education their lifelong career. As I think back, I respect their spirit even more today than I did then.

"After that the student enrollment increased every year, and we now have more than 280 students, a number that would certainly be much greater if we accepted all who apply for admission. But the building is too small so we really cannot accommodate everyone. I have thought of expanding but I have no money. In this out-of-the-way place people still cling to ancient ideas. They don't mind spending large sums of money on superstitious offerings and on useless social events, but they are absolutely averse to donating even one coin to the school. However, I feel satisfied, for many of our graduates are spread throughout Longyan and neighboring villages. As long as the school exists—even for just one more day—I will be able to build on some student's outstanding ability. I dare not harbor any extravagant wishes, but I do hope no misfortune strikes us. I will struggle for the school until my final day."

All the people sitting there were bending their ears to hear this moving story. I felt great interest in this principal so I asked for the school's address. I said I would go to visit his school at nine o'clock the following morning.

"You are most welcome. Please come and enlighten us." His face was piled full of smiles as he said, "Tomorrow morning I will send a student to come and fetch you. You must be quite unfamiliar with the roads, since this is your first time here."

"No, there is no need to interrupt the student's work. I can find my own way to the school."

"Then I will let you. You'll need only to ask for the Equal Rights Girls School and someone will give you directions. Almost all the people in the neighborhood are parents of our students."

The following day was clear and bright. After breakfast I followed the route described to me by the principal, climbing up a low hill through a grove of trees filled with fragrant wildflowers. Butterflies fluttered amid the flowers, darting and dancing. I leaned against a large tree to rest. Far away, below the hill, I saw densely layered buildings. Above one of them flapped our national flag with its colors of blue sky, white sun, and red earth. I decided that there must be the Equal Rights Girls School.

I walked down the hill through the fields, on a jade-green path, and suddenly I found myself on a street. I made inquiries at two corners and at last I arrived at the school.

When the four large words EQUAL RIGHTS GIRLS SCHOOL appeared in front of my eyes, I immediately conjured an image of the crippled principal setting up a small stall at the Huangpu harbor, telling peoples' fortunes. He was like the trained warrior from Shandong Province who used the money that he received from begging to run a school. The word *great* cannot sufficiently describe his spirit.

When a common person who is also half disabled is nonetheless able to establish such a good school—isn't this a human miracle? Just when I was thinking this, a woman in her fifties, dressed like a servant, bowed to me and asked, "What is your honorable name, and what is your business here?"

Her manner was unusually humble and respectful. In all ways, I thought, this school is special, for even an old amah has manners.

"My name is Xie. I came to visit your school."

"Ah! You are the teacher from Shanghai? Welcome, welcome!"

Immediately she hastened inside. I stood by the door of the visitors' lounge. The lounge also served as an office. I noticed lists, charts, and maps hanging on either side of the doorway, all neatly displayed. The furniture in the room, though very old, was wiped absolutely clean and showed not a single trace of dust.

"Please come in and sit. Are you tired from your walk?" The principal suddenly appeared in front of me, just as I was absorbed in my observations. He earnestly introduced me to the woman who was dressed like a servant. It turned out that she was his hardworking wife.

"Ah—so this is the principal's wife. Just now I was impolite." I felt very embarrassed.

But she answered in a natural manner. "Don't mention it. But we apologize for not coming out to welcome you."

After she poured me a cup of tea she promptly looked at the clock. It was time for classes to be dismissed so she hurriedly took up the bell and left the room to ring it.

I asked him softly, "Is it still your honorable wife who is responsible for all these petty chores?"

"She alone, yes—and now the workload is even heavier than it was before. More than twenty students live here now, and she must cook their meals and wash their clothes, though the students in each class take turns sweeping the classrooms. Students who are forged in this kind of environment are actually very easy to manage. The only difficulty is that we have trouble hiring good teachers, for the simple reason that our funds are so tight that the salaries we pay are very low. Also, this place is quite isolated. Our big problem, whenever we try to hire a teacher from the outside, is that—even apart from the cost of travel—no one wants to come."

By now the classes had been dismissed and many students from the lower grades had run to the door of the office. They watched us with great interest. They did not talk, merely gazed at me steadily and intensely. The principal gave a single wave of his hand and they all quietly walked away.

"I will assemble the entire student body during this hour, for I would like you to say a few words to them."

I felt myself in a difficult position and did not know how best to answer him. I feared that the children might not understand my accent, yet if I refused his kindness, I would feel ungrateful. Hesitantly, I replied, "There will be another opportunity some other time. Today I must return early to take care of a small matter, so I must refuse your offer."

"No! This is such a rare opportunity. No matter what, I must ask you to say a few words to them."

Actually, by then the students had already assembled. I was greatly surprised when the teacher on duty for the day came to report to the principal that the students had all lined up. They were sharp and nimble in their movements, yet also quiet and serious, which was quite beyond what I had expected.

Because I was afraid that they would not understand my accent, I spoke only a few customary words of encouragement. I especially praised the principal and his wife by saying that China has countless schools but that this school was the only one that was established with such difficulty, in an environment of ten thousand hardships. I encouraged them to study especially hard and to reward the founder of this school by achieving excellence.

Hearing this, the principal was naturally extremely happy. The children gave thunderous applause, as if they had been injected with stimulants. Following the ringing of the bell for the second time, they all went into their classrooms. The principal gave me a tour of seven classrooms. In one of these a twelve- or thirteen-year-old girl was playing the organ while several other students surrounded her and watched. When they saw us coming into the room they quickly found their own seats and, one by one, sat down.

"Originally, this was the hour for music instruction in this class, but because we could not find a teacher, we can only let them practice by themselves."

As the principal explained this, I suddenly had an idea. I asked, "Are they taught to read the five-line staff or the simplified system?"

"They are taught by Arabic numbers."

I almost laughed when I heard this, for the simplified system uses Arabic numbers. Luckily, I warned myself at once that I absolutely could not laugh at this earnest village educator.

"Then I will recommend myself to teach music at your honorable school, though I must first make it clear that my playing is not good, and it is perhaps not too different from that of a student. Also, my throat is very coarse. But I do remember many songs, and I can introduce them to the students." This was not humbleness on my part, but my honest confession.

"There, there—you are too polite. It will be our great honor if our school can benefit from your teaching." He spoke very politely.

I actually became a music teacher the next day. I remember the first song I taught them was "Spring Flower":

> Red clouds are as brilliant as piled brocade,
> Peaches and plums and red almonds displayed;
> On flowery branches the bright birds sing,
> And flowers are opening to trumpet the spring.
> Youthful days are springtime flowers—
> Youth, oh, cling to your withering hours!

This had been my favorite song when I was very young, and I felt I had been restored to my childhood as now I taught it to the students. These village girls were honest, modest, and innocent. They treated their teachers even more affectionately than they treated their own parents. I liked children very much and now I was among troops of them; my spirit felt indescribably satisfied.

A few days later I also took up teaching Chinese literature to the sixth grade and teaching music to the entire school. Each day I spent my time on the road to school and inside classrooms. In addition to correcting my students' compositions and diaries, in the evenings I wrote essays and sent them to the "free discussion" column of the *Shanghai News*. Several of those essays were later collected in *Hunan's Wind*, a small volume published by Beixin Bookstore.

It was the time of the Dragon Boat Festival. All families were busily wrapping the three-cornered dumplings. I was living with Little Hang and his wife, who was a good and virtuous hostess. She had told me earlier that I should not go out to eat on festival day, so I refused the invitation to a banquet given by the principal. I never expected that he would send a student to me, bringing an earthenware cooking pot and ten dumplings with pureed red beans. The student arrived at eleven o'clock. The pot was still steaming, clearly just off the stove. I opened the cover to look, and there I saw a fat hen and a few small eggs floating above the golden broth.

"The principal said that Teacher is unable to go to his house to eat, probably because of another engagement. Therefore he sends over the chicken and asks you to please accept it." The student spoke very politely.

I really didn't know how to reply. It would be rather embarrassing for me to take it, yet if I refused it he would think I didn't value his gift. I finally accepted his goodwill. When it was time to eat, Little Hang and his wife said that the affection that came with the chicken was more precious than ten ounces of gold.

Three months later I left Longyan and was forever parted from that group of lovable children. Even today the scene of their crying when they saw me off is still playing in my mind. Sometimes I can almost hear the sound of their crying. Other times I can hear them calling from inside the forest, "Do not forget us, Teacher. You must come again."

I have never forgotten them. But I am afraid that "come again" will never come true.

A PLACE ABOUT thirteen miles west of Longyan called Gutian produced an unusual person. A farmer by birth, he could not read a single word, but he had a merciful heart. His thinking was socialistic. He espoused using peaceful means to solve all society's disputes and dispel all society's confusions, instead of advocating violent methods to eliminate farm owners or confiscate their land. Some people said that he was a reformist. Others opposed his style and called it unworkable. But strangely, his town had already established a system of peasant-owned land and equal land rights for all. And there was not one person—neither male nor female, neither old nor young, neither rich farmer nor poor farmer nor rent farmer—who did not support him. To overstate a little, the people in Gutian actually compared him to a god: words only had to come from his mouth to be honored. The country people were not the only ones who felt this way. Even the bandits in the nearby mountains and woods never caused disturbances in Gutian, though they robbed and looted in other places. When the Communist New Fourth Army came here, it did not dare attack the Earth Emperor. Instead, the army did its utmost to work with him. It was not clear exactly when the people from outside Gutian bestowed on him the honorable title of Earth Emperor, but whenever people called him by this title he was neither happy nor angry. He only smilingly shook his head and said modestly, "Not at all, you're joking."

Actually, this was not a joke. Though he did not have the majesty of an emperor, he had the emperor's power and influence. Whatever the command might be, it was immediately acted upon, as long as it had come from him. His name was Fu Bocui and he was nearly sixty years old, but his energy and strength were still like those of a young man. When he walked he looked exactly like a person who lifted a sedan chair or pulled a cart, and he moved faster than the average coolie. He liked to walk and did not care to ride horses. He was totally against sitting in a sedan chair, for he said that for one person to carry another was a most unreasonable and inhumane act. So when we went to visit him we either rode on horses or walked, to avoid making him feel uneasy. Though he did not sit in sedan chairs himself, he did not oppose others' doing so. He said it was entirely a matter of individual choice and had no bearing on the problems of society.

All visitors to western Fujian Province knew that an earth emperor was living in Gutian, and all were curious to meet him and to admire his style. Quite unexpectedly I had an opportunity to go to Gutian: Wugou and Shanshan, tired of life in Shanghai, came to visit me in the ancient farming village of Longyan, and I took time out to roam with them through all the scenic places close by. Afterward we traveled swiftly (each of us riding a fine horse) to the Earth Emperor's native village.

On the way we passed countless steep and lofty mountain ranges. Sometimes we moved through forests of ancient trees that penetrated clouds and seemed to reach toward heaven, and sometimes we could not see sunlight or anything around us in any direction, and then, overwhelmed by a layer of green, we thought we had lost our way in the deep woods. Once in a while we stopped to let our horses rest their hooves a bit. Then the ear-pleasing sound of sighing wind in pines seemed like roaring surf, and the clear, crisp sounds of birds playing nature's music made us drunk and dreamy. We would have loved to have jumped off our horses and lain on the downy green grass and slept luxuriously.

Sometimes on faraway mountains we saw silvery-white chains dangling. As we drew nearer, those chains grew clearer, and when we drew closer still we heard the immense, heroic sounds of waterfalls that made our horses stomp and linger. Once they had heard the sound, our horses refused to go on.

The scenery became lovelier as we got closer to Gutian. This was truly an out-of-the-world Arcadia. When we climbed over a high mountain and saw a golden wheat field, we all gave a cry, for here the water was exceptionally clear, the mountains exquisite, the rocks beautiful, and even the sky unusually bright.

"Is it possible that this is really a fairyland? Why is it that as soon as we entered Gutian my mind suddenly became light and free?" I turned my head to ask Wugou this question.

She was staring at the sea-blue sky.

As she answered me, Wugou spoke in the tone of one reciting a poem: "Jade-green water under jade-green mountain—what a lovely, quiet and peaceful place. Let us live here forever and never return to Shanghai."

Shanshan was bouncing like a child on the back of her horse. "It is so enjoyable here. We will ask the Earth Emperor to divvy up some land for us to farm. Honestly, let's not go back."

At last we reached our destination. Two big fat yellow dogs were the first to welcome us. They did not bite, only happily wagged their tails. Following behind them came a friend of ours from Beijing, named Kangkang, and the Earth Emperor himself, Mr. Fu Bocui.

To us, three guests fresh from Shanghai, everything seemed new and strange and interesting. At meals we sat at the same table with farmers who had bare feet and shaved heads. Kangkang, a writer, had now completely changed the way he dressed. He wore straw shoes and a straw hat. His skin had been tanned very dark, and he was much stronger now than he had been when he lived in Beijing.

"This is perhaps the first time you have eaten unhulled rice, and I am afraid that perhaps you cannot swallow it. I am sorry that today we were not ready for you. Tomorrow I will have hulled rice made for your meal." The Earth Emperor spoke to us very apologetically.

Wugou replied quickly, "No, Mr. Fu, you are too generous. The unhulled rice not only tastes good but is richly nutritious. We enjoy eating it."

I certainly would not have guessed that this pampered young lady, grown up spoiled in a hothouse of luxury, could endure this sort of hardship. She ate two bowls of the rice without looking the least uncomfortable.

The next day we changed our clothes. Each of us bought a large straw hat and put on straw shoes. As if we had returned to a primitive time, we ran like a band of savages from field dikes to mountain slopes, flinging our bodies into nature's arms, and all day long we were companions of green mountains and jade-tinted water. Sometimes we forgot the time, forgot even to eat until the Earth Emperor dispatched someone to fetch us.

In front of the building where we stayed was a small creek with large rocks on either side. We would lie on top of the rocks, gazing at the deep blue sky and at the mountains far and near. We made it a habit every day after supper to lie on the rocks and watch the sunset. Sometimes when we saw people approaching we sat up and greeted them, and always they smiled and nodded their heads in such a way that made us feel not at all like strangers. Still, conversing with them was difficult and took a lot of effort. But they all seemed to us like lovable old friends. Perhaps they had been influenced by the Earth Emperor. He was a model for the farmers—not proud and not pretentious, his heart full of kindness, his face reflecting his sincerity, dignity, and courtesy. Because they all acted as he did, we came to look at all farmers as the people of the Earth Emperor.

The Earth Emperor led a simple life. No matter how hot the weather, he always wore an old outfit made of coarse blue cloth and always had his feet slipped into a pair of straw shoes. Whenever he went out he liked to put on either a leaf hat or a straw hat. He ate two meals every day, each consisting only of rice and a dish of vegetables. He did not like to talk much and he disliked socializing even more. Whenever he was invited to eat at a restaurant he would feel a headache coming on, and he would try again and again to decline the invitation. When it was an invitation that he could not refuse, he would force himself to attend and would make a perfunctory appearance. He was not eloquent before a group and as a rule he did not speak at public gatherings. But if it was absolutely necessary for him to speak, his words were simple and honest, like those spoken by a plain and upright farmer—every phrase he uttered was truthful and practical.

Once in Longyan I witnessed the Earth Emperor flying into a rage. Unlike people who roar when they are angry, he raised his voice only a little, while at the same time saying decisively, "No good. Definitely no compromise—it must be done this way." People told us he always used these same words to enforce his views, whatever the problem under discussion.

He was tall and thin. He had a sparse yellow moustache and a beard. His eyes were not large but were full of spirit. When he smiled, the warm gleam of his eyes was sincere. Even though he was the actual leader of the people in the village of Gutian, and the Earth Emperor for the whole of western Fujian's special district, he never put on airs. Like an old woman, he was forever mixing with people. Each day he was visited by at least twenty or thirty people. As soon as these visitors had seated themselves he would ask about this and that, as if they were all in a family gathering. They would even tell him news about which family's hen had hatched little chicks, which family's plowing ox had died—matters as large as sesame seeds.

One day a woman of thirty or so ran breathlessly in to have a meeting with the Earth Emperor. He stood up right away to give her his seat. "What is the emergency?"

"My husband and I are divorced because we have different ideas. Our divorce procedure has already been taken care of at the district office, but I still owe him twenty yuan and he is forcing me to pay him back immediately. But I don't have the money. I thought of repaying him by installments, but he won't agree to it. So I have come here today to ask for Mr. Fu's help. Perhaps you can persuade him not to press me to pay—or perhaps you could lend me the money so that I can pay him back right away. I will repay you in installments."

This woman was poised and spoke in a natural manner. She actually looked as if she had noble aspirations, the sort of person who would never repudiate a debt. She did not chatter on and on but spoke resolutely, each phrase precise.

"All right. Since your husband is pressing you, take twenty yuan from me and repay him. As for my money, you don't need to hurry—wait until you have some extra funds and then we will talk. It will be all right if you don't have the money to pay me back. Now, tell me, what are your plans for the future?"

"Me? I don't plan to get married. I will use my pair of hands to support myself. This will make me feel satisfied, and I won't have to suffer bullying or to bear the burden of having children." She answered the Earth Emperor straightforwardly, without the least hesitation—which made us all smile.

"Do you think she is wise or not?" asked the Earth Emperor, looking at us and smiling.

"If she were educated, she would surely be able to accomplish great things for society," I replied, just as she stood up to leave.

The expression on her face remained as it had been, perhaps because she did not understand what I had said.

The Earth Emperor gave her twenty yuan. She said many thank-yous and bowed to each of us. We quickly stood up and walked her to the door.

I asked in surprise, "Is it this easy for a husband and wife to get a divorce here?"

"Marriage is absolutely free. Divorce is allowed only if both parties agree or if one person has shortcomings. Because every woman can be financially independent, her life is not affected in the least after she leaves her husband. Besides, because of her financial independence, her husband does not dare to repress her. So her status is raised to the level of a man, and she is equal to a man."

After seeing all this, I truly envied the women who lived in Gutian. I rejoiced for the whole world of women. After all, here in one isolated corner of the earth was a new land that treated women as humans.

ONE DAY GENERAL Cai Tingkai came to Gutian, and we took part in a mass meeting for the people.

He and his troops had coined a slogan: "Strike the Northeast!" They did not forget the bloody stain of January Twenty-eighth, and they stirred the people to resist the Japanese. The general had come to Gutian on this occasion to awaken the people and to help them recognize that the Japanese imperialists were China's biggest enemy. People who attended the meeting were very enthusiastic. We were particularly fond of those barefoot women who wore wide-brimmed bamboo hats. All of them had strong bodies, and their healthy steps made them look as if they were flying. Having been trained for four or five years, they speedily and uniformly performed basic drills such as standing at attention, standing at ease, turning left, turning right. Each held in her hand a stick and was as full of spirit as if she were a soldier holding a gun.

The meeting was scheduled for eight o'clock in the morning, but before seven o'clock the men and women, old and young, began arriving from four surrounding villages. No director was on hand but the womenfolk kept order. We arrived early to take pictures. We also intended to talk to the women, but because we couldn't understand their dialect, we could only stand on the side and watch the bustle.

I felt like a foreigner. The Earth Emperor wanted me to give a speech and he even found a translator for me. I was so excited that I was nearly in tears. I particularly respected the people's spirit when the heavy rain poured down and the crowd stood there, solemn and unmovable as a mountain. What could I say on this kind of occasion? Language and words are dead and it is only these brave fighters who can, with the courage of dragons and tigers, give power to the country and give light and joy to mankind.

After I stepped down from the platform, I hurried to where Wugou and Shanshan were standing. I said quietly, "We should be ashamed. Look at them, those copper-muscled and iron-boned bodies. Usually they are looked down on by city people, who call them ignorant and uncivilized villagers. But when it is time to protect our nation's soil, how we need them! Our bodies are useless. We can only hold a pen and write a few essays. Let me ask you, what use are we?"

"Especially me," said Wugou. "When I stand in front of them, I actually become a person from the country of dwarfs. I am both short and small—it really makes me mad."

We all laughed.

DURING THE PREVIOUS twenty years, the most serious change in China had been in politics. Parties increased in number by the day, and the problems of ideology had become more and more complex. I was a lover of freedom and did not wish to join any party whatever, or to be swept into any political whirlpool. I utterly disdained those politicians who hung up a sheep's head to sell dog meat, and those opportunist revolutionaries who supported this party today and purged that party tomorrow. In newspapers and magazines we had been reading only about infighting—I purge you, you overthrow me—and we never saw anyone writing about setting aside private opinions and working hard for the future of the country and our people. I grieved and suffered bitterly, but I could only drop my head and quietly sigh. I remember that in Shanghai I got into a big mess because I was suspected of leaning to the Left. But I never joined their battle lines and I was never used by any one of them to give credence to their meaningless and idle writings.

I had gone to Fujian because I had been deeply hurt and wished to use the beautiful surroundings to readjust my life. After my body had been nourished, I intended to devote myself to writing. What is more, I went there with no particular destination in mind, with no particular purpose, just to travel for travel's sake as the spirit moved me. It was only when I accepted a contract from the middle school at Xiamen that I decided to once again take up the chalk to earn a livelihood. I never imagined that those types who always wear tinted glasses would bother making up false rumors about me, but they did. They said I was the head of the Women's Ministry in the People's Government of the Social Democratic Party. The truth was that I did not join any party and that I was never a minister of any kind. I was only a teacher at Xiamen Middle School. But because those senseless people made up this rumor, my students were provoked to react. They were eager to make a proclamation to explain my innocence, but I persuaded them not to. I used the argument that facts will prevail over debate. It has always been my character not to beg people to understand me but to let the facts prove my worth.

In the fall of 1934, with the People's Government newly established, every school in Xiamen chose a representative to go to the Fujian Provincial Government to request more funds. I was one of them. Yet when I arrived in Fuzhou, I actually did not perform my duties as a representative but instead secretly slipped away and traveled to visit Gushan. I was just two days in Fuzhou, and I spent all my time delighting in the city's porcelain and visiting the surrounding mountain-and-water scenery. I knew that such opportunities are rare. I did not want to waste even one hour. Who could have foreseen the unfortunate incident that occurred when I returned from Fuzhou?

At the outset it was Hong's idea that I should go to work in Fuzhou, but I replied, "I would rather die of hunger. I absolutely will not be an official."

Seeing that my attitude was so stubborn and unyielding, he said no more. And later, when someone else mentioned the matter of my taking charge of the Women's Ministry, I said, "Please do not joke—or some newspaper reporter may use your talk as material for a story."

In fact, someone did read in the newspaper that I had become the head of the Women's Ministry. Heavens—this was a false charge on an unlucky day. I did not see the paper, only heard about it from someone. I did not want to dispute the lie, and anyway I would not have known how to begin, so I merely buried my head in my teaching and my writing. My colleagues felt aggrieved on my behalf, but I stayed free of the emotions stirred up by the situation. I answered them, "It doesn't matter. Facts will be my witnesses."

It was a winter evening. Already the bedtime bell had rung. Suddenly a messenger came to me and said there was a soldier outside who was looking for me and wished to speak with me. I had no time to consider who this might be and even less time to consider whether I should go to meet him. With quick steps I went outside and there I saw a military man I had never seen before. He was standing at the doorway of the reception office. After a courteous salute he felt in his pocket for a letter. He handed it to me, saying, "This is from the secretary general.* He asks that you please leave Xiamen tonight."

Heavens! What could be so serious that I must leave Xiamen this very night? I had not participated in any political work. Was it possible that I had committed a crime? I was an innocent teacher—why must I be forced to leave Xiamen?

"Do you know why he wants me to leave Xiamen?" Stupidly, I asked this of the soldier who had brought the letter.

---

*Hong was the secretary general.—trans.

"Times and situations have changed. Everybody is preparing to escape. This evening the secretary general followed General Cai and left Fuzhou."

"Their departure is their business. What does it have to do with me?"

Like a fool I asked him this. But that comrade in uniform merely saluted me and then fled.

Holding the letter, with heavy footsteps I dragged myself back to my bedroom. I opened the letter and found the message that I had been told it contained. But there was another phrase at the end: "We will meet again; hope you will take care of yourself." I was stupefied for about ten minutes. Then I took the letter to show Kuizhang. He suggested that I leave Xiamen that night.

"Can it be so serious? I never participated in their work. It does not concern me in the least."

"Perhaps someone thought you had worked for them. Only the teachers and students of our school, and some of your friends in Xiamen, believe in you. I am afraid it is difficult to say that about people elsewhere."

"Then, according to you, what will happen if I don't leave?"

Actually, at that moment I was not afraid for myself, but I was worried that the school would be implicated if something happened to me. That thought made me very uneasy.

"It is very difficult to say. The tone of this letter seems quite serious. I think you had better leave."

After hesitating a little, I answered him, "Of course, if it were not serious, Hong certainly would not have dispatched someone to me with a letter."

"Leave. I advise you not to consider it any longer."

At that moment my heart was awhirl with indignation. I had no idea who was against me, who was making it impossible for me to find peace no matter where I went. I could not believe that God would single me out to treat me with such cold cruelty. Was it mere chance? Why did the evil power of circumstance look for only me to destroy? I was truly like a lone vessel without a rudder, floating on giant waves in a rolling sea. At any moment I might run against hidden rocks and sink, destroyed by violent wind and rain. Like a lamb lost deep in thorny mountains amid tigers and wildcats, I could see no way out. I could only wait for my final fate to descend.

I returned to my room, and the more I thought about the situation, the angrier I became. How could this be? Must I secretly run off without telling my students? How was this possible? No, I could not do it. I must struggle with the situation. I would not submit.

With this thought, I went to find the principal. He was talking with another colleague, and he appeared very nervous when he saw me come in. Immediately he stood up and said, "Gather your things quickly—we will see you to the ship."

"What are you saying? I will not go. If you are afraid that the school will be implicated, I can go to visit Xiamen University or Jimei to enjoy myself for a few days." I put on an angry look.

"It is not a problem for the school; it is a matter of your own safety."

Already I had reached the stage where I was no longer in charge of my decision. They treated me as if I were a thief, and they secretly took me to the steamship headed for Shanghai.

ON THE SHIP I became ill. I had a high fever; my head ached. I could not eat, only wanted to drink water. The atmosphere aboard ship was very tense because of the ongoing war and all the political turmoil, and the ship was full of special staff who carefully interrogated every passenger and inspected everyone's luggage. I feared that they might find out my real name and put me in jail. That would be just too unjust, and pointless.

My situation became more serious when I arrived in Shanghai. I saw my name listed in the paper as one of the Fujian rebels whose arrest had been ordered. This made me laugh but also made me furious. I went to see Mr. Liu Yazi. He said, "You had better quickly hide for a while. The recent situation has become very tense. Though you did not join their organization, you did participate in the resistance work of the Nineteenth Army. And you have been to Longyan. After all, you are still young. You do not understand society's many tricks. Clearly, you have been wrongly judged. At the moment there is no one who will speak reasonably with you. You cannot stay long in Shanghai. Why don't you quietly return to your native village, rest for a while, and then come out again?"*

---

*The Chinese Nineteenth Army had made a gallant attempt (which Xie Bingying has described) to defend Shanghai against the attacking Japanese in early 1933. Afterward, the Nineteenth Army was

Mr. Liu Yazi was someone who was concerned about me and took care of me. Naturally, I was willing to listen to his words.

I returned to Changsha and told my youngest brother that I planned to go to Japan to continue my studies. He was very much in favor of it. Soon afterward I carried out that plan. Meanwhile, I lived with my youngest brother's wife at Green Mountain Temple. I will never forget her kindness and consideration. She was afraid that I found it hard to bear the accusations against me, so every day she went out with me to walk, fly kites, and watch movies. She always made two or three of my favorite dishes at every meal and paid special attention to my nutrition. At that time chicken eggs were very cheap in Changsha. One yuan would buy 160 eggs and you could choose the large ones yourself. Needless to say, I ate eggs every day. Yet my body was still thin and weak. I lived an unusually quiet, satisfying, and physically comfortable life, and it was in those perfect days that I began to write my autobiography, *A Woman Soldier's Own Story*. My sister-in-law was afraid that I would overtax my brains and injure my health, so she kept thinking up different ways to amuse me. The two of us—and we were both then older than twenty—would still fly our kite, and I don't know how many people followed us and laughed at us, but we were not the least bashful. We tied the string to the back of the kite and no matter what we did it would not take off. Children would watch us and laugh loudly. They told us how to follow the wind to send the kite up, how to let loose the string, and so on. Because I did not have any financial responsibility, I felt very free and content.

Just at this time a few inconsequential small papers did their utmost to publish articles that attacked me. I still remember that one day at twilight we were upstairs keeping warm by the fire when suddenly we heard someone shouting outside, "Buy the evening newspaper! Buy the evening newspaper! Quickly read the news about Xie!"

My sister-in-law flew downstairs, bought the evening paper, and came back gasping for breath. As soon as we opened the paper, a banner headline struck my eyes: XIE BINGYING TAKES REFUGE IN HONG KONG. We then

---

transferred to Fujian Province. The army's leaders, particularly General Cai Tingkai, became dissatisfied with Chiang Kai-shek, and took steps to create an alliance with the Red Army to fight against Chiang and the Japanese. In November 1933 Cai Tingkai imposed martial law in Fujian Province. By the end of January 1934, however, Chiang and his troops had put down the rebellion.—trans.

read the small print, which was even more preposterous and false. My sister-in-law was so angry that she slammed the table. "I will find some people to help me pound this damned newspaper office into powder."

It looked as if she had reached the limit of her anger and that she must fight or else.

"Never mind. This only proves again that this newspaper is nonsense, that it only fabricates rumors. Everyone who reads the paper knows that I am living a good life in Changsha, so the plan to injure me with rumors has obviously failed. There is no need to get angry at what does not concern us."

I comforted my sister-in-law, but her anger did not disappear. She asked me angrily, "Do you mean to say that after reading this news you really are not the least angry?"

"Of course I am not angry, not in the least. I am quite used to small newspapers fabricating rumors. How else would they push the sale of their newspaper, except through such vulgar tactics?"

"You are broad-minded. You even forgive them for creating rumors. But I certainly cannot bear this sort of insult. I am going to find the person responsible."

She picked up her purse and started running downstairs. I stopped her with my hand. I told her that it was absolutely impossible for her to do any good because she would only provide them with additional news. But as long as we took no notice of them, the paper's sales would decrease day by day.

She listened to me and did not go. I pretended that I had not seen the fabricated news story. My mind was peaceful and calm as I continued with my writing.

But I never forgot my child, Little Soldier, who was growing up in poverty.* She was now already three and a half years old. My friends gave

---

*The passage beginning with this sentence and ending on page 259 is the only one in our translation that does not come from the first edition of volume 1 or volume 2 of Xie Bingying's autobiography. We include it to help complete the story of her first daughter.—trans.

me word that Qi's mother had said that she would not give the child back to me, no matter what happened, because my child was her only comfort when Qi was in prison. She told my friends, "If Bingying thinks about coming back to take the child away, I will fight her to the death."

Yet I decided that I must live with my child from then on. I truly hated to be apart from her.

ON A SNOWY MORNING, I crossed the river from Hankou to Wuchang. As I walked along a street I saw a small child wearing a red hat and a red quilted jacket that had been mended—just like the ones I had sent to my child. I knew this must be she. I hugged her. She didn't cry or smile. She only opened her two big eyes and stared at me.

"Child, I am your mother." I said, crying.

She hesitated, and then called, "Mother." But suddenly it was as if she felt that this was not right. She tried to struggle out of my arms, to run away. I held her so tightly that she almost began to cry.

Then I looked up and saw Qi's sister Yi standing next to us. She said to the child, "Little Soldier, this really is your mother."

We hired a ricksha to go to Qi's home together. I held Little Soldier on my knees. I kissed her forehead, her cheeks, her mouth, her hands.

"Dear child, why don't you recognize me? I really am your mother," I said.

"Mother, why are you not living with me?" She held on to my neck as she talked, as if she had just been awakened from a bad dream. She was very excited. She very happily patted me with her little hands and said, "Mother, take me to Shanghai—don't give me up again."

I could only nod. My eyes were full of tears. I was still holding her as we entered the door, and she also held me tightly. When Qi's mother saw us like this, she said sadly, "For the child's sake, you really should come here to live with her. This poor child is truly pitiful. She has often begged for her mother. I know Qi's temper is very bad, and perhaps he mistreated you, but you should eventually forgive him."

I didn't have words to answer her. I knew that I should have come back earlier. Yet I knew that it was impossible for me to get back with Qi. I didn't love him. How could I live with him?

I looked at the room where I had lived before. It was dark like a prison. There was only a small window, obscured by the shadow of eaves. The bed had collapsed. The table was heaped with unwashed bowls and cups. On the western wall hung a picture of me, Qi, and four other friends: I was sitting in the middle, wearing a male student's uniform, and the rest of them were standing on either side. The old lady told me that Little Soldier often climbed up onto the table to look at this picture. Hanging on a wall was a picture of Little Soldier, taken when she was three months old. She was lying naked on the table and her little body was fat, her eyes jet black. She was no longer as chubby as she was in the picture, and her face was already more beautiful. Her features were delicate, her cheeks rosy. Her voice was clear and melodious like music. Whether she was happy or angry, her voice was lovely to listen to. I had never seen such a lovable child as she.

I held her while we ate. After our meal the old lady took her out to wash her face, while I opened my suitcase and looked for the clothes I had brought her. Then Yi let me see a bunch of letters that Qi had sent to his family from prison. Yi earnestly hoped that I would make up with Qi. I read the letters in silence, filled with a million contradictory feelings.

The old lady and child had not returned. I ran out to look for them. I looked for half a day but could not find them.

I cried out, "Sister Yi, we must go look for them. Where did your mother take her in this cold weather?"

Yi answered casually, "Perhaps my mother took her to buy candy."

Despite the heavy snow, I went out again and randomly searched for them along big streets and in small alleys. Darkness fell and I still had found no trace. I felt full of anger. I hated the old lady. I thought of going to the police and reporting that this woman had kidnapped my child. But I feared making matters worse. I restrained my anger and returned to the dark house to wait.

They didn't come back.

I loudly scolded Yi, "Why is she hiding my child? What kind of a person is she that she dares to forcibly take my child? I have the right to be her guardian—who can interfere with me?"

But it was as if it had all been planned. Yi ignored my cries and uproar. Finally, she said, "Bing, don't be so angry. After all, the child will be yours. But you will have to wait until she grows up."

My breast was filled with hatred. I left that house, alone.
When will we two, mother and daughter, meet again?*

RED LEAVES IN Japan rival the beauty of cherry blossoms in spring. When I first saw those crimson, pink, orange, reddish-orange, and pale yellow leaves congregated on trees, I cried out with joy.

Hisao Honma was my professor at the Literature Research Institute of Waseda University in Tokyo. Many years earlier I had read his translation of *Trends of Thought in European Literature*. His writing was fluent and forceful, and he was one of the writers I respected most. A very cultivated scholar, he had a most sincere manner and in no way did he put on the air of being a professor. He treated the Chinese students with special courtesy. For example, if we happened to discuss the problem of the Northeast, he would always say, "Ah—this is an unfortunate incident. I hope the Northeast will soon be returned to China. Imperialism is wrong."

His wife always received us with a smile and, although she had a maid, she was not at ease unless she herself handed us the various refreshments and cups of tea. Because I was frequently in contact with Japanese people, my skill with the language improved day by day. I began to learn how to translate novels, which, because of their numerous dialects and their complicated grammar, I considered far more difficult to translate than essays. My plan was to study the Japanese language diligently for several years in Tokyo. I would then introduce China to the complete works of the writers I most respected—writers such as Tolstoy, Dickens, Romain Rolland, and Balzac—by translating their works from Japanese to Chinese. I did not have a firm enough foundation in English to translate from the English, so I was forced to take this comparatively easier route. The Tokyo publishing world was very current: no matter what the famous book might be, a translation would be out within two weeks after it was shipped to Tokyo. And the books were very cheap. No wonder so many people, especially the literati, came from abroad to study in Tokyo.

---

*Xie Bingying met her daughter, Fu Bing, in Guilin when the child was thirteen. The young girl refused to go away with her mother. Fu Bing died in Beijing in 1966. She was thirty-six.—trans.

During this period I spent my time, day and night, studying Japanese writings and speaking the Japanese language. Mr. Yoshio at the language school often said, "You are studying so hard that I guarantee within two years you will finish your study and return to your country."

Who could have guessed that before I could finish my studies I would be falsely charged and made a prisoner in the Muhei Police Station?

WHO WOULD HAVE IMAGINED this? Quite unexpectedly, I was sitting in a Japanese prison.

The moment I mention this topic I feel bitterness and hatred, for as a result of the cruelties I suffered in Japanese prison, my head now throbs—throbs as if it is being hit by a hammer—every time I write more than one or two thousand words or read an hour too long. What makes me angrier still is that from that moment on my memory began to deteriorate. Suddenly I found myself unable to recall names of friends, and when I tried to write the previous day's events in my diary, I could not even remember what had happened.

On the evening of April 12, 1935, I had just returned home from the house of Yasuzumi Takeda, who had given me an extra lesson in Japanese. Suddenly, I was arrested by the police and taken to the police station in Muhei District. Even before this happened I had been questioned two or three times by detectives who had come to ask me whether I would be able to go to welcome Puyi on the day he arrived in Tokyo.* I felt this was too insulting. What a thing was Puyi? Only a traitor who was spit on and cursed by all the Chinese people. Why would I go to welcome him?

"Not only will I not go to welcome him, but I fundamentally oppose him and I do not recognize the 'Manchurian Nation.'"

My words, naturally, only induced in them feelings of resentment for me and increased their hatred for me. So on that evening a car took me to the ice-cold prison.

---

*The Japanese had convinced the twenty-five-year-old Puyi, the last emperor of the Qing dynasty, that they would restore him to power by making him "chief executive" of a new independent state called Manchukuo in the Chinese province of Manchuria.—trans.

Though I spent only three weeks in prison, to me it felt longer than three years. I suffered every possible insult and pain. With a round post as wide as a rice bowl, they struck my head as if they wanted to beat my brains out. They also inserted three square bamboo sticks between the four fingers of my right hand and pressed with such force that the joints of my bones were almost broken, and several times the pain knocked me unconscious. Yet even then they would not quit. I described all these experiences in detail in my book *Inside Japanese Prison*, and I do not wish to repeat them here.*

But here I do want to especially mention one thing: the Japanese militarists confiscated eight years of diaries that I had written every day without fail. They also refused to return many of my precious photos and manuscripts. I will never forget this tragically painful scar—just as I will forever remember my hatred for them.

THE JAPANESE IMPERIALISTS not only wantonly propagandized my imprisonment in every newspaper in their own country but let the news travel to Shanghai, saying that I was such and such. There was no mention of my patriotism. Instead, they willfully charged me with being a reactionary who would be put to death. As a result, every paper in Shanghai also published this news. Many of my friends read it and became anxious for me, worrying that my life was in danger. Later, the consulate and the office for supervision of overseas students sent deputies to bail me out, after they had received a telegram from Mr. Liu Yazi. That was when I was released.

When I came out of the prison I lived in the Japanese-Chinese Literary Society, an espionage agency organized by Japanese militarists and Chinese traitors. My movements were still being watched and I did not have the least freedom. Luckily, Shigeko Takenaka sympathized with me and helped me quickly escape the tiger's mouth and return to the bosom of my motherland.

But Shanghai, at that time, was not a place I could stay long. A group of people there did not sympathize with my mishap, did not understand that

---

*Inside Japanese Prison (Shanghai: Far East Books, 1940).—trans.

I was in jail for my patriotism, and looked at me as if I were an enemy on the same level as the Japanese militarists. So I could only leave Shanghai quickly and return, by way of Hong Kong, to Guilin, where I rested for a while at my third brother's place.

I SPENT A very comfortable summer vacation in Guilin. In July 1935 I received a telegram and a contract from the Nanning Senior Middle School.* I left Guilin unwillingly and resumed making my livelihood with the chalk.

At Nanning Senior Middle School I was responsible for teaching the fifteenth and sixteenth classes of Chinese literature. Miss Chen Chuheng and I lived in two rooms on the upper floor of a small two-story building. From our window we could see a wide field where once several families with leprosy had lived, before the police had chased them away and burned down their houses. Often when I felt lonesome I would push open the windows and stare at the neatly lined electricity poles, until I could not see any more of them. There was also a small forest with several ancient trees so proud and dignified and towering that it made a person want to worship them as they rose straight up toward heaven. Perhaps they were related to evergreens, for I never saw any fallen leaves. No sooner was it twilight than a group of crows would congregate on the branches, calling *cha-cha* endlessly. Other than these things, I could see only numerous grave mounds covered with dense and dying grass. Every few days there would suddenly be a new grave, and when I heard the crying of the relatives of the deceased, my heart would be moved to play a similar sad tune and my tears would fall.

Living in that sort of lonely and desolate environment, I was lucky that young men and women often came to talk with me and discuss their problems. Otherwise, I would perhaps have been as lifeless as if living in a grave.

The women of Guangxi Province were lovable, and their fortitude in enduring hardship made a person admire them greatly. The coolies I saw

---

*Nanning, about four hundred miles west of Hong Kong, is the capital of Guangxi Province in southeastern China.—trans.

at the harbor of Wuzhou were all women. Some wore straw shoes; some were barefoot. They all wore wide rain hats with pointed tops. Their hands grasped the flat carrying pole as on their shoulders they effortlessly carried loads weighing one hundred or two hundred pounds. They walked so fast that even a rider in a ricksha could not overtake them. They not only were financially independent but supported their entire families. Many husbands of these women would hide at home and not go out all year. The good ones would help their wives by taking care of the children; the bad ones only lay in bed all day, leading the opium life of swallowing clouds and breathing out mists. Contrary to expectation, the women did not complain at all, just lowered their heads and worked like cows and horses. Truly, they were a rare sort of people.

Because the female laborers had made such a wonderful impression on me, I wanted to be close to all the women in Guangxi Province, and naturally the female students became my favorites. Having been so often with children, I was easily able to turn myself into a child, and on the second day after a Miss Hu came to visit me from Hong Kong, she and I went to the exercise field to use the swings. Some of my students were there, and I told them that when I was little I had loved to swing more than anything else. I had just finished talking when I stood up on the swing to pump hard and swing high—and suddenly my two hands let go of the large ropes and my body lightly floated toward the sky. Then I fell and knew nothing. When I had somewhat recovered my senses, I could hear Hu calling by my ear, "You wake up, you wake up, quickly open your eyes and look at me." The students also said, "Teacher, Teacher, wake up quickly, you cannot die."

I would have very much liked to have opened my eyes and looked at them and to have told them that I had not died, but my eyes would not open no matter what, and my mouth would not make a sound, and I could not tell them what I wanted to say. I heard continuous cries of *wu-wu* in my ears, and I was afraid that I had suddenly changed into a deaf mute—wouldn't that be a mess?

After a little while my brain again lost all sensation and I slept as if I were a dead person. They later told me that my entire body had been ice cold for more than ten minutes. When they revived me, I slowly became clearheaded. Yet for several days my head was so dizzy that I was unable to get out of bed. After I had recovered sufficiently, I forced myself to go and teach my classes. But when I wrote one word on the blackboard, it would suddenly become two words, and two words would become countless words. When I was correcting students' compositions in the evening, my head would become dizzy and my eyes would become blurred even before I had finished the fourth booklet. Then I could not continue.

After I had recuperated at the provincial hospital for a week, I was much better, but I still could not teach my classes. I had no alternative but to ask my third brother to substitute for me.

All this was the result of the tortures I had suffered in Japan. My heart ached and I was filled with anger. I cannot forgive the wickedness of the Japanese militarists. I will risk my life to oppose them as long as I live.

THOUGH MY FRIENDS in Nanning affectionately asked me to remain, and though my lovable students were determined not to allow me to leave them, I was concerned about my health. I loaded the editorial responsibilities of *Guangxi Women's Weekly* onto Wenlan's shoulders and, carrying the emotions of a regretful farewell in my bosom, I left my lonesome little dwelling, left my third brother and his wife, and again returned to Changsha.

Perhaps I had suffered too many blows, for my body was indeed getting worse day by day. During this time I put my *Hunan's Wind* in order for publication, and I, in one breath, completed the first volume of *A Woman Soldier's Own Story*, which I had promised the Liangyou Publishing Company.

I was now living in a room with plenty of sunlight and fresh air at Miaogao Peak. As a rule, I wrote for at least four hours every day, and sometimes I wrote for six hours. I put all my emotion into my writing: smiles would float in the corners of my mouth when I wrote about happy events, and tears would involuntarily drop from my eyes when I wrote about sad things.

At this time Big Sister Tie returned from Tianjin. She had spent four full years in prison. When she went in she had a big belly, and when she came out the child was already almost four years old.

"Because my child, Sha, had never in her whole life seen trolleys or automobiles, she was actually terrified and cried when she first came in contact with these things on the street. Another funny thing was that we had gotten used to eating black steamed buns while we were in prison, and when she saw white rice she refused to eat it, no matter what."

Big Sister Tie and I had been schoolmates at the First Provincial Girls Teacher Training School. Though she had not had any formal education, she still was accepted into the school. Needless to say, her great effort, determination, and fortitude helped her. She was more than thirty years old, so both male and female schoolmates called her Big Sister Tie. She had been accepted into the military school by passing the entrance test, but because she opposed taking the second exam, she was, unfortunately, expelled.

She was an extraordinary person and, if she had received more education, would certainly have made a big contribution to society. She performed her tasks with vigor and determination. She was not afraid of difficulty, danger, or failure. In her mind, it was as if there were no tasks under the sky that could not be accomplished as long as one had determination and unflagging energy. Average people, with the stunted ideas of a village schoolmaster hunkering over his stove in winter, all jeered at her and called her a monstrosity, but she was completely indifferent to all this.

"So what if I am a strange creature?" she would say. "Anyway, I will not surrender to outside pressure."

I really never imagined that Big Sister Tie, who was so full of vitality, would at last become downhearted and wither away. All day, taking her daughter, Sha, with her, she led the life of a peddler, selling cigarettes, seeds, and peanuts. Her husband, who had been a minor socialist leader, no longer sang the high tunes of democracy and emancipation. He objected to Big Sister Tie for being too old and ugly, and he often struck and kicked her. Finally, he abandoned her because he wanted to find a younger and more beautiful woman. This blow almost made Big Sister Tie want to stop living. I heard later that she became blind. No one knows whether she is still among the mortals of this world, but in the memories of her friends her image will remain forever.

IN THE WINTER of 1936 my mother had a stroke. I received a telegram and returned home to see her. She was lying on the cane chair by the door, gazing out. Her tears began to flow as soon as she saw me.

"Child, you have come back."

At once I rushed to embrace her, and I grasped her two hands tightly.

"I cannot move. My right hand and right foot are already paralyzed. I have become an invalid. If you had not come back, perhaps you would not ever have seen Ma again."

Her tears swelled. Quickly I pulled out a handkerchief and wiped her eyes dry, and I put into her hand a package of candy.

"Give them to the others to eat, my teeth are gone," Mother said, suffering.

I had not seen her in four years. She was indeed much older and grayer. Seeing how she looked, with half her body paralyzed, I felt indescribable sorrow. It was true: Mother had become crippled. She, who so loved to work, was suddenly living a life of total dependence on others. So of course she was depressed.

Our past alienation was now completely forgotten. She constantly showed extraordinary motherly love, inquiring in detail about my recent circumstances, never mentioning a word about the past. She wanted me to bring back all my published works for her to read. Often she would caress my head and face with her good left hand. Unfortunately, after barely a week I again left her and went back to Changsha.

When I received a telegram for the second time saying that Mother was ill and in danger, I hurried home during the night. She was lying on the bed, already unable to speak. I held back my tears as I knelt beside her on the bed. I could hear a very feeble sound coming from her throat: "Child, you have returned."

Then two bright, bean-size tears rolled down her face. My sister and I started to cry too, but we quickly wiped dry our tears, for Mother would be heartbroken if she saw us weeping.

I asked the cause of her illness.

My third sister-in-law said what had happened was very peculiar: "Three evenings ago, at about midnight, we suddenly heard Mama crying loudly, 'Come quickly! You come quickly!' I was staying in the next room, so I right away got up and ran to her. Mama's entire forehead was sweating profusely, and she grabbed me with one hand and said, 'Terrible! Terrible! An old man with a very long beard came to grab me. I did not want to go, but he insisted on dragging me away. I called you but you did not answer. Oh! I'm finished! Finished!' After she spoke these words, Mama sighed a long sigh and then she was mute. Since then she has been unable to speak."

It was as if I were listening to a myth. I could not believe that such strange things actually happened in this world, but it was a fact that Mother could not speak. We invited a doctor to stay in our home to treat her, but even then we did not see any improvement. Her illness became more and more serious from one day to the next, and my heart was getting more and more anxious.

I did not leave Mother day or night for a whole week. During the day I sat by her side and waited on her and fed her soup and medicine. At night I took her temperature and her pulse every half hour, and I recorded everything in a small book. Once, when Mother had to urinate in the middle of the night, she suddenly touched my face and said, "Child, you have grown thin." Then she asked, "Is your third brother back yet?"

If I had not watched her lips move, I would not have been able to make out what she was saying. I had thought she would be better soon, but from then on her illness worsened. On the next day she suddenly sat up and used hand gestures to ask Father to sit on her bed. At the same time she pointed to my fountain pen and, with much effort, she uttered a very, very small sound: "Write."

Father thought for a moment and then—as if suddenly he understood her—he said, "Rest your mind. The land for Minggang has already been recorded. It definitely will be given to her."

Mother nodded. She affectionately kissed my face, and then she made known that she wanted Father to come near her. Father only gave her his hand, and Mother kissed it. Then she lay down.

Mother's illness became more and more perilous. Her pulse grew fainter and fainter, and her temperature was lower every time I measured it. I touched Mother's legs and they were like two ice pillars. Though I had not watched a person die before, I knew Mother's life would soon end. Quietly, I told my big brother and my sister not to leave her on any account. But what were we to do about my third brother? The telegram had been sent ten days earlier and still we saw no sign of him. Was the transportation in Guangxi really this slow? I held Mother's hand tightly and watched her eyes. Her hands gradually became freezing cold, her eyelids opened and closed, and there was an unceasing *hu-lu, hu-lu* sound in her throat. I saw on Mother's face a most painful expression. Quickly, I asked Father to go and sit in the reception room, and he asked me, "What do you mean?"

I replied, "There are too many people in this room. The air is not good and it could be harmful to Mother." At the same time I told him that my third brother was coming back that night and that we should let Mother have a good rest.

"Why did your mother's illness suddenly become worse?" he asked, suspiciously. He did not want to leave the room.

"She is not so bad. She was worse last night. I am used to seeing how she looks. You have not seen her at her worst, to make a comparison. I know there is no danger. Please, Father, go to the reception room to rest a little."

Since Mother had become ill, Father and my sister's husband had been sleeping in the reception room. After he heard what I said, he went to sleep. I asked my sister to bring in all the rest of the family to sit by Mother's side. My heart hurt as if it had been cut by a knife. I knew that in a split second Mother's life would melt from my arms. I held her tightly and would not let loose. The *hu-lu, hu-lu* sound became more and more urgent, and the color of her face became more and more miserably white. I touched her body to check for warmth; already she was cold to her belly. My tears suddenly poured out like the rushing tide, but I turned my face away so Mother would not see me. My sister and sister-in-law finally let out their cries, but I stopped them instantly with a stern face and severe words, "You must not cry. Ma will be better very soon."

As if she understood my words, Mother opened her eyes. She gazed at us and extended three fingers, meaning to ask if third brother had returned. I answered her, "Ma, my third brother has returned."

Her eyes swept all around the room, and then she deeply sighed and shook her head twice to show that she did not believe me. My heart sank.

Mother's expression was becoming more painful to watch, and her breathing sounded more urgent and mournful. It broke my heart to see how she was struggling with death. Finally, I could not bear it and began to cry out loud. This time my uncle gave us stern orders to stop. Seeing how Mother was suffering, my big brother said loudly, "Ma, Third Brother might not be back tonight. If you are unable to wait, then rest your heart and depart."

He had just finished speaking when Mother opened her eyes to look at us. Then she deeply sighed a long sigh and closed her eyes forever in a deep sleep. Immediately, two tears flowed from the corners of her eyes.

I was shattered. So Mother's life had ended like this. During sixty years she had lived days of weariness, distress, and bustle. Now her sons and daughters were all grown up, and this should have been a time for her to live a few comfortable days. Who would have thought that her life would be so cruelly snatched away by an unfeeling creator? How can I describe my grief?

Right after Mother died, my uncle said that she was exactly like someone sleeping and we should not make noise that would disturb her. He did not allow us to cry. He alone chanted softly in grief, "Amida, Amida, Amida Buddha Amida . . ."

He burned paper money as he chanted; the light of the fire shone on Mother's kind face. She looked as if she were sleeping in peace. I tightly held her ice-cold hand—I wanted to snatch back her life. I blamed my eldest brother for having said such cruel words, for if Mother's life were extended for even one more minute, it would have meant another minute's blessing for her children. My tears dropped on Mother's body. Uncle dragged me away. At this moment pitiful Father still was waiting in the parlor for my third brother to return. When I told Father the dreadful news, he wailed and wept bitterly, as if he did not want to live.

Aye! I did not do right by my father and even less by my mother. Why was I so stupid and so cruel? I clearly knew that Mother's death was near. Why didn't I let Father see her? I was concerned only that Father would find it difficult to bear if he watched Mother stop breathing. I did not think how this was going to be the eternal farewell between the affectionate husband and wife. I should have let Father escort her to the end.

From then on I became a motherless orphan. I would never again receive the tender love of my mother. In the past I had not done right by Mother. Now I could only kneel before Mother's soul and weep tears of repentance and pray for her repose in the underworld beneath the Nine Springs.

After Mother's death the faces of all of us in the family were covered with masks of grief. Each time I saw the sad and bitter expression on my old father's teary face, my heart ached and my tears poured like rain.

At night, under a vegetable-oil lamp, relatives and I silently kept company with Mother's body. Our neighbors, men and women, all came to mourn her, to cry, to speak of Mother's goodness, of her virtues, of her contributions to the village.

Mother! Your body has left this world. Your soul will live forever in people's hearts.

PART 10 Days of War

I RETURNED TO CHANGSHA AND I IMMEDIATELY BEGAN MOBILIZING women to assist injured soldiers at the front line. My program was no sooner announced in the newspaper than many nurses and female students got in touch with me—and thus the Hunan Women's War Zone Service Corps was established in four days flat.

We all wore gray military uniforms, bound our legs in puttees, and provided our own green shoes and socks. We received no official support for this project because some people said women should work only behind the lines, at home. We, on the contrary, seized the opportunity to rush to the front lines. In fact, everywhere in China women were beginning to mobilize.

Changsha roared with anger. Every night the radio broadcast war reports and heroic marches. Many groups donated flags to us, and the women workers at the long-distance telephone company helped us raise money. The number of requests to join the women's service corps were increasing day by day. I alone had all the responsibility for organizing this group, but I really did not have the resources to accommodate many people.

How can I possibly describe my excitement? I went almost crazy when at two o'clock one afternoon I received the news that we could set forth at four o'clock. I felt that sitting in a ricksha would be too slow, so I combined three steps into one and quickly walked back to Chuyingyuan, where I instructed several of our corps members to split up and find those comrades who did not know that we were setting out. To my surprise, we were able to locate sixteen people before four o'clock. Several women lived so far away that we could not notify them, so we could only leave them behind.

I was overwhelmed with happiness. It had been a full ten years since I had taken off my uniform, and during all that time not a day had passed that I did not remember the meaningful and satisfying life I had lived in those army days, and not a day had passed that I did not long for that life, so full of hardship and tragedy, yet so very pleasant and amusing as one marched with the troops. I never believed that I would actually be able to relive that dream of ten years earlier. I was able not only to put on my military uniform and set off once more for war but, single-handedly, to bring sixteen young women to the front. This would be a day for me to feel honored, glorious.

I walked at the very front of our group, holding the corps flag high. As seventeen of us loudly sang songs of war and resistance, all the people along the road turned to look at us. Children and many students returning home from school followed us and joined us in singing and in shouting the slogan "Down with Japanese imperialism! Long live the people of the liberated Chinese nation!" The entire city of Changsha was stirred with emotion by us women soldiers. When we arrived at the train station we were hemmed in on all sides by a huge crowd. Soon a large troop of soldiers arrived, and we again raised our voices and sang even louder. News reporters arrived in a rush, took photos, did interviews, kept us all very busy. We held a simple but powerful ceremony in which we took our oath to fight the enemies in the North. Suddenly, a few minutes before the train was about ready to move, an old man with a full head of white hair came up to me and said, "I am Fu Enping's father. I am old and cannot go to serve at the battlefield, so I am handing my daughter over to you to take to the front line. You must urge her to work hard at all times. And if she should be injured, or die, I will not be sad. I will feel proud." He then turned his face to his left and said to his daughter, "Enping, remember my words. I will not feel anxious about you. And you need not feel anxious about me. I can read news about the front line in the newspaper every day. So you need not write to me. If only you can protect and nurse the many injured soldiers, I will receive great comfort."

We were all moved. We applauded his speech.

WE BEGAN OUR train journey at two o'clock in the morning on September 14. We arrived in Anting at five-thirty on the morning of the nineteenth. As we got off the train, we each carried a simple backpack. We followed the troops to the mountain ridge outside Jiading. That evening the army at the firing line began to fight and we began our work in the field hospital.*

Because we had to adapt ourselves to army life and to the battlefield environment, our group sacrificed individual freedoms and submitted ourselves to strict military regulations, written in iron:

1. Sacrifice all; fight to the finish.
2. Work with dedication and energy.
3. Live and die with our soldiers, sharing their sweetness and pain.

Though none of our corps members had lived the army life before, all bore the hardship and followed the rules. I divided them into four sections, each with a commander and three members. I sent sections 1 and 2 to serve at the field hospital of the Fifty-ninth Division, sections 3 and 4 to serve at the field hospital of the Ninetieth Division.

In the first two days there weren't many injured soldiers, so we set up a work schedule by dividing the day and night into three shifts: the night shift was six hours and the two day shifts were nine hours each. While we were on each shift our duties changed every three hours. But on the third day the

---

*Xie Bingying arrived at Anting, on the outskirts of Shanghai, on September 19, 1937, and then marched to Jiading, about ten miles away. Two months earlier, far to the north, the July 7 incident at the Marco Polo Bridge near Beijing had touched off war between China and Japan. By the end of July, Japan controlled the entire Beijing–Tianjin area. Chiang Kai-shek decided to mount an offensive farther south. On August 14 his air force bombed Japanese warships at anchor in Shanghai. Though Chinese troops initially outnumbered the Japanese in the Shanghai region, Japan sent reinforcements. Chiang had ordered his troops to prevail over the Japanese at any cost, but they were unable to do so. The Chinese lost 250,000 troops. They began their westward retreat toward Nanjing on November 11. By the time Xie Bingying arrived in the war zone in mid-September, the Chinese were already on the defensive and fighting a losing battle.—trans.

number of injured soldiers brought back from the front lines suddenly began to swell. Now they were lying crowded together in every room and even on the steps and in the central courtyard. Each injured soldier shrank his body and huddled. Sometimes on the leg of a slightly injured soldier lay the head of a man severely wounded. We had to step carefully over the bodies when we went to give them medicine or change their bandages. Some had legs or arms severed by explosions. Others had lost half their brains in bomb blasts. Some had been hit in the stomach by machine guns and their small intestines were spilling out. Some had bullets still lodged in their flesh, and they cried out day and night from the pain. Some were missing two-thirds of the skin and flesh on their thighs. Some had wounds in which multitudes of maggots grew. Some had only a single tendon left in their hands.

Blood. The soldiers' fresh blood flowed from the trenches to the wilderness, from the wilderness to the roads, from the roads to the field hospital. Now we did not distinguish night from day. We lived and worked each twenty-four hours in a bloody pool. At first we felt very uncomfortable when our hands were stained with blood, so we washed whenever it was time to eat. Later, with the blood of more and more injured soldiers dripping on our shoes and our clothes, and smeared all over our hands, we not only were unafraid of blood but regarded it as a badge of honor. Sometimes in slapdash fastion we used only a little cotton soaked in alcohol to wipe our blood-dripping hands before we held up our rice bowls to eat. During that period the food we ate and the water we drank all seemed to carry the smell of blood, yet no one's appetite decreased because of it. On the contrary, we ate more than usual. Because of the increasing urgency of our work, and because Japanese planes were bombing all day long, we did not dare make a fire to cook food during the day. After eating at dawn we went without food until seven or eight o'clock in the evening, when we would have our second meal. And sometimes we ate only one meal a day.

As for our relief work, we held this belief: "Saving one soldier is like killing one enemy." Though we could not carry guns and go directly to the firing line to risk ourselves in battle, we were able to wash, bandage, and apply remedies to the wounds of our soldiers. We poured boiled water for them to drink and we gave them food to eat. We used gentle words to comfort them and stimulating and heroic words to encourage them. We wrote letters to their families for them, and we searched for used clothes to shield them from the cold. We solicited and collected newspapers and books for them to read, and we told them all the current news.

Whomever we treated on the battlefield, officer or soldier, we felt close to him and he to us. Even those few wounded soldiers who were bad tempered did not care to vent their complaints, for we were gentle with them—unlike the male ambulance corps members, who washed wounds rather heavy-handedly and who, if an injured soldier cried out in pain, would stiffly say, "What are you shouting about? Do you know how many have died?"

Our women offered sympathy and comfort, saying, "Comrade, try to stand the pain—it is only for a moment, and soon you will be well. You have suffered honorably for our country, our race. When you are healthy let us hope you can attack the enemy again. . . ."

We often listened to the soldiers tell stories about the war, and as they talked—with great intensity and earnestness—they would forget their pain and distress and hunger. They slept on straw soaked with fresh blood, and sometimes they ate only one meal of rice gruel a day. Yet they did not grumble.

AT FIRST OUR prime goal was to nurse and save soldiers. Later we noticed another need that we could help meet. Civilians in the war zone had not organized themselves to resist. Some of them, on the ridge outside the city, even asked us, "What country are you from?" Perhaps they had simply never received any information from the outside world. They knew nothing about this war of resistance or about why we were fighting the Japanese. We noticed that our own people were being turned into traitors by our enemies, and we saw that we must hurry up and get them organized or the future would be unthinkable.

So I dispatched twelve corps members to work regularly with the Bureau of Instruction at the Ministry of War. In addition, our whole group joined together to go out and inform the people whenever we had a spare moment from our nursing duties. At first our method was to go from door to door, speaking with people individually. We began our visits with conversations about their daily life, and afterward we talked about the terrors of the enemy's planes and huge cannons, and about how cruel the enemy's burning and killing policies were, and how our soldiers were bravely fighting the war of resistance, and how the civilian population should collaborate with the military and help it gain a victory over the enemy—for only then (we said) would our people be able to live in peace, content with their labors. At day's end we always met to examine and critique the work we had done that day. We discussed the tough problems we had encountered, and we gave individual reports on the effects of our propaganda. We also decided on the locations and methods of operation for the following day.

Our organization gradually expanded. Four new comrades from Shanghai and one from Suzhou rushed to join us. They were able to speak the local dialect, so our work progressed even more smoothly. Ordinary village people hid from male soldiers but not from us women, so we were able to give considerable help to the military without having planned it. For example, each time the army arrived at a new destination, tasks such as hiring coolies, hiring boats, finding lodgings, and borrowing necessary items were ones we women easily accomplished after we had explained things to the local people.

ON THE BATTLEFIELD we drank muddy yellow water from the creek, ate coarse rice and cold food, and wore single-layered shirts and trousers. We used thin bedcovers donated by the Shanghai Women's Service Corps. We slept on the floor of a freezing parlor invaded by the north wind, on damp bedding. Even so, our life was extraordinarily happy. Our group of young women, accustomed to living comfortable lives, did not feel the least distressed. When they were ill, they were surrounded by nurses. When they were cold, seven or eight people crowded into a pile. When the cistern was empty, they carried the water with a pole on their shoulders. When the furnace was out of brushwood, they collected wood. As for washing clothes and sweeping floors and cooking meals, these were daily duties that they all performed. We had many talents among us. Two of us knew how to cut hair; three could sew; five could cook tasty dishes; some liked to write old-style or modern poetry; some wrote novels or acted in plays or sang songs. Our lives were filled with joy.

When it was time to work, everyone lowered her head and worked hard.

No one let slip her responsibility, even slightly. If a corps member was found to be negligent in her work, or failing to fulfill her responsibilities, or if she was heavy-handed while washing the wounds of an injured soldier, or if she talked to a soldier in a coarse voice and not in a gentle manner, then she would immediately be criticized by other corps members. In the meetings where we critiqued ourselves and our work, we did not stand on ceremony. We sternly examined and discussed everyone's words and actions. Sometimes the criticisms were so excessive that they actually made someone cry. But we did not treat this colleague leniently, just because she had cried. Instead, we reprimanded her, saying, "Revolutionaries do not shed tears, only blood."

When our work was finished we all either read books or wrote diaries. We looked upon the battlefield as if it were our own home, and so we calmly passed our days.

Then came the night of November 12—a moment I shall never forget, for it was when we received orders to leave Jiading. On the previous day the local officers in charge of several organizations—the division for maintaining public order, the divisional office of instruction, the reserves, and the schools in the war zone—had held a joint conference with our four war-zone service corps to discuss practical problems of collaboration between the military and civilians and to establish an office of joint affairs. Unfortunately, just a day later we had to leave those lovable civilians who had been baptized by our propaganda and the place so blessed with our fighters' blood and flesh.

We followed the military medical unit and retreated with our injured soldiers to Suzhou, where we encountered three days and nights of severe bombing. We went out every day to nurse the wounded and never stopped working. We changed their dressings; we cooked their meals; we boiled their drinking water. We had absolutely no wish to leave them and retreat to a safer place, even though the head of the military medical unit asked us several times to retreat to Wuxi.

At this time Suzhou had become an extremely nervous and terrified city; it was preparing for war. The public roads were jammed with thousands of withdrawing troops. Many injured soldiers lay on public roads and helplessly waited for the moment when enemy planes would come and bombard them, for they could not find a hospital or their own military medical units.

Everywhere were corpses of soldiers and civilians who had been killed by bombing. All the shops were closed, so nothing could be bought, and food had become a big problem. The situation was getting more critical by the moment. The military medical unit again received orders to retreat to Wuxi. There we stopped for two days before we had to retreat to Changzhou.

My spirits were extremely low. Ever since we had set out for the front we had prayed each day for victory. We wanted only to follow the troops and move forward—who could be happy about retreating?

On the night we arrived at Changzhou, I suddenly heard news that the second group of the Hunan Women's War Zone Service Corps had arrived. I immediately went to look for them. Along the road I met an assistant officer from the Ministry of War, who said, "Regiment Commanding Officer Liu has already returned to Hankou, and ten of the corps members left last night for Wuxi to look for you."

I was dumbstruck. I had just come from Wuxi that morning. We had missed each other on the road. Fearing that they would hurry back to Changzhou—which we had again received orders to withdraw from—I could only return to Wuxi that afternoon to look for them. I asked the military commander to tell us the policy on advancing or retreating and to give me the work assignments for the new corps members.

Braving wild wind and lashing rain, I returned to Wuxi alone, riding on a military vehicle. There I found those ten innocent little sisters. They were still thinking about going to Suzhou—which by then had already been occupied by the enemy. The military commander immediately gave Officer Xue one hundred yuan to be used for sending my new group home. As for the original corps members, he suggested that we return to Hankou and serve in the hospital at the home front. He said we could go to the front lines later, after the troops were put in order.

Naturally, I did not wish to accept this order. Though we were forced to leave Wuxi that night, I still hoped to bivouac in Changzhou, especially since there seemed to be hope of returning soon to Suzhou and Jiading. What I did not know was that even as I was arriving in Changzhou, my entire corps had already left for Zhenjiang. I waited for a day, finally managed to find a vehicle, and hurried toward Zhenjiang. Fortunately, I met them on the road. Finally, our group was united except for three members who were still working for the Bureau of Instruction in the Sixtieth Division. All this had made me very anxious and impatient, not knowing where everyone had gone as they followed the troops.

From Jiading we retreated to Nanjing, and our sorry plight while in retreat was indescribable. While we had fought a winning war, the army had treated us excellently, securing vehicles and boats for us and finding coolies to help us carry our bags. Our spirits had been inflamed; our bodies, healthy. But when it was time to retreat, we had to travel night and day, carrying all our own things, and we had trouble finding food to eat, trouble finding places to stay. In addition, every service organization felt that women were tiresome burdens and that we would be an impediment if we moved on with the troops. They all hoped that we would quickly retire to the rear, but we were unwilling to leave the wounded soldiers—more than one hundred of them—who were retreating with us. We never imagined that we would not be allowed to stay for even a few days in Nanjing. The same day that we arrived there we were hurriedly crowded onto the dispatch ship *Jiangan* and set sail for Hankou.*

On board the ship we crowded into piles of three and lay by the side of a narrow corridor. People stepped over our bodies endlessly, day and night, and sometimes in the middle of the night someone stepped on us and hurt our heads or feet. We could not buy food, and no use even talking about buying boiled water. One day, with great difficulty, we managed to buy some rice, which we put in a wash basin and divided among ourselves. We did not wash our faces for three or four days. We arrived in Hankou looking like refugees.

WHEN I RETURNED to Hankou, many schools and civilian groups asked me to give speeches. I remember that when I gave a speech called "Return-

---

*Nanjing is 150 miles west of Jiading. They sailed from Nanjing down the Yangzi to Hankou, 290 miles southwest as the crow flies, along a stretch of river that Xie Bingying had traveled in the opposite direction in 1928 when she and Aizhen sailed from Hankou to Shanghai.

About a month after Xie Bingying passed through Nanjing, the Japanese entered the city and inflicted on the populace an inferno of horror that has seldom been equaled in history. As many as twenty thousand women were raped repeatedly, many until they died. More than forty thousand civilians and fleeing soldiers were murdered. Fires and general destruction reduced much of the city to ruins.—trans.

ing from the Front Line" at Zhonghua University, not only was every corner of the large auditorium jammed with people standing but even the space under the platform was crammed with people. They quietly listened to the true stories written with our soldiers' blood. When I finished speaking, I could not press my way through the crowd, so I let them carry me out.

Many young girls came to the Women's Association to look for me and to ask to join our corps. But because so many troops had died from wounds, we followed the order to shrink our group. Some of the original corps members were being transferred to other army corps. Naturally, we could not add members. But for these girls, learning this was a big shock.

I had lived on the battlefield for more than two months, and my spirits were unbearably weary. Just at this time the *Xinmin News* insisted that I come help out, and I had no alternative but to agree to go to Chongqing to edit a short-term supplementary edition called *Blood Tide*.*

I had trouble getting accustomed to life as it was lived on the home front. When I smelled the perfumed hair of the modern women, I would think of the rank odor of blood on the front line. When I passed a tavern or a restaurant and heard the noises of those inside drinking and playing games, I would think of the soldiers lying in the field hospital, bleeding and moaning. I knew that cultural work on the home front was important, perhaps as important as the tasks on the front line in this war of resistance, yet I wanted to return to the front simply because doing so was satisfying to my spirit. There were too many writers on the home front, too few who participated in work for the military. My third brother was in the fifth war zone, and he had sent a telegram asking me to go there to work. I did not hesitate. I went directly to Xuzhou.†

My arrival coincided with the big victory at Taierzhuang, and more than twenty Chinese and foreign reporters were gathered there.‡ The prizes of war that had been captured by our army were heaped like a hill. Every soldier and every civilian was jubilant, and each face overflowed with joy. We inspected the battlefield, stepped on our soldiers' bloody traces, and felt

---

*Chongqing is about 480 miles southwest of Hankou.—trans.

†Xuzhou is a town about 320 miles northwest of Shanghai.—trans.

‡In April 1938 Li Zongren, one of Chiang Kai-shek's generals, lured the Japanese army into a trap at Taierzhuang, killing about thirty thousand Japanese troops.—trans.

both sad and satisfied when we saw the provision boxes, leather shoes, and bullets left behind by the Japanese as they retreated while alley fighting. During this time I wrote a large number of essays that were collected in my books *The Soldier's Hand, At the Firing Line, New War Diary,* and *Notes in the Army.**

Unfortunately, the enemy soon counterattacked and our weapons were not as good as theirs. Many of our men died from their wounds. Our reinforcements were delayed because of transportation problems. A month later, Taierzhuang, famous in the history of this war, fell again into enemy hands.

Filled with sorrow and disappointment, we followed the troops and returned to Hankou. I rested for only a few days, and then again returned to Changsha to solicit donations for the Association for Child Care. Luckily, I met the dean of internal medicine at Xiangya Hospital, Dr. Yang Qishi, and we made use of two months during the summer vacation to organize another war zone service corps. He wanted me to be the corps' guide, and I brought the members to Xishui, a small town that had already been bombed to bits.† By then my third sister-in-law had put on a military uniform and joined the war effort. And my brother-in-law and niece, Sufang, had also gone to the front.

Of the original service corps members, only Luo Peilan joined me. We resumed our work of assisting the wounded. We were close to the front line and the enemy planes bombed us all day long. Every day more people were injured by bombs and were waiting for us to nurse them. The population of Xishui was thankful to the Xiangya Ambulance Corps, and they even gave Dr. Yang a very large plaque on which was written, in large characters, PEOPLE'S SAVIOR—which shows just how badly the civilians in the war zone needed medical help and spiritual consolation.

Subsequently, we worked a short time in Guangji and Huangmei. Then the enemy assaulted Wuhan, and we again returned to Hankou.

**The Soldier's Hand* (Chongqing: Independence Press, 1938); *At the Firing Line* (Shanghai: Life Books, 1938); *New War Diary* (Shanghai: Tianma Press, 1938); *Notes in the Army* (Guangzhou: Guangzhou Daily, 1937).—trans.

†Xishui is in the mountains sixty miles east of Hankou.—trans.

When the Xiangya Ambulance Corps had returned to Hunan Province, I had originally considered going along with them to Changsha and then on to Xinhua to see my father and my oldest brother and his wife. But I was afraid that it would not be easy to get out, so I did not go. I lived with Peilan in Hankou. Day and night I was like an ant on a hot pot, unable to sit or lie quietly. My friends strongly advised me to return to Chongqing and to use the material I had gathered in each war zone to write essays for the readers at the home front. So I did. Meanwhile, Peilan, who had not wanted to go to the rear, joined the Red Cross.

I wrote a popular novel of more than fifty thousand words for the Bureau of Education. It was about the war of resistance. Half a year later I was again tired of this kind of life. I had to fulfill my oath that I would not stop working in the battlefield until the enemy had been destroyed. Soon after, I led twelve young women to work in hostels for wounded soldiers. We also trained several hundred young men and women to work in the First, Fifth, and Tenth War Zones. I ran all over Henan and northern Hubei and was also at the Yellow River and at the front line in Xiangfan.* In the foothills of the Dabie Mountains we risked our lives, barely escaped being captured, and suffered greatly from hunger and cold. At Laohekou Hospital I fell ill with chronic appendicitis that was so severe I could not even drink one drop of boiled water. I lay there in pain for two weeks. They saved my life, but recovery was slow. I was forced to return to Chongqing for an operation.

As I lay in Haitangxi's Ninth Hospital for the Severely Wounded, I looked out my window at a vast and boundless blue sky in which countless little stars flashed luminously. I forgot my pain, felt only my spirit lightly floating, as if I had been transformed into a small white dove that had escaped from its cage in a mountain city. I sang songs of victory in a high voice, and I spread both my wings, intending to fly straight to that vast northern wilderness that was the front line, where cannon fire touched the sky.

I must struggle to finish the work that is still undone.

---

*Xiangfan is 170 miles northwest of Hankou.—trans.